Key Documents in American History Volume I

1492–1870

by Jonathan D. Kantrowitz, Caitlin Morrison, and D. Claude Morest

Edited by Patricia F. Braccio and Sarah M. Williams

Class Pack ISBN: 978-0-7827-1403-6 • Student Book ISBN: 978-0-7827-1402-9 •

Queue, Inc. • 80 Hathaway Drive • Stratford, CT 06615
(800) 232-2224 • (800) 775-2729 • www.qworkbooks.com

Table of Contents

TO THE STUDENTS

In this workbook, you will read many primary source documents about various topics in our nation's history. You will then answer multiple-choice and open-ended questions about what you have read.

As you read and answer the questions, please remember:

- You may refer back to the text as often as you like.
- Read each question very carefully and choose the **best** answer.
- Indicate the correct multiple-choice answers directly in this workbook. Circle or underline the correct answer.
- Write your open-ended responses directly on the lines provided. If you need more space, use a separate piece of paper to complete your answer.

Here are some guidelines to remember when writing your open-ended answers:

- Organize your ideas and express them clearly.
- Correctly organize and separate your paragraphs.
- Support your ideas with examples when necessary.
- Make your writing interesting and enjoyable to read.
- Check your spelling and use of grammar and punctuation.
- Your answers should be accurate and complete.

Priviledges and Prerogatives Granted by Their Catholic Majesties to Christopher Columbus, April 30, 1492

Christopher Columbus was born at Genoa, Italy either about 1446 or in 1451, the exact date being uncertain. His father was a wool-comber, of some small means, who lived till 1498. According to the life of Columbus by his son Ferdinand, young Christopher was sent to the university of Pavia, where he devoted himself to astronomy, geometry and cosmography. Yet, according to the admiral's own statement, he became a sailor at fourteen. Evidently this statement, however, cannot mean the abandonment of all other employment, for in 1470, 1472, and 1473 we find him engaged in trade at Genoa, following the family business of weaving.

Columbus visited England in 1476. He claims to have made a voyage in the northern seas, and even to have visited Iceland about February 1477. Soon after this he returned to Portugal, where (probably in 1478) he married a lady of some rank, Felipa Moiiiz de Perestrello, daughter of Bartholomew Perestrello, a captain in the service of Prince Henry the Navigator.

About 1479, Columbus was in Portugal. He probably employed his time in making maps and charts for a livelihood, while he pored over the logs and papers of his deceased father-in-law, and talked with old seamen of their voyages, and of the mystery of the western seas. About this time, too, if not earlier, he seems to have arrived at the conclusion that much of the world remained undiscovered, and step by step conceived that design of reaching Asia by sailing west which was to result in the discovery of America. His views, as finally developed and presented to the courts of Portugal and Spain, were supported by three principal lines of argument, derived from natural reasons, from the theories of geographers, and from the reports and traditions of mariners. He believed the world to be a sphere; he underestimated its size; he overestimated the size of the Asiatic continent. And the farther that continent extended towards the east, the nearer it came towards Spain. Nor were these theories the only supports of his idea. Martin Vicente, a Portuguese pilot, was said to have found, four hundred leagues to the westward of Cape St Vincent, and after a westerly gale of many days duration, a piece of strange wood, wrought, but not with iron; Pedro Correa, Columbus's own brother-in-law, was said to have seen another such wood, with great canes capable of holding four quarts of wine between joint and joint, and to have heard of two men being washed up at Flores very broadfaced, and differing in aspect from Christians. In his northern journey, too, some vague and formless traditions may have reached the explorer's ear of the voyages of Leif Ericson and of the coast of Vinland. All were hints and rumors to bid the bold mariner sail towards the setting sun, and this he at length determined to do.

The concurrence of some state or sovereign, however, was necessary for the success of this design. Columbus submitted to King John of Portugal the scheme he had now matured for reaching Asia by a western route across the ocean. The king was deeply interested in the rival scheme (of an eastern or southeastern route round Africa to India) which had so long held the field, which had been initiated by the Genoese in 1291, and which had been revived, for Portugal, by Prince Henry the Navigator; but he listened to the Genoese, and referred him to a committee of council for geographical affairs. The council's report was adverse; but the king, who was yet inclined to favor the theory of Columbus, assented to the suggestion of the bishop of Ceuta that the plan should be carried out in secret and without its author's knowledge. A caravel was dispatched; but it returned after a brief absence, the sailors having lost heart, and refused to venture farther. Upon discovering this treachery, Columbus left Lisbon for Spain (1484).

Columbus was finally invited to meet Queen Isabella at the court at Cordova (1486). It was an ill moment for the navigator's fortune. Castile and Leon were in the thick of that struggle which resulted in the final conquest of the Granada Moors; and neither Ferdinand nor Isabella had time as yet to give due consideration to Columbus's proposals. The adventurer was still kindly received. But the committee that had been appointed to consider the new project reported that it was vain and impracticable.

In 1488, Columbus was invited by the king of Portugal, his especial friend, to return to that country, and was assured of protection against arrest or proceedings of any kind (March 20th): he had probably made fresh overtures to King John shortly before; and in the autumn of 1488 we find him in Lisbon, conferring with his brother Bartholomew and laying plans for the future. We have no record of the final negotiations of Columbus with the Portuguese government, but they clearly did not issue in anything definite, for Christopher now returned to Spain (though not till he had witnessed the return of Bartholomew Diaz from the discovery of the Cape of Good Hope and his reception by King John), while Bartholomew proceeded to England with a mission to interest King Henry VII in the Columbian schemes. If the London enterprise was unsuccessful (as indeed it proved), it was settled that Bartholomew should carry the same invitation to the French court. He did so; and here he remained until summoned to Spain in 1493. In the meantime, Christopher, unable throughout 1490 to get a hearing at the Spanish court, was in 1491 again referred to a junta, presided over by Cardinal Mendoza; but this junta, to Columbus's dismay, once more rejected his proposals; the Spanish sovereigns merely promised him that when the Granada war was over, they would reconsider what he had laid before them.

Columbus reached Granada in time to witness the surrender of the city (January 2, 1492), and negotiations were resumed. Columbus believed in his mission, and held out for high terms: he asked for the rank of admiral at once (Admiral of the Ocean in all those islands, seas, and continents that he might discover), the vice-royalty of all he should discover, and a tenth of the precious metals discovered within his admiralty. These conditions were rejected, and the negotiations were again interrupted. An interview with Mendoza appears to have followed; but nothing came of it, and before the close of January 1492, Columbus actually set out for France. At length, however, on the entreaty of the queen's confidante, the Marquesa de Moya, of Luis de Santangel, receiver of the ecclesiastical revenues of the crown of Aragon, and of other courtiers, Isabella was induced to determine on the expedition. A messenger was sent after Columbus, and overtook him near a bridge called Pinos, 6 m. from Granada. He returned to the camp at Santa Fe, and on the 17th of April 1492, the agreement between him and their Catholic majesties was signed and sealed.

FERDINAND and ELIZABETH, by the Grace of God, King and Queen of Castile, of Leon, of Arragon, of Sicily, of Granada, of Toledo, of Valencia, of Galicia, of Majorca, of Minorca, of Sevil, of Sardinia, of Jaen, of Algarve, of Algezira, of Gibraltar, of the Canary Islands, Count and Countess of Barcelona, Lord and Lady of Biscay and Molina, Duke and Duchess of Athens and Neopatria. Count and Countess of Rousillion and Cerdaigne, Marquess and Marchioness of Oristan and Gociano, &c.

For as much of you, Christopher Columbus, are going by our command, with some of our vessels and men, to discover and subdue some Islands and Continent in the ocean, and it is hoped that by God's assistance, some of the said Islands and Continent in the ocean will be discovered and conquered by your means and conduct, therefore it is but just and reasonable, that since you expose yourself to such danger to serve us, you should be rewarded for it. And we being willing to honour and favour You for the reasons aforesaid: Our will is, That you, Christopher Columbus, after discovering and conquering the said Islands and Continent in the said ocean, or any of them, shall be our Admiral of the said Islands and Continent you shall so discover and conquer; and that you be our Admiral, Vice-Roy, and Governor in them, and that for the future, you may call and stile yourself, D. Christopher Columbus, and that your sons and successors in the said employment, may call themselves Dons, Admirals, Vice-Roys, and Governors of them; and that you may exercise the office of Admiral, with the charge of Vice-Roy and Governor of the said Islands and Continent, which you and your Lieutenants shall conquer, and freely decide all causes, civil and criminal, appertaining to the said employment of Admiral, Vice-Roy, and Governor, as you shall think fit in justice, and as the Admirals of our kingdoms use to do; and that you have power to punish offenders; and you and your Lieutenants exercise the employments of Admiral, Vice-Roy, and Governor, in all things belonging to the said offices, or any of them; and that you enjoy the perquisites and salaries belonging to the said employments, and to each of them, in the same manner as the High Admiral of our kingdoms does.

GIVEN at Granada, on the 30th of April, in the year of our Lord, 1492.—

I, THE KING, I, THE QUEEN.

By their Majesties Command . . .

1. The king and queen hope that Columbus will
    a. find and conquer some land.
    b. Christianize the natives.
    c. one day become the ruler of his own kingdom.
    d. prove that the world is round.

2. The king and queen plan to reward Columbus with
    a. boats and men.
    b. possession of any newly-discovered lands.
    c. titles and a job.
    d. a portion of the profits.

3. The king and queen are willing to reward Columbus because
    a. they think he will discover a new land.
    b. he is their High Admiral.
    c. he is using their ships and sailors.
    d. of the risk involved.

4. Based on the document above, what do you infer to be the king and queen's—and Columbus's—primary motives for entering into this agreement?

The Mayflower Compact (1620)

The settlers who came to the New World brought with them a great deal of baggage in the form of ideas and beliefs they had held dear in England. Indeed, many of them, such as the Puritans, came to America so they could live in stricter accord with those beliefs. The Pilgrims, a branch of the Puritans, arrived off the coast of Massachusetts in November 1620, determined to live sacred lives according to biblical commands, and in so doing to build a "city upon a hill" that would be a beacon to the rest of the world.

But aside from their religious enthusiasm, the Pilgrims also knew that the English settlement founded a few years earlier at Jamestown in Virginia had practically foundered because of the lack of a strong government and leadership. They would not make that mistake, and agreed that once a government had been established, they would obey the commands of its leaders.

In making this compact, the Pilgrims drew upon two strong traditions. One was the notion of a social contract, which dated back to biblical times and which would receive fuller expression in the works of Thomas Hobbes and John Locke later in the century. The other was the belief in covenants. Puritans believed that covenants existed not only between God and man, but also between man and man. The Pilgrims had used covenants in establishing their congregations in the Old World. The Mayflower Compact is such a covenant in that the settlers agreed to form a government and be bound by its rules.

The Compact is often described as America's first constitution, but it is not a constitution in the sense of being a fundamental framework of government. Its importance lies in the belief that government is a form of covenant, and that for government to be legitimate, it must derive from the consent of the governed. The settlers recognized that individually they might not agree with all of the actions of the government they were creating; but they, and succeeding generations, understood that government could be legitimate only if it originated with the consent of those it claimed to govern. The document follows:

We whose names are underwritten, the loyal subjects of our dread Sovereign Lord King James, by the Grace of God of Great Britain, France and Ireland, King, Defender of the Faith, etc.

Having undertaken, for the Glory of God and advancement of the Christian Faith and Honour of our King and Country, a Voyage to plant the First Colony in the Northern Parts of Virginia, do by these presents solemnly and mutually in the presence of God and one of another, Covenant and Combine ourselves together into a Civil Body Politic, for our better ordering and preservation and furtherance of the ends aforesaid; and by virtue hereof to enact, constitute and frame such just and equal Laws, Ordinances, Acts, Constitutions and Offices, from time to time, as shall be thought most meet and convenient for the general good of the Colony, unto which we promise all due submission and obedience. In witness whereof we have hereunder subscribed our names at Cape Cod, the 11th of November, in the year of the reign of our Sovereign Lord King James, of England, France and Ireland the eighteenth, and of Scotland the fifty-fourth. Anno Domini 1620.

1. Why did the Puritans leave England?

a. to create a better government
b. to follow their strict religious beliefs
c. to bring Christianity to the heathens
d. to free Jamestown from the Native Americans

2. The Pilgrims originally planned to settle in an area nearest to which of the following modern American cities?

a. Boston
b. New York City
c. Philadelphia
d. Washington, D.C.

3. Which of the following explanations is given in the document for why the Pilgrims undertook their voyage?

a. religious freedom
b. political freedom
c. patriotic reasons
d. economic reasons

4. The Mayflower Compact does all of the following **except** it does not

a. give the government of the colony the authority to make laws.
b. specify the democratic structure of the colony's government.
c. recognize that the government should benefit the colony as a whole.
d. promise that all signers will be law-abiding citizens.

5. The social contract is an understanding

a. between two people.
b. among ancient religions.
c. between man and God.
D. among society, man, and God.

6. Why did does the Mayflower Compact refer to the plantation as "a Civil Body Politic"?

a. It aptly describes the role the church should play in government.
b. It refers to the Pilgrims who became a political group under a government.
c. It shows the subordination of the Compact to the throne.
D. It illustrates the freedom of the people in the plantation.

7. What is implicit in this document? In other words, if you were a Pilgrim signing the Mayflower Compact, what assumptions—that are not explicitly stated—could you make about the colony?

8. Why did the Pilgrims create the Mayflower Compact and what did it signify? Use examples from the text.

Connecticut Blue Laws (1648)

The Connecticut Blue Laws, enacted by the people of the "Dominion of New Haven," became known as the blue laws because they were printed on blue paper.

The governor and magistrates convened in general assembly are the supreme power, under God, of the independent dominion.

From the determination of the assembly no appeal shall be made.

No one shall be a freeman or have a vote unless he is converted and a member of one of the churches allowed in the dominion.

Each freeman shall swear by the blessed God to bear true allegiance to this dominion and that Jesus is the only king.

No dissenter from the essential worship of this dominion shall be allowed to give a vote for electing of magistrates or any officer.

No food or lodging shall be offered to a heretic.

CONCERNING THE SABBATH:

No one shall cross a river on the Sabbath but authorized clergymen.

No one shall travel, cook victuals, make beds, sweep houses, cut hair, or shave on the Sabbath Day.

No one shall kiss his or her children on the Sabbath or feasting days.

The Sabbath Day shall begin at sunset Saturday.

Whoever wears clothes trimmed with gold, silver, or bone lace above one shilling per yard shall be presented by the grand jurors and the selectmen shall tax the estate 300 pounds.

Whoever brings cards or dice into the dominion shall pay a fine of 5 pounds.

No one shall eat mince pies, dance, play cards, or play any instrument of music except the drum, trumpet, or jewsharp.

A man who strikes his wife shall be fined 10 pounds.

A woman who strikes her husband shall be punished as the law directs.

No man shall court a maid in person or by letter without obtaining the consent of her parents; 5 pounds penalty for the first offense; 10 pounds for the second, and for the third imprisonment during the pleasure of the court.

1. Which of the following **best** describes the Dominion of New Haven's government in 1648?

   a. fundamentalist monarchy
   b. autocratic theocracy
   c. religious democracy
   d. theocratic republic

2. Which of the following were you allowed to do in New Haven on a Saturday night in 1648?

   a. square dancing
   b. play your trumpet
   c. kiss your children good night
   d. sweep up after dinner

3. According to the document, for which of the following would a resident of New Haven in 1648 have been fined?

   a. wearing clothing trimmed with lace
   b. not being a member of a church
   c. not fasting on the Sabbath
   d. hitting one's spouse

4. Discuss the hypothetical constitutionality of the Connecticut blue laws in the document above. Which laws would be deemed unconstitutional today? Which laws do not conflict with the Constitution?

The Maryland Toleration Act, September 21, 1649

Maryland had been established as a refuge for Roman Catholics. When Lord Baltimore appointed a Protestant as governor Protestants were attracted to the colony in increasing numbers. They insisted upon a guarantee of liberty of conscience. The Maryland Assembly of 1649 was composed of Puritans, Church of England men, and a few Roman Catholics. It was this body of a majority of Protestants that passed the Toleration Act of which so much has been written. That act seems to have been an outgrowth of statutes passed by the British Parliament in 1645 and 1647. It was adopted by the Maryland legislature under the pressure of the strong Puritan influence then existing there.

By that act, every believer in Jesus Christ and the Trinity was allowed the free exercise of his or her religious opinions, but from this "toleration" Jews and Unitarians were alike excluded. No man was allowed to reproach another on account of his peculiar religious doctrines, excepting under the penalty of a fine to be paid to the person so insulted.

The persecuted in other colonies now flocked to Maryland in order to enjoy this broader freedom—Churchmen from New England, Puritans from Virginia, and Roman Catholics from all. That act is the pride and glory of Maryland's early legislation, yet it was not the first act of the kind (as has been often alleged) passed by a colonial assembly in America. In May, 1647—two years before—the General Assembly of Rhode Island adopted a code of laws which closed with the declaration that "all men may walk as their consciences persuaded them, without molestation—every one in the name of his God." This would include Jew or Mohammedan, Buddhist or Pagan. It was absolute toleration.

The Maryland Toleration Act (1649)

An Act Concerning Religion

Forasmuch as in a well governed and Christian Commonwealth matters concerning Religion and the honor of God ought in the first place to be taken, into serious consideration and endeavoured to be settled, be it therefore ordered and enacted by the Right Honourable Cecilius Lord Baron of Baltemore absolute Lord and Proprietary of this Province with the advise and consent of this Generall Assembly:

That whatsoever person or persons within this Province and the Islands thereunto belonging shall from henceforth blaspheme God, that is Curse him, or deny our Saviour Jesus Christ to be the son of God, or shall deny the holy Trinity the father son and holy Ghost, or the Godhead of any of the said three persons of the Trinity or the Unity of the Godhead, or shall use or utter any reproachfull speeches, words or language concerning the said Holy Trinity, or any of the said three persons thereof, shall be punished with death and confiscation or forfeiture of all his or her lands and goods to the Lord Proprietary and his heires.

And be it also enacted by the authority and with the advise and assent aforesaid, that whatsoever person or persons shall from henceforth use or utter any reproachfull words or speeches concerning the blessed Virgin Mary the Mother of our Saviour or the holy apostles or evangelists or any of them shall in such case for the first offence forfeit to the said Lord Proprietary and his heirs Lords and proprietaries of this province the summe of five pound Sterling or the value thereof to be levyed on the goods and chattells of every such person soe offending, but in case such offender or offenders, shall not then have goods and chattells sufficient for the satisfyeing of such forfeiture, or that the same bee not otherwise speedily satisfyed that then such offender or offenders shalbe publically whipped and be imprisoned during the pleasure of the Lord Proprietary or the lieutenant or chief governor of this Province for the time being. And that every such offender or offenders for every second offence shall forfeit tenne pound sterling or the value thereof to bee levyed as aforesaid, or in case such offender or offenders shall not then have goods and chattells within this Province sufficient for that purpose then to be publically and severely whipped and imprisoned as before is expressed. And that every person or persons before mentioned offending herein the third time, shall for such third offence forfeit all his lands and goods and be for ever banished and expelled out of this Province.

And be it also further enacted by the same authority advise and assent that whatsoever person or persons shall from henceforth uppon any occasion of offence or otherwise in a reproachful manner or Way declare call or denominate any person or persons whatsoever inhabiting, residing, traffiqueing, trading or comerceing within this Province or within any the ports, harbors, creeks or havens to the same belonging an heritick, scismatick, idolator, puritan, independant, Prespiterian popish prest, Jesuite, Jesuited papist, Lutheran, Calvenist, Anabaptist, Brownist, Antinomian, Barrowist, Roundhead, Separatist, or any other name or terme in a reproachfull manner relating to matter of religion shall for every such offence forfeit and loose the somme of tenne shillings sterling or the value thereof to bee levyed on the goods and chattells of every such offender and offenders, the one half thereof to be forfeited and paid unto the person and persons of whom such reproachfull words are or shalbe spoken or uttered, and the other half thereof to the Lord Proprietary and his heires Lords and Proprietaries of this Province. But if such person or persons who shall at any time utter or speake any such reproachfull words or language shall not have goods or chattells sufficient and overt within this Province to be taken to satisfie the penalty aforesaid or that the same bee not otherwise speedily satisfyed, that then the person or persons so offending shall be publically whipped, and shall suffer imprisonment without bail or maineprise [bail] untill he, she or they respectively shall satisfy the party so offended or greived by such reproachfull language by asking him or her respectively forgivenes publically for such his offence before the Magistrate of chief officer or officers of the town or place where such offence shal be given.

And be it further likewise enacted by the authority and consent aforesaid that every person and persons within this Province that shall at any time hereafter prophane the Sabbath or Lords day called Sunday by frequent swearing, drunkennes or by any uncivil or disorderly recreacion, or by working on that day when absolute necessity doth not require it shall for every such first offence forfeit 2*s* 6*d* sterling or the value thereof, and for the second offence 5*s* sterling or the value thereof, and for the third offence and so for every time he shall offend in like manner afterwards 10*s* sterling or the value thereof. And in case such offender and offenders shall not have sufficient goods or chattells within this Province to satisfy any of the said Penalties respectively hereby imposed for prophaning the Sabbath or Lords day called Sunday as aforesaid, That in Every such case the partie so offending shall for the first and second offence in that kind be imprisoned till he or she shall publickly in open Court before the chief Commander Judge or Magistrate, of that County Town or precinct where such offence shall be committed acknowledge the scandall and offence he hath in that respect given against God and the good and civil governement of this Province, And for the third offence and for every time after shall also bee publically whipped.

And whereas the enforcing of the conscience in matters of religion hath frequently fallen out to be of dangerous consequence in those commonwealthes where it hath been practised, and for the more quiet and peaceable governement of this Province, and the better to preserve mutual love and amity among the inhabitants thereof, be it therefore also by the Lord Proprietary with the advise and consent of this Assembly ordered and enacted (except as in this present Act is before declared and set forth) that no person or persons whatsoever within this Province, or the islands, ports, harbors, creekes, or havens thereunto belonging professing to beleive in Jesus Christ, shall from henceforth be any waies troubled, molested or discountenanced for or in respect of his or her religion nor in the free exercise thereof within this Province or the islands thereunto belonging nor any way compelled to the beleif or exercise of any other religion against his or her consent, so as they be not unfaithfull to the Lord Proprietary, or molest or conspire against the civil governement established or to be established in this Province under him or his heires. And that all and every person and persons that shall presume contrary to this Act and the true intent and meaning thereof directly or indirectly either in person or estate willfully to wrong disturbe trouble or molest any person whatsoever within this Province professing to beleive in Jesus Christ for or in respect of his or her religion or the free exercise thereof within this Province other than is provided for in this Act that such person or persons so offending, shall be compelled to pay treble damages to the party so wronged or molested, and for every such offence shall also forfeit 20*s* sterling in money or the value thereof, half thereof for the use of the Lord Proprietary, and his heires Lords and Proprietaries of this Province, and the other half for the use of the party so wronged or molested as aforesaid, or if the partie so offending as aforesaid shall refuse or be unable to recompense the party so wronged, or to satisfy such fine or forfeiture, then such offender shall be severely punished by public whipping and imprisonment during the pleasure of the Lord Proprietary, or his Lieutenant or chief Governor of this Province for the time being without baile or maineprise.

And be it further also enacted by the authority and consent aforesaid that the sheriff or other officer or officers from time to time to be appointed and authorized for that purpose, of the county towne or precinct where every particular offence in this present Act conteyned shall happen at any time to be committed and whereupon there is hereby a forfeiture fine or penalty imposed shall from time to time distraine and seise the goods and estate of every such person so offending as aforesaid against this present Act or any part thereof, and sell the same or any part thereof for the full satisfaccion of such forfeiture, fine, or penalty as aforesaid, Restoring unto the partie so offending the remainder or overplus of the said goods or estate after such satisfaccion so made as aforesaid.

The freemen have assented.

1. All of the following were outlawed by the Maryland Toleration Act **except**

   a. practicing any religion one wants to.
   b. discussing religious beliefs in public speeches.
   c. speaking negatively about the apostles.
   d. swearing on Sundays.

2. Of which of the following was the Maryland Toleration Act most tolerant?

   a. free speech
   b. Christians
   c. diverse religious beliefs
   d. Catholics

3. Which of the following violations of the Maryland Toleration Act incurred the most severe penalty?

   a. saying that one does not believe in the Holy Trinity
   b. insulting the Virgin Mary
   c. using a religious slur against a Christian
   d. profaning the Sabbath

4. The Maryland Toleration Act does all of the following **except**

   a. specifying the penalties for breaking the law.
   b. explaining why religious toleration is desirable.
   c. listing the religions people may not practice.
   d. outlawing certain activities on Sundays.

5. Do you think the Maryland Toleration Act was a liberal or conservative law for its time and place? Explain your reasoning.

Colonial Laws of Massachusetts (1651)

Sumptuary Laws (Laws Regarding What One May or May Not Wear)

ALTHOUGH SEVERAL DECLARATIONs and orders have been made by this Court against excess in apparell, both of men and women, which have not taken that effect as were to be desired, but on the contrary, we cannot but to our grief take notice that intolerable excess and bravery have crept in upon us, and especially among people of mean condition, to the dishonor of God, the scandal of our profession, the consumption of estates, and altogether unsuitable to our poverty. And, although we acknowledge it to be a matter of much difficulty, in regard of the blindness of men's minds and the stubbornness of their wills, to set down exact rules to confine all sorts of persons, yet we cannot but account it our duty to commend unto all sorts of persons the sober and moderate use of those blessings which, beyond expectation, the Lord has been pleased to afford unto us in this wilderness. And also to declare our utter detestation and dislike that men and women of mean condition should take upon them the garb [of] gentlemen by wearing gold or silver lace, or buttons, or points at their knees, or to walk in great boots; or women of the same rank to wear silk or tiffany hoods, or scarves which, though allowable to persons of greater estates or more liberal education, we cannot but judge it intolerable. . . .

It is therefore ordered by this Court, and authority thereof, that no person within the jurisdiction, nor any of their relations depending upon them, whose visible estates, real and personal, shall not exceed the true and indifferent value of £200, shall wear any gold or silver lace, or gold and silver buttons, or any bone lace above 2s. per yard, or silk hoods, or scarves, upon the penalty of 10s. for every such offense and every such delinquent to be presented to the grand jury. And forasmuch as distinct and particular rules in this case suitable to the estate or quality of each perrson cannot easily be given: It is further ordered by the authority aforesaid, that the selectmen of every town, or the major part of them, are hereby enabled and required, from time to time to have regard and take notice of the apparel of the inhabitants of their several towns respectively; and whosoever they shall judge to exceed their ranks and abilities in the costliness or fashion of their apparel in any respect, especially in the wearing of ribbons or great boots (leather being so scarce a commodity in this country) lace, points, etc., silk hoods, or scarves, the select men aforesaid shall have power to assess such persons, so offending in any of the particulars above mentioned, in the country rates, at £200 estates, according to that proportion that such men use to pay to whom such apparel is suitable and allowed; provided this law shall not extend to the restraint of any magistrate or public officer of this jurisdiction, their wives and children, who are left to their discretion in wearing of apparel, or any settled militia officer or soldier in the time of military service, or any other whose education and employment have been above the ordinary degree, or whose estate have been considerable, though now decayed.

1. Which of the following is a reason given for restricting what certain people can wear?
   a. It tempts members of the opposite sex.
   b. It distracts people from getting their work done.
   c. Some people are spending too much money on their clothes.
   d. It is hard to tell the upper, middle and lower classes apart.

2. People can wear ornate clothes if they

   a. can afford them.
   b. get permission from the town selectmen.
   c. own estates valued at or above £200.
   d. are people of mean condition.

3. Which of the following groups is exempt from the Sumptuary Laws?

   a. children
   b. clergy
   c. college students
   d. people who used to be wealthy

4. How is present-day America similar to and different from Colonial Massachusetts with respect to the issue of what clothing people of certain socio-economic classes wear?

6. All Students shall be slow to speake and eschew and in as much as in them lies, shall take care, that others may avoid all sweareing, lieing, curseing, needless asseverations, foolish talkeing. scurrility, babling, filthy speakeing, chideing, strife, raileing, reproacheing, abusive jesting, uncomely noise, uncertaine rumors, divulging secrets, and all manner of troublesome and offensive gestures, as being the [document torn] should shine before others in exemplary life.

7. No scholler shall goe out of his chamber without coate, gowne, cloake, and every one every where shall weare modest and sober habit, without strange ruffian like or new fangled fashions, without all lavish dress, or excess of apparel what soever: nor shall any weare gold and silver or such ornaments, except to whome upon just ground the President shall permit the same, neither shall it be lawfull for any to weare long haire, locks, or foretops, nor to use curling, crispeing, parteing or powdering theire haire.

8. No undergraduate upon any pretence of recreation or any other cause whatsoever, (unless allowed by the President or his Tutor) shall be absent from his studies or appointed exercises in the Colledge, except halfe an houre at breakefast, an houre and halfe at dinner, and after evening prayer untill nine of the clock: but while he is in the Colledge he shall studiously redeeme his time, both observing the houres common to all the Students to meet in the hall, and those that are appointed to theire own lectures, where unto he shall diligently attend, being inoffensive in word and gesture.

9. No Student shall goe into any Taverne, vittaileing house, or Inne to eate or drink, unless he be called by his parents, Guardians, or without some sufficient reason such as the President or his Tutor may approve of: neither shall any one entertaine any stranger to lodge or abide in the Colledge, unless by the leave of the President or his Tutor, or in case of theire absence of one of the fellows: neither shall he without sufficient reason such as the President or his Tutor shall approve, either take Tobacco or bring or permit to be brought into his chamber strong beare, wine, or strong water or any other enebriateing drink, to the end that all excess and abuse thereof may be prevented.

10. No Student shall under any pretence whatever use the company or familiar acquaintance of persons of ungirt and dissolute life, [4] intermeddle with other mens buisiness, nor Intrude himselfe into chambers, neither may any undergraduate goe out of the town, nor be present at any Courts, Elections, Faires, Traineings, or any such like assemblies, except upon leave obtained of the President or his Tutor, or two of his fellows in theire absence.

11. No Student shall board or lie out of the Colledge, without just cause allowed by the President, nor shall any stay out of the Colledge after nine of the clock at night, nor watch after eleven, nor have a light before four in the morning, except upon extraordinary occasions.

12. Every undergraduate shall be called onely by his sur name unless he be the son of a nobleman, or a knights eldest son, or a fellow commoner.

1. The document above regulated all of the following **except**

   a. what the students could wear.
   b. the way students should address their professors.
   c. how the students could speak.
   d. whom the students could associate with.

2. Which of the following does the document above state that a student could do with the permission of the president?

   a. make uncomely noises
   b. be addressed by his first name
   c. wear long hair
   d. bring tobacco into his room

3. Which of the following **best** describes the laws of Harvard College in 1655?

   a. a list of things students may not do
   b. an explanation of how students should behave and why
   c. a rulebook that lists the consequences of misbehavior
   d. a document that communicates to students their rights and responsibilities

4. How could these rules potentially have been abused by either students or college officials?

The Albany Plan of Union (1754)

Knowing that a war with France was imminent, Benjamin Franklin and Massachusetts governor Thomas Hutchinson drafted a proposal for colonial unity. The plan called for the creation of a new government. A president-general would be appointed by the Crown. He would exercise broad powers over relationships with the Native Americans, making war and governing the frontier areas until new colonies were created. A grand council was also proposed. Its members would be appointed by the existing colonial assemblies. Representation would be based on the amount of financial contribution paid to the organization, rather than on population.

The plan for a federated colonial government never got off the ground. The delegates at Albany approved it. However, not a single colonial assembly ratified it. It was doubtful, even if approved by the assemblies, that royal officials would have approved of this consolidation of power in America.

Instead, the creation of a colonial council composed of one representative from each colony was proposed. That body would be responsible for raising militia forces and apportioning the cost among the membership. This idea elicited little enthusiasm in America. The colonists preferred to have British regulars fight their battles with money raised on the other side of the Atlantic.

The Albany Plan of Union set an example that would later be followed by such gatherings as the continental congresses.

It is proposed that humble application be made for an act of Parliament of Great Britain, by virtue of which one general government may be formed in America, including all the said colonies, within and under which government each colony may retain its present constitution, except in the particulars wherein a change may be directed by the said act, as hereafter follows.

1. That the said general government be administered by a President-General, to be appointed and supported by the crown; and a Grand Council, to be chosen by the representatives of the people of the several Colonies met in their respective assemblies.

2. That within ___ months after the passing such act, the House of Representatives that happen to be sitting within that time, or that shall be especially for that purpose convened, may and shall choose members for the Grand Council, in the following proportion, that is to say,

Massachusetts Bay	7
New Hampshire	2
Connecticut	5
Rhode Island	2
New York	4
New Jersey	3
Pennsylvania	6
Maryland	4
Virginia	7
North Carolina	4
South Carolina	+ 4
	48

3. ___ who shall meet for the first time at the city of Philadelphia, being called by the President-General as soon as conveniently may be after his appointment.

4. That there shall be a new election of the members of the Grand Council every three years; and, on the death or resignation of any member, his place should be supplied by a new choice at the next sitting of the Assembly of the Colony he represented.

5. That after the first three years, when the proportion of money arising out of each Colony to the general treasury can be known, the number of members to be chosen for each Colony shall, from time to time, in all ensuing elections, be regulated by that proportion, yet so as that the number to be chosen by any one Province be not more than seven, nor less than two.

6. That the Grand Council shall meet once in every year, and oftener if occasion require, at such time and place as they shall adjourn to at the last preceding meeting, or as they shall be called to meet at by the President-General on any emergency; he having first obtained in writing the consent of seven of the members to such call, and sent duly and timely notice to the whole.

7. That the Grand Council have power to choose their speaker; and shall neither be dissolved, prorogued, nor continued sitting longer than six weeks at one time, without their own consent or the special command of the crown.

8. That the members of the Grand Council shall be allowed for their service ten shillings sterling per diem, during their session and journey to and from the place of meeting; twenty miles to be reckoned a day's journey.

9. That the assent of the President-General be requisite to all acts of the Grand Council, and that it be his office and duty to cause them to be carried into execution.

10. That the President-General, with the advice of the Grand Council, hold or direct all Indian treaties, in which the general interest of the Colonies may be concerned; and make peace or declare war with Indian nations.

11. That they make such laws as they judge necessary for regulating all Indian trade.

12. That they make all purchases from Indians, for the crown, of lands not now within the bounds of particular Colonies, or that shall not be within their bounds when some of them are reduced to more convenient dimensions.

13. That they make new settlements on such purchases, by granting lands in the King's name, reserving a quitrent to the crown for the use of the general treasury.

14. That they make laws for regulating and governing such new settlements, till the crown shall think fit to form them into particular governments.

15. That they raise and pay soldiers and build forts for the defence of any of the Colonies, and equip vessels of force to guard the coasts and protect the trade on the ocean, lakes, or great rivers; but they shall not impress men in any Colony, without the consent of the Legislature.

16. That for these purposes they have power to make laws, and lay and levy such general duties, imposts, or taxes, as to them shall appear most equal and just (considering the ability and other circumstances of the inhabitants in the several Colonies), and such as may be collected

with the least inconvenience to the people; rather discouraging luxury, than loading industry with unnecessary burdens.

17. That they may appoint a General Treasurer and Particular Treasurer in each government when necessary; and, from time to time, may order the sums in the treasuries of each government into the general treasury; or draw on them for special payments, as they find most convenient.

18. Yet no money to issue but by joint orders of the President-General and Grand Council; except where sums have been appropriated to particular purposes, and the President-General is previously empowered by an act to draw such sums.

19. That the general accounts shall be yearly settled and reported to the several Assemblies.

20. That a quorum of the Grand Council, empowered to act with the President-General, do consist of twenty-five members; among whom there shall be one or more from a majority of the Colonies.

21. That the laws made by them for the purposes aforesaid shall not be repugnant, but, as near as may be, agreeable to the laws of England, and shall be transmitted to the King in Council for approbation, as soon as may be after their passing; and if not disapproved within three years after presentation, to remain in force.

22. That, in case of the death of the President-General, the Speaker of the Grand Council for the time being shall succeed, and be vested with the same powers and authorities, to continue till the King's pleasure be known.

23. That all military commission officers, whether for land or sea service, to act under this general constitution, shall be nominated by the President-General; but the approbation of the Grand Council is to be obtained, before they receive their commissions. And all civil officers are to be nominated by the Grand Council, and to receive the President-General's approbation before they officiate.

24. But, in case of vacancy by death or removal of any officer, civil or military, under this constitution, the Governor of the Province in which such vacancy happens may appoint, till the pleasure of the President-General and Grand Council can be known.

25. That the particular military as well as civil establishments in each Colony remain in their present state, the general constitution notwithstanding; and that on sudden emergencies any Colony may defend itself, and lay the accounts of expense thence arising before the President-General and General Council, who may allow and order payment of the same, as far as they judge such accounts just and reasonable.

1. Which of the following statements about the Albany Plan of Union is probably **not** true?

   a. The plan was to be submitted to Parliament in Great Britain.
   b. The plan would have to be approved by Parliament.
   c. The "general government" of the plan included all of the colonies.
   d. The plan replaced the constitutions of all colonies.

2. The individual who would lead the government created under the plan was called the

   a. crown.
   b. president-general.
   c. member.
   d. representative.

3. The men who would represent the colonies at meetings under the plan would be chosen by the

   a. Parliament in Great Britain.
   b. assemblies of their respective colonies.
   c. men who wrote the plan.
   d. voters in the colonies.

4. The plan called for the first meeting of the new government to be held in

   a. Albany.
   b. Massachusetts Bay.
   c. Philadelphia.
   d. Great Britain.

5. How long would members of the Grand Council serve according to the plan?

   a. three years
   b. one year
   c. one month
   d. six weeks

6. According to point five, the number of representatives to the Grand Council from each colony would be determined by the

   a. population of that colony.
   b. crown and the Parliament.
   c. money contributed by each colony.
   d. house of representatives in each colony.

7. According to the plan, delegates would receive __________ for serving on the Grand Council.

   a. ten shillings per day
   b. no travel expenses
   c. purchases from Native Americans
   d. land grants

8. Under the plan, the Grand Council could **not** ________ Native American tribes.

   a. make treaties with
   b. make trade agreements with
   c. declare war on
   d. seize land that belonged to

9. According to the plan, the Grand Council could raise an army but it could not "impress" men. A man who is "impressed" into an army is most likely

   a. paid a large bonus to join.
   b. given an officer's rank.
   c. forced to serve against his will.
   d. eager to volunteer.

10. According to the plan, the final approval of all laws passed by the Grand Council had to be given by

   a. "a majority of the Colonies."
   b. "the King and his Council."
   c. "the Speaker of the Grand Council."
   d. "twenty-five members."

11. According to point eight, members of the Grand Council were paid for travel to meetings, with "twenty miles to be reckoned a day's journey." What conclusions can be drawn from that figure?

12. Points sixteen though eighteen of the plan detailed how the money needed by the Grand Council would be raised and withdrawn. Write a brief summary explaining the financial structure of the government under the Albany Plan of Union.

The Stamp Act, March 22, 1765

The Stamp Act was enacted by Parliament as a means of raising colonial tax revenues to help defray the cost of the French and Indian War in North America. The colonists' reaction was strong. They asserted that the Stamp Act was an attempt to raise money in the colonies without the approval of colonial legislatures. Resistance to the act was demonstrated through debates in the colonial legislatures, written documents (including legislative resolves, prints, and songs), and mob/crowd actions such as tarring and feathering tax collectors. The reaction was the beginning of the end of British rule in the thirteen colonies.

An act for granting and applying certain stamp duties, and other duties, in the British colonies and plantations in America, towards further defraying the expences of defending, protecting, and securing the same; and for amending such parts of the several acts of parliament relating to the trade and revenues of the said colonies and plantations, as direct the manner of determining and recovering the penalties and forfeitures therein mentioned.

WHEREAS by an act made in the last session of parliament, several duties were granted, continued, and appropriated, towards defraying the expences of defending, protecting, and securing, the British colonies and plantations in America: and whereas it is just and necessary, that provision be made for raising a further revenue within your Majesty's dominions in America, towards defraying the said expences: we, your Majesty's most dutiful and loyal subjects, the commons of Great Britain in parliament assembled, have therefore resolved to give and grant unto your Majesty the several rates and duties herein after mentioned; and do most humbly beseech your Majesty that it may be enacted, and be it enacted by the King's most excellent majesty, by and with the advice and consent of the lords spiritual and temporal, and commons, in this present parliament assembled, and by the authority of the same, That from and after the first day of November, one thousand seven hundred and sixty five, there shall be raised, levied, collected, and paid unto his Majesty, his heirs, and successors, throughout the colonies and plantations in America which now are, or hereafter may be, under the dominion of his Majesty, his heirs and successors,

For every skin or piece of vellum or parchment, or sheet or piece of paper, on which shall be ingrossed, written or printed, any declaration, plea, replication, rejoinder, demurrer, or other pleading, or any copy thereof, in any court of law within the British colonies and plantations in America, a stamp duty of three pence. . . .

For every such pamphlet and paper (being larger than half a sheet, and not exceeding one whole sheet) which shall be so printed, a stamp duty of one penny, for every printed copy thereof.

For every pamphlet and paper being larger than one whole sheet, and not exceeding six sheets in octavo, or in a lesser page, or not exceeding twelve sheets in quarto, or twenty sheets in folio, which shall be so printed, a duty after the rate of one shilling for every sheet of any kind of paper which shall be contained in one printed copy thereof.

For every advertisement to be contained in any gazette, news paper, or other paper, or any pamphlet which shall be so printed, a duty of two shillings.

For every almanack or calendar, for any one particular year, or for any time less than a year, which shall be written or printed on one side only of any one sheet, skin, or piece of paper parchment, or vellum, within the said colonies and plantations, a stamp duty of two pence.

For every other almanack or calendar for any one particular year, which shall be written or printed within the said colonies or plantations, a stamp duty of four pence.

And for every almanack or calendar written or printed within the said colonies and plantations, to serve for several years, duties to the same amount respectively shall be paid for every such year.

For every skin or piece of vellum or parchment, or sheet or piece of paper, on which any instrument, proceeding, or other matter or thing aforesaid, shall be ingrossed, written, or printed, within the said colonies and plantations, in any other than the English language, a stamp duty of double the amount of the respective duties being charged thereon . . .

III. And be it further enacted by the authority aforesaid, That every deed, instrument, note, memorandum, letter, or other instrument or writing, for or relating to the payment of any sum of money, or for making any valuable consideration for or upon the loss of any ship, vessel, goods, wages, money, effects, or upon any loss by fire, or for any other loss whatsoever, or for or upon any life or lives, shall be construed, deemed, and adjudged to be policies of assurance, within the meaning of this act: and if any such deed, instrument, note, memorandum, letter, or other minument or writing, for insuring, or tending to insure, any more than one ship or vessel for more than any one voyage, or any goods, wages, money, effects, or other matter or thing whatsoever, for more than one voyage, or in more than one ship or vessel, or being the property of, or belonging to, any more than one person, or any more than one body politick or corporate, or for more than one risk; then, in every such case, the money insured thereon, or the valuable consideration thereby agreed to be made, shall become the absolute property of the insured, and the insurer shall also forfeit the premium given for such insurance, together with the sum of one hundred pounds.

IV. And be it further enacted by the authority aforesaid, That every deed, instrument, note, memorandum, letter, or other minument or writing, between the captain or master or owner of any ship or vessel, and any merchant, trader, or other person, in respect to the freight or conveyance of any money, goods, wares, merchandizes, or effects, laden or to be laden on board of any such ship or vessel, shall be deemed and adjudged to be a charter party within the meaning of this act . . .

1. A word in paragraph one that has about the same meaning as "taxes" is

   a. "duties."
   b. "expences."
   c. "penalties."
   d. "act."

2. Which part of the British government was responsible for writing the Stamp Act?

   a. "British colonies and plantations"
   b. "the commons of Great Britain in parliament"
   c. "the King's most excellent majesty"
   d. "the lords spiritual and temporal"

3. Which of the following statements about the Stamp Act is probably **not** true?

   a. It was the first tax act passed on the colonies.
   b. It was intended to raise money from the colonies.
   c. The money was used to pay for the colonies' defense.
   d. The act had to be approved by the king.

4. The first tax listed in the Stamp Act of three pence was placed on all

   a. newspapers.
   b. parchments.
   c. letters.
   d. legal documents.

5. The tax on any printed copy of a document was

   a. three pence.
   b. one shilling.
   c. one penny.
   d. four pence.

6. The total tax on a pamphlet that contained six pages would be

   a. one shilling.
   b. six shillings.
   c. three pence.
   d. six pence.

7. Which of the following statements about newspaper owners was probably **true**?

   a. They had to charge more for ads to pay the new taxes.
   b. They did not charge for printing advertisements.
   c. They were not affected by the Stamp Act.
   d. They approved of the Stamp Act.

8. For which "almanack or calendar" would the taxes be lowest?

   a. several years printed on many pages
   b. a single year printed on two pages
   c. one printed on vellum or parchment
   d. a single year printed on one page

9. Taxes would be highest on an "almanack or calendar" printed

   a. on one side of vellum.
   b. in French or Spanish.
   c. to cover several years.
   d. on two sides of paper parchment.

10. Part III of the Stamp Act prohibited colonists from

   a. getting insurance for ocean voyages.
   b. buying insurance from companies in Great Britain
   c. paying more than one hundred pounds for insurance.
   d. insuring more than one ship for one ocean voyage.

11. Why would colonists who owned businesses be among the people who would have had the strongest objections to the Stamp Act?

The Declaration of Independence (1776)

Acting under the instruction of the Virginia Convention, Richard Henry Lee on June 7, 1776, introduced a resolution in the Second Continental Congress proposing independence for the colonies. The Lee Resolution contained three parts: a declaration of independence, a call to form foreign alliances, and "a plan for confederation."

On June 11, 1776, the Congress appointed three concurrent committees in response to the Lee Resolution.

Because many members of the Congress believed action such as Lee proposed to be premature or wanted instructions from their colonies before voting, approval was deferred until July 2nd. On that date, Congress adopted the first part (the declaration). New York cast no vote until the newly elected New York Convention upheld the Declaration of Independence on July 9, 1776.

The plan for making treaties was not approved until September 1776; the plan of confederation was delayed until November 1777.

Resolution introduced in the Continental Congress by Richard Henry Lee (Virginia) proposing a Declaration of Independence, June 7, 1776

Resolved, That these United Colonies are, and of right ought to be, free and independent States, that they are absolved from all allegiance to the British Crown, and that all political connection between them and the State of Great Britain is, and ought to be, totally dissolved.

That it is expedient forthwith to take the most effectual measures for forming foreign Alliances.

That a plan of confederation be prepared and transmitted to the respective Colonies for their consideration and approbation.

The Declaration of Independence (1776)

When in the course of human events, it becomes necessary for one people to dissolve the political bands which have connected them with another, and to assume the Powers of the earth, the separate and equal station to which the Laws of Nature and of Nature's God entitle them, a decent respect to the opinions of mankind requires that they should declare the causes which impel them to the separation.

We hold these truths to be self-evident, that all men are created equal, that they are endowed by their Creator with certain unalienable rights, that among these are Life, Liberty, and the pursuit of Happiness. That to secure these rights, Governments are instituted among Men, deriving their just powers from the consent of the governed. That whenever any Form of Government becomes destructive of these ends, it is the Right of the People to alter or to abolish it, and to institute new Government, laying its foundation on such principles and organizing its powers in such form, as to them shall seem most likely to effect their Safety and Happiness. Prudence, indeed, will dictate that Governments long established should not be changed for light and transient causes; and accordingly all experience hath shown, that mankind are more disposed to suffer, while evils are sufferable, than to right themselves by abolishing the forms to which they are accustomed. But when a long train of abuses and usurpations, pursuing invariably the same Object evinces a design to reduce them under absolute Despotism, it is their right, it is their duty, to throw off such Government, and to provide new Guards for their future security.—Such has been the patient sufferance of these Colonies; and such is now the necessity which constrains them to alter their former Systems of Government. The history of the present King of Great Britain is a history of repeated injuries and usurpations, all having in direct object the establishment of an absolute Tyranny over these States. To prove this, let Facts be submitted to a candid world. He has refused his Assent to Laws, the most wholesome and necessary for the public good.

He has forbidden his Governors to pass Laws of immediate and pressing importance, unless suspended in their operation till his Assent should be obtained; and when so suspended, he has utterly neglected to attend to them.

He has refused to pass other Laws for the accommodation of large districts of people, unless those people would relinquish the right of Representation in the Legislature, a right inestimable to them and formidable to tyrants only.

He has called together legislative bodies at places unusual, uncomfortable and distant from the depository of their public Records, for the sole purpose of fatiguing them into compliance with his measures.

He has dissolved Representative Houses repeatedly, for opposing with manly firmness his invasions on the rights of the people.

He has refused for a long time, after such dissolutions, to cause others to be elected; whereby the Legislative powers, incapable of Annihilation, have returned to the People at large for their exercise; the State remaining in the mean time exposed to all dangers of invasion from without, and convulsions within.

He has endeavoured to prevent the population of these States; for that purpose obstructing the Laws of Naturalization of Foreigners; refusing to pass others to encourage their migrations hither, and raising the conditions of new Appropriations of Lands.

He has obstructed the Administration of Justice, by refusing his Assent to Laws for establishing Judiciary powers.

He has made Judges dependent on his Will alone, for the tenure of their offices, and the amount and payment of their salaries. He has erected a multitude of New Offices, and sent hither swarms of Officers to harass our People, and eat out their substance. He has kept among us, in times of peace, Standing Armies without the Consent of our legislature.

He has affected to render the Military independent of and superior to the Civil Power.

He has combined with others to subject us to a jurisdiction foreign to our constitution, and unacknowledged by our laws; giving his Assent to their Acts of pretended Legislation:

For quartering large bodies of armed troops among us:

For protecting them, by a mock Trial, from Punishment for any Murders which they should commit on the Inhabitants of these States: For cutting off our Trade with all parts of the world:

For imposing taxes on us without our Consent:

For depriving us of many cases, of the benefits of Trial by Jury: For transporting us beyond Seas to be tried for pretended offences:

For abolishing the free System of English Laws in a neighbouring Province, establishing therein an Arbitrary government, and enlarging its Boundaries so as to render it at once an example and fit instrument for introducing the same absolute rule into these Colonies:

For taking away our Charters, abolishing our most valuable Laws, and altering fundamentally the Forms of our Governments: For suspending our own Legislatures, and declaring themselves invested with Power to legislate for us in all cases whatsoever. He has abdicated Government here, by declaring us out of his Protection and waging War against us.

He has plundered our seas, ravaged our Coasts, burnt our towns, and destroyed the lives of our people.

He is at this time transporting large armies of foreign mercenaries to compleat the works of death, desolation, and tyranny, already begun with circumstances of Cruelty & perfidy scarcely paralleled in the most barbarous ages, and totally unworthy the Head of a civilized nation.

He has constrained our fellow Citizens taken Captive on the high Seas to bear Arms against their Country, to become the executioners of their friends and Brethren, or to fall themselves by their Hands.

He has excited domestic insurrections amongst us, and has endeavoured to bring on the inhabitants of our frontiers, the merciless Indian savages, whose known rule of warfare, is an undistinguished destruction of all ages, sexes, and conditions.

In every stage of these Oppressions We have Petitioned for Redress in the most humble terms: Our repeated Petitions have been answered only by repeated injury. A Prince, whose character is thus marked by every act which may define a Tyrant, is unfit to be the ruler of a free people.

Nor have We been wanting in attention to our British brethren. We have warned them from time to time of attempts by their legislature to extend an unwarrantable jurisdiction over us. We have reminded them of the circumstances of our emigration and settlement here. We have appealed to their native justice and magnanimity, and we have conjured them by the ties of our common kindred to disavow these usurpations, which, would inevitably interrupt our connections and correspondence. They too must have been deaf to the voice of justice and of consanguinity. We must, therefore, acquiesce in the necessity, which denounces our Separation, and hold them, as we hold the rest of mankind, Enemies in War, in Peace Friends.

We, therefore, the Representatives of the United States of America, in General Congress, Assembled, appealing to the Supreme Judge of the world for the rectitude of our intentions, do, in the Name, and by Authority of the good People of these Colonies, solemnly publish and declare, That these United Colonies are, and of Right ought to be free and independent states; that they are Absolved from all Allegiance to the British Crown, and that all political connection between them and the State of Great Britain, is and ought to be totally dissolved; and that as Free and Independent States, they have full Power to levy War, conclude Peace, contract Alliances, establish Commerce, and to do all other Acts and Things which Independent States may of right do. And for the support of this Declaration, with a firm reliance on the Protection of Divine Providence, we mutually pledge to each other our Lives, our Fortunes, and our sacred Honor.

1. The authors' purpose in the first paragraph of the Declaration of Independence is to

   a. list the complaints that colonists have against the king.
   b. explain the reasons for issuing the declaration.
   c. declare war against Great Britain.
   d. explain the new form of government in the colonies

2. According to the authors of the declaration, when people are ruled by an abusive government, they generally

   a. suffer rather than revolt.
   b. revolt rather than suffer.
   c. are unaware of the abuse.
   d. complain to the leaders of the government.

3. The authors of the declaration most likely listed the offenses of the king because

   a. few colonists understood what the king had done.
   b. the king was going to be put on trial for his offenses.
   c. they were the specific reasons for declaring independence.
   d. the king was unaware of the way he had treated the colonists.

4. The word, "usurpations," appears several times in the declaration. "Usurpations" are most likely actions that occur when

   a. people refuse to obey the laws of a ruler.
   b. a ruler takes away the rights of the people.
   c. one nation declares war on another nation.
   d. a ruler gives up some of his power to his subjects.

5. The declaration states that "Governments" derive "their just powers from the consent of the governed." Why would that have been a revolutionary idea at the time? How would King George III most likely have reacted to that statement?

6. What two phrases in the final section of the Declaration are used to refer to an absolute power that might be called God? In what context are the terms used?

7. Perhaps the most famous phrase from the Declaration of Independence is: " . . . all men are created equal . . . " In what ways was that statement flawed at the time it was written? Do you think it is flawed today? Support your answer.

"The American Crisis" (1777)
by Thomas Paine

THESE are the times that try men's souls. The summer soldier and the sunshine patriot will, in this crisis, shrink from the service of their country; but he that stands it now, deserves the love and thanks of man and woman. Tyranny, like hell, is not easily conquered; yet we have this consolation with us, that the harder the conflict, the more glorious the triumph. What we obtain too cheap, we esteem too lightly: it is dearness only that gives every thing its value. Heaven knows how to put a proper price upon its goods; and it would be strange indeed if so celestial an article as FREEDOM should not be highly rated. Britain, with an army to enforce her tyranny, has declared that she has a right (not only to TAX) but "to BIND us in ALL CASES WHATSOEVER," and if being bound in that manner, is not slavery, then is there not such a thing as slavery upon earth. Even the expression is impious; for so unlimited a power can belong only to God.

Whether the independence of the continent was declared too soon, or delayed too long, I will not now enter into as an argument; my own simple opinion is, that had it been eight months earlier, it would have been much better. We did not make a proper use of last winter, neither could we, while we were in a dependent state. However, the fault, if it were one, was all our own; we have none to blame but ourselves. But no great deal is lost yet. All that Howe has been doing for this month past, is rather a ravage than a conquest, which the spirit of the Jerseys, a year ago, would have quickly repulsed, and which time and a little resolution will soon recover.

I have as little superstition in me as any man living, but my secret opinion has ever been, and still is, that God Almighty will not give up a people to military destruction, or leave them unsupportedly to perish, who have so earnestly and so repeatedly sought to avoid the calamities of war, by every decent method which wisdom could invent. Neither have I so much of the infidel in me, as to suppose that He has relinquished the government of the world, and given us up to the care of devils; and as I do not, I cannot see on what grounds the king of Britain can look up to heaven for help against us: a common murderer, a highwayman, or a house-breaker, has as good a pretence as he.

'Tis surprising to see how rapidly a panic will sometimes run through a country. All nations and ages have been subject to them. Britain has trembled like an ague at the report of a French fleet of flat-bottomed boats; and in the fourteenth [fifteenth] century the whole English army, after ravaging the kingdom of France, was driven back like men petrified with fear; and this brave exploit was performed by a few broken forces collected and headed by a woman, Joan of Arc. Would that heaven might inspire some Jersey maid to spirit up her countrymen, and save her fair fellow sufferers from ravage and ravishment! Yet panics, in some cases, have their uses; they produce as much good as hurt. Their duration is always short; the mind soon grows through them, and acquires a firmer habit than before. But their peculiar advantage is, that they are the touchstones of sincerity and hypocrisy, and bring things and men to light, which might otherwise have lain forever undiscovered. In fact, they have the same effect on secret traitors, which an imaginary apparition would have upon a private murderer. They sift out the hidden thoughts of man, and hold them up in public to the world. Many a disguised Tory has lately shown his head, that shall penitentially solemnize with curses the day on which Howe arrived upon the Delaware.

As I was with the troops at Fort Lee, and marched with them to the edge of Pennsylvania, I am well acquainted with many circumstances, which those who live at a distance know but little or nothing of. Our situation there was exceedingly cramped, the place being a narrow neck of land between the North River and the Hackensack. Our force was inconsiderable, being not one-fourth so great as Howe could bring against us. We had no army at hand to have relieved the garrison, had we shut ourselves up and stood on our defence. Our ammunition, light artillery, and the best part of our stores, had been removed, on the apprehension that Howe would endeavor to penetrate the Jerseys, in which case Fort Lee could be of no use to us; for it must occur to every thinking man, whether in the army or not, that these kind of field forts are only for temporary purposes, and last in use no longer than the enemy directs his force against the particular object which such forts are raised to defend. Such was our situation and condition at Fort Lee on the morning of the 20th of November, when an officer arrived with information that the enemy with 200 boats had landed about seven miles above; Major General [Nathaniel] Green, who commanded the garrison, immediately ordered them under arms, and sent express to General Washington at the town of Hackensack, distant by the way of the ferry = six miles. Our first object was to secure the bridge over the Hackensack, which laid up the river between the enemy and us, about six miles from us, and three from them. General Washington arrived in about three-quarters of an hour, and marched at the head of the troops towards the bridge, which place I expected we should have a brush for; however, they did not choose to dispute it with us, and the greatest part of our troops went over the bridge, the rest over the ferry, except some which passed at a mill on a small creek, between the bridge and the ferry, and made their way through some marshy grounds up to the town of Hackensack, and there passed the river. We brought off as much baggage as the wagons could contain, the rest was lost. The simple object was to bring off the garrison, and march them on till they could be strengthened by the Jersey or Pennsylvania militia, so as to be enabled to make a stand. We staid four days at Newark, collected our out-posts with some of the Jersey militia, and marched out twice to meet the enemy, on being informed that they were advancing, though our numbers were greatly inferior to theirs. Howe, in my little opinion, committed a great error in generalship in not throwing a body of forces off from Staten Island through Amboy, by which means he might have seized all our stores at Brunswick, and intercepted our march into Pennsylvania; but if we believe the power of hell to be limited, we must likewise believe that their agents are under some providential control.

I shall not now attempt to give all the particulars of our retreat to the Delaware; suffice it for the present to say, that both officers and men, though greatly harassed and fatigued, frequently without rest, covering, or provision, the inevitable consequences of a long retreat, bore it with a manly and martial spirit. All their wishes centered in one, which was, that the country would turn out and help them to drive the enemy back. Voltaire has remarked that King William never appeared to full advantage but in difficulties and in action; the same remark may be made on General Washington, for the character fits him. There is a natural firmness in some minds which cannot be unlocked by trifles, but which, when unlocked, discovers a cabinet of fortitude; and I reckon it among those kind of public blessings, which we do not immediately see, that God hath blessed him with uninterrupted health, and given him a mind that can even flourish upon care.

I shall conclude this paper with some miscellaneous remarks on the state of our affairs; and shall begin with asking the following question, Why is it that the enemy have left the New England provinces, and made these middle ones the seat of war? The answer is easy: New England is not infested with Tories, and we are. I have been tender in raising the cry against these men, and used numberless arguments to show them their danger, but it will not do to sacrifice a world either to their folly or their baseness. The period is now arrived, in which either they or we must change our sentiments, or one or both must fall. And what is a Tory? Good God! what is he? I should not be afraid to go with a hundred Whigs against a thousand Tories, were they to attempt to get into arms. Every Tory is a coward; for servile, slavish, self-interested fear is the foundation of Toryism; and a man under such influence, though he may be cruel, never can be brave.

But, before the line of irrecoverable separation be drawn between us, let us reason the matter together: Your conduct is an invitation to the enemy, yet not one in a thousand of you has heart enough to join him. Howe is as much deceived by you as the American cause is injured by you. He expects you will all take up arms, and flock to his standard, with muskets on your shoulders. Your opinions are of no use to him, unless you support him personally, for 'tis soldiers, and not Tories, that he wants.

I once felt all that kind of anger, which a man ought to feel, against the mean principles that are held by the Tories: a noted one, who kept a tavern at Amboy, was standing at his door, with as pretty a child in his hand, about eight or nine years old, as I ever saw, and after speaking his mind as freely as he thought was prudent, finished with this unfatherly expression, "Well! give me peace in my day." Not a man lives on the continent but fully believes that a separation must some time or other finally take place, and a generous parent should have said, "If there must be trouble, let it be in my day, that my child may have peace;" and this single reflection, well applied, is sufficient to awaken every man to duty. Not a place upon earth might be so happy as America. Her situation is remote from all the wrangling world, and she has nothing to do but to trade with them. A man can distinguish himself between temper and principle, and I am as confident, as I am that God governs the world, that America will never be happy till she gets clear of foreign dominion. Wars, without ceasing, will break out till that period arrives, and the continent must in the end be conqueror; for though the flame of liberty may sometimes cease to shine, the coal can never expire.

America did not, nor does not want force; but she wanted a proper application of that force. Wisdom is not the purchase of a day, and it is no wonder that we should err at the first setting off. From an excess of tenderness, we were unwilling to raise an army, and trusted our cause to the temporary defence of a well-meaning militia. A summer's experience has now taught us better; yet with those troops, while they were collected, we were able to set bounds to the progress of the enemy, and, thank God! they are again assembling. I always considered militia as the best troops in the world for a sudden exertion, but they will not do for a long campaign. Howe, it is probable, will make an attempt on this city [Philadelphia]; should he fail on this side the Delaware, he is ruined. If he succeeds, our cause is not ruined. He stakes all on his side against a part on ours; admitting he succeeds, the consequence will be, that armies from both ends of the continent will march to assist their suffering friends in the middle states; for he cannot go everywhere, it is impossible. I consider Howe as the greatest enemy the Tories have; he is bringing a war into their country, which, had it not been for him and partly for themselves, they had been clear of. Should he now be expelled, I wish with all the devotion of a Christian, that the names of Whig and Tory may never more be mentioned; but should the Tories give him encouragement to come, or assistance if he come, I as sincerely wish that our next year's arms may expel them from the continent, and the Congress appropriate their possessions to the relief of those who have suffered in well-doing. A single successful battle next year will settle the whole. America could carry on a two years' war by the confiscation of the property of disaffected persons, and be made happy by their expulsion. Say not that this is revenge, call it rather the soft resentment of a suffering people, who, having no object in view but the good of all, have staked their own all upon a seemingly doubtful event. Yet it is folly to argue against determined hardness; eloquence may strike the ear, and the language of sorrow draw forth the tear of compassion, but nothing can reach the heart that is steeled with prejudice.

COMMON SENSE.

December 23, 1776.

1. Paine uses the phrase, "summer soldier and sunshine patriot," to describe a person who

   a. remains loyal to Great Britain.
   b. is from the southern colonies.
   c. does not want to fight hard for freedom.
   d. will not fight in bad weather.

2. Paine describes fighting that has taken place in

   a. New England.
   b. New York.
   c. New Jersey.
   d. Philadelphia.

3. Paine is writing at a time when the American army

   a. has forced the British army to retreat.
   b. has been retreating from the British army.
   c. has marched to New England.
   d. has rebelled against George Washington.

4. Paine compares King George III to

   a. "a common murderer."
   b. "Joan of Arc."
   c. "George Washington."
   d. "King William."

5. Paine expresses gratitude that ________ has been blessed with "uninterrupted health."

   a. General Howe
   b. King George III
   c. the "summer solder"
   d. George Washington

6. The people Paine labels as "Tories" are most likely

   a. colonists who supported the American army.
   b. regular soldiers in the British army.
   c. members of the colonial militia.
   d. colonists who remained loyal to King George III.

7. Paine believes that a militia is

   a. the only force colonists need to fight the British.
   b. not trained well enough to fight the British.
   c. filled with men who do not want to fight.
   d. best-suited for a lengthy war.

8. What does Paine believe should happen to Tories once the British have been defeated?

9. Why does Paine call his document "The American Crisis"? What was Paine's purpose in writing this document?

The Virginia Statute for Religious Freedom (1786)

In Virginia, the American Revolution led to the disestablishment of the Anglican Church, which had been tied closely to the royal government. Then the question arose as to whether the new state should continue to impose taxes to be used for the support of all recognized churches. The proposal had a number of supporters who, even if they no longer accepted an established church, still believed that religion should be supported by the public purse.

For some Virginians, however, imposing religion on people smacked of tyranny. Thomas Jefferson and James Madison, both of whom would later be presidents of the United States, argued that religious beliefs should be solely matters of individual conscience and completely immune from any interference by the state. Moreover, religious activity of any sort should be wholly voluntary. Not only did they oppose taxing people to support an established church, but they also objected to forcing people to pay taxes even for their own church. To Jefferson, a high wall of separation should always keep church and state apart.

Jefferson drafted the following measure, but it was Madison who skillfully secured its adoption by the Virginia legislature in 1786. It is still part of modern Virginia's constitution, and it has not only been copied by other states but was also the basis for the Religion Clauses in the Constitution's Bill of Rights. Both men considered this bill one of the great achievements of their lives, and Jefferson directed that on his tombstone he should not be remembered as president of the United States or for any of the other high offices he held, but as the author of the Declaration of Independence and the Virginia Statute for Religious Freedom, and as the founder of the University of Virginia.

Whereas Almighty God hath created the mind free; that all attempts to influence it by temporal punishments or burthens, or by civil incapacitations, tend only to beget habits of hypocrisy and meanness, and are a departure from the plan of the Holy author of our religion, who being Lord both of body and mind, yet chose not to propagate it by coercions on either, as it was in his Almighty power to do; that the impious presumption of legislators and rulers, civil as well as ecclesiastical, who being themselves but fallible and uninspired men, have assumed dominion over the faith of others, setting up their own opinions and modes of thinking as the only true and infallible, and as such endeavouring to impose them on others, hath established and maintained false religions over the greatest part of the world, and through all time; that to compel a man to furnish contributions of money for the propagation of opinions which he disbelieves, is sinful and tyrannical; that even the forcing him to support this or that teacher of his own religious persuasion, is depriving him of the comfortable liberty of giving his contributions to the particular pastor, whose morals he would make his pattern, and whose powers he feels most persuasive to righteousness, and is withdrawing from the ministry those temporary rewards, which proceeding from an approbation of their personal conduct, are an additional incitement to earnest and unremitting labours for the instruction of mankind; that our civil rights have no dependence on our religious opinions, any more than our opinions in physics or geometry; that therefore the proscribing any citizen as unworthy the public confidence by laying upon him an incapacity of being called to offices of trust and emolument, unless he profess or renounce this or that religious opinion, is depriving him injuriously of those privileges and advantages to which in common with his fellow-citizens he has a natural right; that it tends only to corrupt the principles of that religion it is meant to encourage, by bribing with a monopoly of worldly honours and emoluments, those who will externally profess and conform to it; that though indeed these are criminal who do not withstand such temptation, yet neither are those innocent who lay the bait in their way; that to suffer the civil magistrate to intrude his powers into the field of opinion, and to restrain the profession or propagation of principles on supposition of their ill tendency, is a dangerous fallacy, which at once destroys all religious liberty, because he being of course judge of that tendency will make his opinions the rule of judgment, and approve or condemn the sentiments of others only as they shall square with or differ from his own; that it is time enough for the rightful purposes of civil government, for its officers to interfere when principles break out into overt acts against peace and good order; and finally, that truth is great and will prevail if left to herself, that she is the proper and sufficient antagonist to error, and has nothing to fear from the conflict, unless by human interposition disarmed of her natural weapons, free argument and debate, errors ceasing to be dangerous when it is permitted freely to contradict them:

Be it enacted by the General Assembly, That no man shall be compelled to frequent or support any religious worship, place, or ministry whatsoever, nor shall be enforced, restrained, molested, or burthened in his body or goods, nor shall otherwise suffer on account of his religious opinions or belief; but that all men shall be free to profess, and by argument to maintain, their opinion in matters of religion, and that the same shall in no wise diminish enlarge, or affect their civil capacities.

And though we well know that this assembly elected by the people for the ordinary purposes of legislation only, have no power to restrain the acts of succeeding assemblies, constituted with powers equal to our own, and that therefore to declare this act to be irrevocable would be of no effect in law; yet we are free to declare, and do declare, that the rights hereby asserted are of the natural rights of mankind, and that if any act shall be hereafter passed to repeal the present, or to narrow its operation, such act shall be an infringement of natural right.

1. The phrase, "civil incapacitations," most likely means

   a. legal punishment.
   b. widespread disease.
   c. community effort.
   d. religious persecution.

2. The word that **best** describes Jefferson's opinion of the people he refers to as "legislators" is

   a. religious.
   b. free.
   c. hypocritical.
   d. criminal.

3. Which of the following statements about Jefferson's religious views is probably **true**?

   a. God exists only in the minds of people.
   b. All colonists should belong to the same church.
   c. All legislators must follow the same religion.
   d. God does not favor one religion over another.

4. Which of the following statements about the period during which Jefferson wrote this document is probably **not** true?

   a. People attended church on a regular basis.
   b. People were judged by their religious opinions.
   c. People did not believe that the government should support churches.
   d. People voted for legislators based on their religious beliefs.

5. In the final section of the document, Jefferson declared that future legislators

   a. have no powers to revoke the act.
   b. can revoke the act but not the principles expressed.
   c. should establish a state religion.
   d. will need to raise taxes on religions institutions.

6. Write a summary of the actual law that is stated in paragraph two of this document.

7. What does Jefferson mean by the phrase, “natural rights”? How do “natural rights” differ from “civil rights”? Give examples in your answer.

The Articles of Confederation (1777–1781)

The Articles of Confederation were a "firm league of friendship" among 13 semi-independent States, and did not provide for a truly sovereign national Government. The principal governmental body was a single-house Congress, in which each State held one vote. No independent executive, to carry out the laws, or autonomous court system, to administer the legal and judicial system or to adjudicate disputes between the Federal Government and the States, were provided. The approval of a minimum of seven States, who elected and paid their delegates, was required for any legislation; "nine, to wage war or pass certain other measures"; and all 13, to alter or amend the Articles themselves. The Continental Congress was empowered to declare and wage war, raise an Army and Navy, make treaties and alliances, appoint and receive ambassadors, decide interstate disputes, negotiate loans, emit bills of credit, coin money, regulate weights and measures, manage Native American affairs, and operate a system of interstate post offices.

Severely inhibiting the effectiveness of Congress in carrying out its prerogatives, however, were three major limitations. One was the lack of a most basic governmental power: the right to levy taxes, which would provide an independent source of revenue. Instead, Congress could only requisition, or request, money from the States and could not enforce payment. Suffering from the economic depression and saddled with their own war debts, they furnished only a small part of the money sought from them.

The second serious congressional deficiency was absence of authority to regulate interstate and foreign commerce. The States negotiated separately with foreign powers on commercial matters to the detriment of the overall economy. And, when two states disagreed about trade matters, they dealt directly with each other much like countries did. Fortunately, to facilitate the conduct of legal business, at least the States had agreed to the mutual recognition of official acts.

Thirdly, the Continental Congress could not properly exercise its treaty power because of the autonomy of the states. Their independent conduct of foreign relations and Native American policy not only hampered Congress in its dealings with other nations but also sometimes even jeopardized national security.

The Continental Congress had led the nation through the War for Independence, and in the Ordinances of 1784 and 1785 had established a plan to advance westward expansion by the addition of new States to the Confederation. But in financial matters, foreign affairs, national defense, mediation of interstate disputes, and protecting American sovereignty in the West it was less successful. After the war, the ramifications of political, social, and economic readjustment caught up with it. People blamed it for the failure to solve problems that would have tried stronger governments. The deficiencies of Congress were real, however. By 1787, even its defenders recognized that it had fallen upon evil times.

Financially, the situation was chaotic. Congress could not pay its war debts, foreign or domestic, or meet current obligations. The private financial system of the country was feeble, and the nation lacked a stable and uniform currency. The central government was virtually powerless to correct the conditions.

Because much of the debt—federal, state, and private—was owed to foreign lenders, the future of the United States in international commerce was precarious. A nation that does not pay its debts cannot command respect from other countries. Furthermore, prosperity depended on trade with Europe and the Caribbean colonies, but Congress could not conclude suitable commercial treaties.

Foreign affairs were another area where the Continental Congress had failed. Other nations showed contempt for the United States. Many of them questioned the stability or even the continued existence of the Confederation. One British official remarked that it would be better to make 13 separate treaties with the individual States than to deal with the Continental Congress. American diplomats, whose efforts were hamstrung by the lack of a central authority that could formulate a unified foreign policy, made slight impress in world capitals.

To all to whom these Presents shall come, we the undersigned Delegates of the States affixed to our Names send greeting.

Articles of Confederation and perpetual Union between the states of New Hampshire, Massachusetts-bay Rhode Island and Providence Plantations, Connecticut, New York, New Jersey, Pennsylvania, Delaware, Maryland, Virginia, North Carolina, South Carolina and Georgia.

I. The Stile of this Confederacy shall be

"The United States of America".

II. Each state retains its sovereignty, freedom, and independence, and every power, jurisdiction, and right, which is not by this Confederation expressly delegated to the United States, in Congress assembled.

III. The said States hereby severally enter into a firm league of friendship with each other, for their common defense, the security of their liberties, and their mutual and general welfare, binding themselves to assist each other, against all force offered to, or attacks made upon them, or any of them, on account of religion, sovereignty, trade, or any other pretense whatever.

IV. The better to secure and perpetuate mutual friendship and intercourse among the people of the different States in this Union, the free inhabitants of each of these States, paupers, vagabonds, and fugitives from justice excepted, shall be entitled to all privileges and immunities of free citizens in the several States; and the people of each State shall [have] free ingress and regress to and from any other State, and shall enjoy therein all the privileges of trade and commerce, subject to the same duties, impositions, and restrictions as the inhabitants thereof respectively, provided that such restrictions shall not extend so far as to prevent the removal of property imported into any State, to any other State, of which the owner is an inhabitant; provided also that no imposition, duties or restriction shall be laid by any State, on the property of the United States, or either of them.

If any person guilty of, or charged with, treason, felony, or other high misdemeanor in any State, shall flee from justice, and be found in any of the United States, he shall, upon demand of the Governor or executive power of the State from which he fled, be delivered up and removed to the State having jurisdiction of his offense.

Full faith and credit shall be given in each of these States to the records, acts, and judicial proceedings of the courts and magistrates of every other State.

V. For the most convenient management of the general interests of the United States, delegates shall be annually appointed in such manner as the legislatures of each State shall direct, to meet in Congress on the first Monday in November, in every year, with a power reserved to each State to recall its delegates, or any of them, at any time within the year, and to send others in their stead for the remainder of the year.

No State shall be represented in Congress by less than two, nor more than seven members; and no person shall be capable of being a delegate for more than three years in any term of six years; nor shall any person, being a delegate, be capable of holding any office under the United States, for which he, or another for his benefit, receives any salary, fees or emolument of any kind.

Each State shall maintain its own delegates in a meeting of the States, and while they act as members of the committee of the States.

In determining questions in the United States in Congress assembled, each State shall have one vote.

Freedom of speech and debate in Congress shall not be impeached or questioned in any court or place out of Congress, and the members of Congress shall be protected in their persons from arrests or imprisonments, during the time of their going to and from, and attendence on Congress, except for treason, felony, or breach of the peace.

VI. No State, without the consent of the United States in Congress assembled, shall send any embassy to, or receive any embassy from, or enter into any conference, agreement, alliance or treaty with any King, Prince or State; nor shall any person holding any office of profit or trust under the United States, or any of them, accept any present, emolument, office or title of any kind whatever from any King, Prince or foreign State; nor shall the United States in Congress assembled, or any of them, grant any title of nobility.

No two or more States shall enter into any treaty, confederation or alliance whatever between them, without the consent of the United States in Congress assembled, specifying accurately the purposes for which the same is to be entered into, and how long it shall continue.

No State shall lay any imposts or duties, which may interfere with any stipulations in treaties, entered into by the United States in Congress assembled, with any King, Prince or State, in pursuance of any treaties already proposed by Congress, to the courts of France and Spain.

No vessel of war shall be kept up in time of peace by any State, except such number only, as shall be deemed necessary by the United States in Congress assembled, for the defense of such State, or its trade; nor shall any body of forces be kept up by any State in time of peace, except such number only, as in the judgement of the United States in Congress assembled, shall be deemed requisite to garrison the forts necessary for the defense of such State; but every State shall always keep up a well-regulated and disciplined militia, sufficiently armed and accoutered, and shall provide and constantly have ready for use, in public stores, a due number of filed pieces and tents, and a proper quantity of arms, ammunition and camp equipage.

No State shall engage in any war without the consent of the United States in Congress assembled, unless such State be actually invaded by enemies, or shall have received certain advice of a resolution being formed by some nation of Indians to invade such State, and the danger is so imminent as not to admit of a delay till the United States in Congress assembled can be consulted; nor shall any State grant commissions to any ships or vessels of war, nor letters of marque or reprisal, except it be after a declaration of war by the United States in Congress assembled, and then only against the Kingdom or State and the subjects thereof, against which war has been so declared, and under such regulations as shall be established by the United States in Congress assembled, unless such State be infested by pirates, in which case vessels of war may be fitted out for that occasion, and kept so long as the danger shall continue, or until the United States in Congress assembled shall determine otherwise.

VII. When land forces are raised by any State for the common defense, all officers of or under the rank of colonel, shall be appointed by the legislature of each State respectively, by whom such forces shall be raised, or in such manner as such State shall direct, and all vacancies shall be filled up by the State which first made the appointment.

VIII. All charges of war, and all other expenses that shall be incurred for the common defense or general welfare, and allowed by the United States in Congress assembled, shall be defrayed out of a common treasury, which shall be supplied by the several States in proportion to the value of all land within each State, granted or surveyed for any person, as such land and the buildings and improvements thereon shall be estimated according to such mode as the United States in Congress assembled, shall from time to time direct and appoint.

The taxes for paying that proportion shall be laid and levied by the authority and direction of the legislatures of the several States within the time agreed upon by the United States in Congress assembled.

IX. The United States in Congress assembled, shall have the sole and exclusive right and power of determining on peace and war, except in the cases mentioned in the sixth article—of sending and receiving ambassadors—entering into treaties and alliances, provided that no treaty of commerce shall be made whereby the legislative power of the respective States shall be restrained from imposing such imposts and duties on foreigners, as their own people are subjected to, or from prohibiting the exportation or importation of any species of goods or commodities whatsoever—of establishing rules for deciding in all cases, what captures on land or water shall be legal, and in what manner prizes taken by land or naval forces in the service of the United States shall be divided or appropriated—of granting letters of marque and reprisal in times of peace—appointing courts for the trial of piracies and felonies commited on the high seas and establishing courts for receiving and determining finally appeals in all cases of captures, provided that no member of Congress shall be appointed a judge of any of the said courts.

The United States in Congress assembled shall also be the last resort on appeal in all disputes and differences now subsisting or that hereafter may arise between two or more States concerning boundary, jurisdiction or any other causes whatever; which authority shall always be exercised in the manner following. Whenever the legislative or executive authority or lawful agent of any State in controversy with another shall present a petition to Congress stating the matter in question and praying for a hearing, notice thereof shall be given by order of Congress to the legislative or executive authority of the other State in controversy, and a day assigned for the appearance of the parties by their lawful agents, who shall then be directed to appoint by joint consent, commissioners or judges to constitute a court for hearing and determining the matter in question: but if they cannot agree, Congress shall name three persons out of each of the United States, and from the list of such persons each party shall alternately strike out one, the petitioners beginning, until the number shall be reduced to thirteen; and from that number not less than seven, nor more than nine names as Congress shall direct, shall in the presence of Congress be drawn out by lot, and the persons whose names shall be so drawn or any five of them, shall be commissioners or judges, to hear and finally determine the controversy, so always as a major part of the judges who shall hear the cause shall agree in the determination: and if either party shall neglect to attend at the day appointed, without showing reasons, which Congress shall judge sufficient, or being present shall refuse to strike, the Congress shall proceed to nominate three persons out of each State, and the secretary of Congress shall strike in behalf of such party absent or refusing; and the judgement and sentence of the court to be appointed, in the manner before prescribed, shall be final and conclusive;

and if any of the parties shall refuse to submit to the authority of such court, or to appear or defend their claim or cause, the court shall nevertheless proceed to pronounce sentence, or judgement, which shall in like manner be final and decisive, the judgement or sentence and other proceedings being in either case transmitted to Congress, and lodged among the acts of Congress for the security of the parties concerned: provided that every commissioner, before he sits in judgement, shall take an oath to be administered by one of the judges of the supreme or superior court of the State, where the cause shall be tried, 'well and truly to hear and determine the matter in question, according to the best of his judgement, without favor, affection or hope of reward': provided also, that no State shall be deprived of territory for the benefit of the United States.

All controversies concerning the private right of soil claimed under different grants of two or more States, whose jurisdictions as they may respect such lands, and the States which passed such grants are adjusted, the said grants or either of them being at the same time claimed to have originated antecedent to such settlement of jurisdiction, shall on the petition of either party to the Congress of the United States, be finally determined as near as may be in the same manner as is before presecribed for deciding disputes respecting territorial jurisdiction between different States.

The United States in Congress assembled shall also have the sole and exclusive right and power of regulating the alloy and value of coin struck by their own authority, or by that of the respective States—fixing the standards of weights and measures throughout the United States—regulating the trade and managing all affairs with the Indians, not members of any of the States, provided that the legislative right of any State within its own limits be not infringed or violated—establishing or regulating post offices from one State to another, throughout all the United States, and exacting such postage on the papers passing through the same as may be requisite to defray the expenses of the said office—appointing all officers of the land forces, in the service of the United States, excepting regimental officers—appointing all the officers of the naval forces, and commissioning all officers whatever in the service of the United States—making rules for the government and regulation of the said land and naval forces, and directing their operations.

The United States in Congress assembled shall have authority to appoint a committee, to sit in the recess of Congress, to be denominated 'A Committee of the States', and to consist of one delegate from each State; and to appoint such other committees and civil officers as may be necessary for managing the general affairs of the United States under their direction—to appoint one of their members to preside, provided that no person be allowed to serve in the office of president more than one year in any term of three years; to ascertain the necessary sums of money to be raised for the service of the United States, and to appropriate and apply the same for defraying the public expenses—to borrow money, or emit bills on the credit of the United States, transmitting every half-year to the respective States an account of the sums of money so borrowed or emitted—to build and equip a navy—to agree upon the number of land forces, and to make requisitions from each State for its quota, in proportion to the number of white inhabitants in such State; which requisition shall be binding, and thereupon the legislature of each State shall appoint the regimental officers, raise the men and cloath, arm and equip them in a solid-like manner, at the expense of the United States; and the officers and men so cloathed, armed and equipped shall march to the place appointed, and within the time agreed on by the United States in Congress assembled. But if the United States in Congress assembled shall, on consideration of circumstances judge proper that any State should not raise men, or should raise a smaller number of men than the quota thereof, such extra number shall be raised, officered, cloathed, armed and equipped in the same manner as the quota of each State, unless the legislature of such State shall judge that such extra number cannot be safely spread out in the same, in which case they shall raise, officer, cloath, arm and equip as many of such extra number as they judeg can be safely spared. And the officers and men so cloathed, armed, and equipped, shall march to the place appointed, and within the time agreed on by the United States in Congress assembled.

The United States in Congress assembled shall never engage in a war, nor grant letters of marque or reprisal in time of peace, nor enter into any treaties or alliances, nor coin money, nor regulate the value thereof, nor ascertain the sums and expenses necessary for the defense and welfare of the United States, or any of them, nor emit bills, nor borrow money on the credit of the United States, nor appropriate money, nor agree upon the number of vessels of war, to be built or purchased, or the number of land or sea forces to be raised, nor appoint a commander in chief of the army or navy, unless nine States assent to the same: nor shall a question on any other point, except for adjourning from day to day be determined, unless by the votes of the majority of the United States in Congress assembled.

The Congress of the United States shall have power to adjourn to any time within the year, and to any place within the United States, so that no period of adjournment be for a longer duration than the space of six months, and shall publish the journal of their proceedings monthly, except such parts thereof relating to treaties, alliances or military operations, as in their judgement require secrecy; and the yeas and nays of the delegates of each State on any question shall be entered on the journal, when it is desired by any delegates of a State, or any of them, at his or their request shall be furnished with a transcript of the said journal, except such parts as are above excepted, to lay before the legislatures of the several States.

X. The Committee of the States, or any nine of them, shall be authorized to execute, in the recess of Congress, such of the powers of Congress as the United States in Congress assembled, by the consent of the nine States, shall from time to time think expedient to vest them with; provided that no power be delegated to the said Committee, for the exercise of which, by the Articles of Confederation, the voice of nine States in the Congress of the United States assembled be requisite.

XI. Canada acceding to this confederation, and adjoining in the measures of the United States, shall be admitted into, and entitled to all the advantages of this Union; but no other colony shall be admitted into the same, unless such admission be agreed to by nine States.

XII. All bills of credit emitted, monies borrowed, and debts contracted by, or under the authority of Congress, before the assembling of the United States, in pursuance of the present confederation, shall be deemed and considered as a charge against the United States, for payment and satisfaction whereof the said United States, and the public faith are hereby solemnly pleged.

XIII. Every State shall abide by the determination of the United States in Congress assembled, on all questions which by this confederation are submitted to them. And the Articles of this Confederation shall be inviolably observed by every State, and the Union shall be perpetual; nor shall any alteration at any time hereafter be made in any of them; unless such alteration be agreed to in a Congress of the United States, and be afterwards confirmed by the legislatures of every State.

And Whereas it hath pleased the Great Governor of the World to incline the hearts of the legislatures we respectively represent in Congress, to approve of, and to authorize us to ratify the said Articles of Confederation and perpetual Union. Know Ye that we the undersigned delegates, by virtue of the power and authority to us given for that purpose, do by these presents, in the name and in behalf of our respective constituents, fully and entirely ratify and confirm each and every of the said Articles of Confederation and perpetual Union, and all and singular the matters and things therein contained: And we do further solemnly plight and engage the faith of our respective constituents, that they shall abide by the determinations of the United States in Congress assembled, on all questions, which by the said Confederation are submitted to them. And that the Articles thereof shall be inviolably observed by the States we respectively represent, and that the Union shall be perpetual.

In Witness whereof we have hereunto set our hands in Congress. Done at Philadelphia in the State of Pennsylvania the ninth day of July in the Year of our Lord One Thousand Seven Hundred and Seventy-Eight, and in the Third Year of the independence of America.

Agreed to by Congress 15 November 1777. In force after ratification by Maryland, 1 March 1781.

1. Under the Articles, the delegates from each state would meet

   a. on the first Monday in November.
   b. in the capital of each state.
   c. every six years.
   d. every three months.

2. From reading the text, it is most likely that the number of delegates to the Congress was determined by a state's

   a. wealth.
   b. geographic size.
   c. white population.
   d. political parties.

3. Which of the following statements about voting among state delegations in Congress is probably **true**?

   a. The largest delegations had the most power.
   b. All votes in Congress had to be unanimous.
   c. Each state had one vote in each legislative matter.
   d. Each state delegation's vote had to be unanimous.

4. Under the Articles, states could enagage in war without congressional approval when they

   a. disagreed with another state over boundaries.
   b. wanted to invade a foreign country.
   c. wanted to be independent of the Confederation.
   d. were threatened by pirates or Native Americans.

5. Which of the following statements about the Committee of the States is probably **true**?

   a. It met during sessions of Congress.
   b. State delegations had between two and seven members each.
   c. It represented the Confederation during Congressional recesses.
   d. State delegations were appointed by Congress.

6. Which of the following issues did **not** require the votes of at least nine states?

   a. raising an armed force
   b. coining money
   c. declaring war
   d. admitting Canada to the Confederation

7. Which of the following government functions was not addressed under the Articles of Confederation?

   a. the post office
   b. standards of weight and measures
   c. foreign diplomacy
   d. the judiciary

8. The term, "alteration," in the articles has about the same meaning as the word

   a. amendment.
   b. legislation.
   c. treaty.
   d. militia.

9. Why was the inability of the Congress to coin money a weakness in the Articles of Confederation's outline for national unity?

10. Why do you think the Articles of Confederation focused primarily on the legislative branch of government while overlooking the executive branch and the court system?

THE NORTHWEST ORDINANCE (1787)

Because the Articles of Confederation, adopted by the states in 1781 as the country's first constitution, have often been considered a failure, it is all too easy to overlook the significant accomplishments of the American government under the Articles. The Confederation negotiated a peace treaty ending the war with Great Britain, carried on diplomatic relations with foreign countries, settled land disputes with the Native American tribes and, in two brilliant pieces of legislation, established a far-reaching policy for the settlement and incorporation of western lands.

After first providing for the survey of the land west of the Appalachian mountains, the so-called Northwest Territory, Congress enacted the Northwest Ordinance of 1787, the single most important piece of legislation in the Confederation period. The Ordinance provided the means by which new states would be created out of the western lands and then admitted into the Union. Governors and judges appointed by Congress would rule a territory until it contained 5,000 free male inhabitants of voting age; then the inhabitants would elect a territorial legislature, which would send a non-voting delegate to Congress. When the population reached 60,000, the legislature would submit a state constitution to Congress and, upon its approval, the state would enter the Union.

The importance of the statute, aside from providing for orderly westerly settlement, is that it made clear that the new states would be equal to the old; there would be no inferior or superior states in the Union. Moreover, in the Ordinance Congress compacted with the settlers of the territories that they would be equal citizens of the United States, and would enjoy all of the rights that had been fought for in the Revolution. Where the Articles of Confederation lacked a bill of rights, the Ordinance provided one that included many of the basic liberties the colonists had considered essential, such as trial by jury, habeas corpus, and religious freedom. Habeas corpus, which literally means "you have the body," is one of the fundamental rights in Anglo-American law. Through the writ of habeas corpus, a prisoner may challenge the legality of his or her imprisonment, and if the state cannot present adequate evidence to justify the jailing, the court may order the prisoner's release. One should also note, however, the important role that property still played in government, a holdover from British theory that only those with a tangible stake in society should partake in its governance.

The Northwest Ordinance would, with minor adjustments, remain the guiding policy for the admission of all future states into the Union.

Be it ordained by the authority aforesaid, That there shall be appointed from time to time by Congress, a governor, whose commission shall continue in force for the term of three years, unless sooner revoked by Congress; he shall reside in the district, and have a freehold estate therein in 1,000 acres of land, while in the exercise of his office.

There shall be appointed from time to time by Congress, a secretary, whose commission shall continue in force for four years unless sooner revoked; he shall reside in the district, and have a freehold estate therein in 500 acres of land, while in the exercise of his office. It shall be his duty to keep and preserve the acts and laws passed by the legislature, and the public records of the district, and the proceedings of the governor in his executive department, and transmit authentic copies of such acts and proceedings, every six months, to the Secretary of Congress: There shall also be appointed a court to consist of three judges, any two of whom to form a court, who shall have a common law jurisdiction, and reside in the district, and have each therein a freehold estate in 500 acres of land while in the exercise of their offices; and their commissions shall continue in force during good behavior.

The governor and judges, or a majority of them, shall adopt and publish in the district such laws of the original States, criminal and civil, as may be necessary and best suited to the circumstances of the district, and report them to Congress from time to time: which laws shall be in force in the district until the organization of the General Assembly therein, unless disapproved of by Congress; but afterwards the Legislature shall have authority to alter them as they shall think fit.

The governor, for the time being, shall be commander-in-chief of the militia, appoint and commission all officers in the same below the rank of general officers; all general officers shall be appointed and commissioned by Congress.

Previous to the organization of the general assembly, the governor shall appoint such magistrates and other civil officers in each county or township, as he shall find necessary for the preservation of the peace and good order in the same: After the general assembly shall be organized, the powers and duties of the magistrates and other civil officers shall be regulated and defined by the said assembly; but all magistrates and other civil officers not herein otherwise directed, shall, during the continuance of this temporary government, be appointed by the governor.

For the prevention of crimes and injuries, the laws to be adopted or made shall have force in all parts of the district, and for the execution of process, criminal and civil, the governor shall make proper divisions thereof; and he shall proceed from time to time as circumstances may require, to lay out the parts of the district in which the Indian titles shall have been extinguished, into counties and townships, subject however to such alterations as may thereafter be made by the legislature.

So soon as there shall be five thousand free male inhabitants of full age in the district, upon giving proof thereof to the governor, they shall receive authority, with time and place, to elect representatives from their counties or townships to represent them in the general assembly:

Provided, That, for every five hundred free male inhabitants, there shall be one representative, and so on progressively with the number of free male inhabitants shall the right of representation increase, until the number of representatives shall amount to twenty-five; after which, the number and proportion of representatives shall be regulated by the legislature:

Provided, That no person be eligible or qualified to act as a representative unless he shall have been a citizen of one of the United States three years, and be a resident in the district, or unless he shall have resided in the district three years; and, in either case, shall likewise hold in his own right, in fee simple, two hundred acres of land within the same;

Provided, also, That a freehold in fifty acres of land in the district, having been a citizen of one of the states, and being resident in the district, or the like freehold and two years residence in the district, shall be necessary to qualify a man as an elector of a representative.

The representatives thus elected, shall serve for the term of two years; and, in case of the death of a representative, or removal from office, the governor shall issue a writ to the county or township for which he was a member, to elect another in his stead, to serve for the residue of the term.

The general assembly or legislature shall consist of the governor, legislative council, and a house of representatives. The Legislative Council shall consist of five members, to continue in office five years, unless sooner removed by Congress; any three of whom to be a quorum: and the members of the Council shall be nominated and appointed in the following manner, to wit: As soon as representatives shall be elected, the Governor shall appoint a time and place for them to meet together; and, when met, they shall nominate ten persons, residents in the district, and each possessed of a freehold in five hundred acres of land, and return their names to Congress; five of whom Congress shall appoint and commission to serve as aforesaid; and, whenever a vacancy shall happen in the council, by death or removal from office, the house of representatives shall nominate two persons, qualified as aforesaid, for each vacancy, and return their names to Congress; one of whom Congress shall appoint and commission for the residue of the term. And every five years, four months at least before the expiration of the time of service of the members of council, the said house shall nominate ten persons, qualified as aforesaid, and return their names to Congress; five of whom Congress shall appoint and commission to serve as members of the council five years, unless sooner removed. And the governor, legislative council, and house of representatives, shall have authority to make laws in all cases, for the good government of the district, not repugnant to the principles and articles in this ordinance established and declared. And all bills, having passed by a majority in the house, and by a majority in the council, shall be referred to the governor for his assent; but no bill, or legislative act whatever, shall be of any force without his assent. The governor shall have power to convene, prorogue, and dissolve the general assembly, when, in his opinion, it shall be expedient.

The governor, judges, legislative council, secretary, and such other officers as Congress shall appoint in the district, shall take an oath or affirmation of fidelity and of office; the governor before the president of congress, and all other officers before the Governor. As soon as a legislature shall be formed in the district, the council and house assembled in one room, shall have authority, by joint ballot, to elect a delegate to Congress, who shall have a seat in Congress, with a right of debating but not of voting during this temporary government.

And, for extending the fundamental principles of civil and religious liberty, which form the basis whereon these republics, their laws and constitutions are erected; to fix and establish those principles as the basis of all laws, constitutions, and governments, which forever hereafter shall be formed in the said territory: to provide also for the establishment of States, and permanent government therein, and for their admission to a share in the federal councils on an equal footing with the original States, at as early periods as may be consistent with the general interest: It is hereby ordained and declared by the authority aforesaid, That the following articles shall be considered as articles of compact between the original States and the people and States in the said territory and forever remain unalterable, unless by common consent, to wit:

ART. 1. No person, demeaning himself in a peaceable and orderly manner, shall ever be molested on account of his mode of worship or religious sentiments, in the said territory.

ART. 2. The inhabitants of the said territory shall always be entitled to the benefits of the writ of habeas corpus, and of the trial by jury; of a proportionate representation of the people in the legislature; and of judicial proceedings according to the course of the common law. All persons shall be bailable, unless for capital offenses, where the proof shall be evident or the presumption great. All fines shall be moderate; and no cruel or unusual punishments shall be inflicted. No man shall be deprived of his liberty or property, but by the judgment of his peers or the law of the land; and, should the public exigencies make it necessary, for the common preservation, to take any person's property, or to demand his particular services, full compensation shall be made for the same. And, in the just preservation of rights and property, it is understood and declared, that no law ought ever to be made, or have force in the said territory, that shall, in any manner whatever, interfere with or affect private contracts or engagements, bona fide, and without fraud, previously formed.

ART. 3. Religion, morality, and knowledge, being necessary to good government and the happiness of mankind, schools and the means of education shall forever be encouraged. The utmost good faith shall always be observed towards the Indians; their lands and property shall never be taken from them without their consent; and, in their property, rights, and liberty, they shall never be invaded or disturbed, unless in just and lawful wars authorized by Congress; but laws founded in justice and humanity, shall from time to time be made for preventing wrongs being done to them, and for preserving peace and friendship with them. . . .

ART. 5. There shall be formed in the said territory, not less than three nor more than five States. . . . And, whenever any of the said States shall have sixty thousand free inhabitants therein, such State shall be admitted, by its delegates, into the Congress of the United States, on an equal footing with the original States in all respects whatever, and shall be at liberty to form a permanent constitution and State government: Provided, the constitution and government so to be formed, shall be republican, and in conformity to the principles contained in these articles; and, so far as it can be consistent with the general interest of the confederacy, such admission shall be allowed at an earlier period, and when there may be a less number of free inhabitants in the State than sixty thousand.

ART. 6. There shall be neither slavery nor involuntary servitude in the said territory, otherwise than in the punishment of crimes whereof the party shall have been duly convicted: Provided, always, That any person escaping into the same, from whom labor or service is lawfully claimed in any one of the original States, such fugitive may be lawfully reclaimed and conveyed to the person claiming his or her labor or service as aforesaid.

1. According to the ordinance, the head of a territorial government was

   a. elected by the citizens of the territory.
   b. the largest landholder of the territory.
   c. appointed by the U.S. Congress.
   d. elected by the territorial legislature.

2. Under the ordinance, which public officials were appointed for life?

   a. governor
   b. judges
   c. secretary
   d. legislators

3. Which of the following statements about eligible voters in a territory is probably **not** true?

   a. They had to own at least fifty acres of land.
   b. They had to have lived in the territory for two years.
   c. They could not belong to a Native American tribe.
   d. They could be either men or women.

4. Under the ordinance, there was one representative for every

   a. five hundred people.
   b. five thousand people.
   c. fifteen hundred people.
   d. one thousand people.

5. The members of the legislative council were

   a. appointed by the U.S. Congress.
   b. elected by the territorial representatives.
   c. appointed by the governor.
   d. elected by all eligible voters.

6. Which of the following statements about the territorial representative to Congress in probably **true**?

   a. The representative had one vote in Congress.
   b. The representative was appointed by the governor.
   c. The representative did not have to be a landholder.
   d. The representative could participate in Congressional debates.

7. The first act of the ordinance guaranteed the right to

   a. vote.
   b. bear arms.
   c. religious freedom.
   d. trial by jury.

8. A territory could apply for statehood when its population reached

   a. sixty thousand.
   b. five thousand.
   c. fifteen thousand.
   d. the same population as the smallest state.

9. How did the Northwest Ordinance address relations with Native American tribes? Where were these relations spelled out? What other aspect of territorial life was laid out in the same area?

10. How does the Northwest Ordinance address the issue of slavery? Why would people who were against slavery object to the ordinance?

Constitution of the United States (1787)

By the mid-1780s, the weaknesses of the Articles of Confederation had become clear to many observers. In their reaction to what they considered the authoritarian government of George III, the framers of the Articles had deliberately created a weak government, although they believed that it had sufficient powers to govern. That assumption proved false. Among its other defects, the Articles of Confederation gave the Congress no power to tax or to regulate commerce among the states, it lacked both executive and judicial branches, and amending the Articles required unanimity of all the states.

James Madison of Virginia, working with the blessing of George Washington, led the drive to get Congress to call a convention for the express purpose of revising the Articles of Confederation. But once the delegates had gathered in Philadelphia in the summer of 1787, they took the bit in their teeth and decided to draft an entirely new document, one that would meet what they perceived to be the current and future needs of the country.

Government under the Constitution remained federal in nature, that is, power was shared between the states and the national government. But where under the Articles the states had been the dominant force, under the Constitution the national government would be supreme. The framers saw both state and national governments as active participants in the political process.

One of the key features in the Constitution, and one that would become a critical factor in the nineteenth century, is that the source of sovereignty, the source of the authority for the document, is the citizenry. "We the People of the United States" ordain and establish the Constitution. This is a direct link to the Declaration of Independence, which declared that governments derive their legitimacy from the consent of the governed.

Perhaps the most striking feature of the Constitution was how extensively it implemented the prevailing notions of separation of powers. Clear lines divided the legislative, executive and judicial branches. In a sharp departure from their experience under the Articles, the framers put a great deal of power in the hands of the president. At the same time, a system of checks and balances ensured that no one branch of the government would dominate the others.

In the debate over ratification of the Constitution that took place in the fall and winter of 1787–1788, proponents of the new document—called Federalists—claimed that not only would it remedy the defects of the Articles of Confederation, but it would provide a strong yet limited government that would ensure the peace and security of the new nation. Those opposed to the Constitution—known as Anti-Federalists—operated at a disadvantage, because they recognized and admitted that the government under the Articles had not been a success. They did, however, demand that as a price of ratification a bill of rights should be added. The Federalists believed that no such listing was necessary, because as a government of limited powers, the new government would have no authority to invade the rights of the citizens. But as Thomas Jefferson explained to James Madison, "A bill of rights is what the people are entitled to against every government on earth, general or particular, and what no just government should refuse, or rest upon inferences."

With the ratification of the Constitution, the new government met in the spring of 1789, and Congress immediately adopted and sent to the states a series of proposed amendments. The states ratified ten of them by 1791, and these have since been known as the Bill of Rights. Other amendments have followed, a few of them primarily technical in nature, but for the most part they have expanded the democratic nature of American society—by abolishing slavery, widening suffrage, or making government more responsive to the people, as in the direct election of senators.

The Constitution has served the people of the United States admirably for over 200 years, in part because the framers were wise enough to recognize that they could not foresee every problem. Those who followed them thus had the ability to take the document and adapt it to new needs and new conditions.

We the People of the United States, in Order to form a more perfect Union, establish Justice, insure domestic Tranquility, provide for the common defence, promote the general Welfare, and secure the Blessings of Liberty to ourselves and our Posterity, do ordain and establish this Constitution for the United States of America.

Article I

Section 1. All legislative Powers herein granted shall be vested in a Congress of the United States, which shall consist of a Senate and House of Representatives.

Section 2. The House of Representatives shall be composed of Members chosen every second Year by the People of the several States, and the Electors in each State shall have the Qualifications requisite for Electors of the most numerous Branch of the State Legislature.

No Person shall be a Representative who shall not have attained to the Age of twenty five Years, and been seven Years a Citizen of the United States, and who shall not, when elected, be an Inhabitant of that State in which he shall be chosen.

Representatives and direct Taxes shall be apportioned among the several States which may be included within this Union, according to their respective Numbers, which shall be determined by adding to the whole Number of free Persons, including those bound to Service for a Term of Years, and excluding Indians not taxed, three fifths of all other Persons. The actual Enumeration shall be made within three Years after the first Meeting of the Congress of the United States, and within every subsequent Term of ten Years, in such Manner as they shall by Law direct. The Number of Representatives shall not exceed one for every thirty Thousand, but each State shall have at Least one Representative; and until such enumeration shall be made, the State of New Hampshire shall be entitled to chuse three, Massachusetts eight, Rhode Island and Providence Plantations one, Connecticut five, New York six, New Jersey four, Pennsylvania eight, Delaware one, Maryland six, Virginia ten, North Carolina five, South Carolina five, and Georgia three.

When vacancies happen in the Representation from any State, the Executive Authority thereof shall issue Writs of Election to fill such Vacancies.

The House of Representatives shall chuse their Speaker and other Officers; and shall have the sole Power of Impeachment.

Section 3. The Senate of the United States shall be composed of two Senators from each State, chosen by the Legislature thereof, for six Years; and each Senator shall have one Vote.

Immediately after they shall be assembled in Consequence of the first Election, they shall be divided as equally as may be into three Classes. The Seats of the Senators of the first Class shall be vacated at the Expiration of the second Year, of the second Class at the Expiration of the fourth Year, and of the third Class at the Expiration of the sixth Year, so that one third may be chosen every second Year; and if Vacancies happen by Resignation, or otherwise, during the Recess of the Legislature of any State, the Executive thereof may make temporary Appointments until the next Meeting of the Legislature, which shall then fill such Vacancies.

No Person shall be a Senator who shall not have attained to the Age of thirty Years, and been nine Years a Citizen of the United States, and who shall not, when elected, be an Inhabitant of that State for which he shall be chosen.

The Vice President of the United States shall be President of the Senate, but shall have no Vote, unless they be equally divided.

The Senate shall chuse their other Officers, and also a President pro tempore, in the Absence of the Vice President, or when he shall exercise the Office of President of the United States.

The Senate shall have the sole Power to try all Impeachments. When sitting for that Purpose, they shall be on Oath or Affirmation. When the President of the United States is tried the Chief Justice shall preside: And no Person shall be convicted without the Concurrence of two thirds of the Members present.

Judgment in Cases of Impeachment shall not extend further than to removal from Office, and disqualification to hold and enjoy any Office of honor, Trust or Profit under the United States: but the Party convicted shall nevertheless be liable and subject to Indictment, Trial, Judgment and Punishment, according to Law.

Section 4. The Times, Places and Manner of holding Elections for Senators and Representatives, shall be prescribed in each State by the Legislature thereof; but the Congress may at any time by Law make or alter such Regulations, except as to the Places of chusing Senators.

The Congress shall assemble at least once in every Year, and such Meeting shall be on the first Monday in December, unless they shall by Law appoint a different Day.

Section 5. Each House shall be the Judge of the Elections, Returns and Qualifications of its own Members, and a Majority of each shall constitute a Quorum to do Business; but a smaller Number may adjourn from day to day, and may be authorized to compel the Attendance of absent Members, in such Manner, and under such Penalties as each House may provide.

Each House may determine the Rules of its Proceedings, punish its Members for disorderly Behaviour, and, with the Concurrence of two thirds, expel a Member.

Each House shall keep a Journal of its Proceedings, and from time to time publish the same, excepting such Parts as may in their Judgment require Secrecy; and the Yeas and Nays of the Members of either House on any question shall, at the Desire of one fifth of those Present, be entered on the Journal.

Neither House, during the Session of Congress, shall, without the Consent of the other, adjourn for more than three days, nor to any other Place than that in which the two Houses shall be sitting.

Section 6. The Senators and Representatives shall receive a Compensation for their Services, to be ascertained by law, and paid out of the Treasury of the United States. They shall in all Cases, except Treason, Felony and Breach of the Peace, be privileged from Arrest during their Attendance at the

Session of their respective Houses, and in going to and returning from the same; and for any Speech or Debate in either House, they shall not be questioned in any other Place.

No Senator or Representative shall, during the Time for which he was elected, be appointed to any civil Office under the Authority of the United States, which shall have been created, or the Emoluments whereof shall have been encreased during such time; and no Person holding any Office under the United States, shall be a Member of either House during his Continuance in Office.

Section 7. All Bills for raising Revenue shall originate in the House of Representatives; but the Senate may propose or concur with amendments as on other Bills.

Every Bill which shall have passed the House of Representatives and the Senate, shall, before it become a Law, be presented to the President of the United States; If he approve he shall sign it, but if not he shall return it with his Objections to that House in which it shall have originated, who shall enter the Objections at large on their Journal, and proceed to reconsider it. If after such Reconsiderations two thirds of that House shall agree to pass the Bill, it shall be sent, together with the Objections, to the other House, by which it shall likewise be reconsidered, and if approved by two thirds of that House, it shall become a Law. But in all such Cases the Votes of both Houses shall be determined by Yeas and Nays, and the Names of the Persons voting for and against the Bill shall be entered on the Journal of each House respectively. If any Bill shall not be returned by the President within ten Days (Sunday excepted) after it shall have been presented to him, the Same shall be a Law, in like Manner as if he had signed it, unless the Congress by their Adjournment prevent its Return, in which Case it shall not be a Law.

Every Order, Resolution, or Vote to which the Concurrence of the Senate and House of Representatives may be necessary (except on a question of Adjournment) shall be presented to the President of the United States; and before the Same shall take Effect, shall be approved by him, or being disapproved by him, shall be repassed by two thirds of the Senate and House of Representatives, according to the Rules and Limitations prescribed in the Case of a Bill.

Section 8. The Congress shall have Power To lay and collect Taxes, Duties, Imposts and Excises, to pay the Debts and provide for the common Defence and general Welfare of the United States; but all Duties, Imposts and Excises shall be uniform throughout the United States;

To borrow Money on the credit of the United States;

To regulate Commerce with foreign Nations, and among the several States, and with the Indian Tribes;

To establish an uniform Rule of Naturalization, and uniform Laws on the subject of Bankruptcies throughout the United States;

To coin Money, regulate the Value thereof, and of foreign Coin, and fix the Standard of Weights and Measures;

To provide for the Punishment of counterfeiting the Securities and current Coin of the United States;

To establish Post Offices and post Roads;

To promote the Progress of Science and useful Arts, by securing for limited Times to Authors and Inventors the exclusive Right to their respective Writings and Discoveries;

To constitute Tribunals inferior to the supreme Court;

To define and punish Piracies and Felonies committed on the high Seas, and Offenses against the Law of Nations;

To declare War, grant Letters of Marque and Reprisal, and make Rules concerning Captures on Land and Water;

To raise and support Armies, but no Appropriation of Money to that Use shall be for a longer Term than two Years;

To provide and maintain a Navy;

To make Rules for the Government and Regulation of the land and naval Forces;

To provide for calling forth the Militia to execute the Laws of the Union, suppress Insurrections and repel Invasions;

To provide for organizing, arming, and disciplining, the Militia, and for governing such Part of them as may be employed in the Service of the United States, reserving to the States respectively, the Appointment of the Officers, and the Authority of training the Militia according to the discipline prescribed by Congress;

To exercise exclusive Legislation in all Cases whatsoever, over such District (not exceeding ten Miles square) as may, by Cession of particular States, and the Acceptance of Congress, become the Seat of the Government of the United States, and to exercise like Authority over all Places purchased by the Consent of the Legislature of the State in which the Same shall be, for the Erection of Forts, Magazines, Arsenals, dock-Yards, and other needful Buildings;—And

To make all Laws which shall be necessary and proper for carrying into Execution the foregoing Powers, and all other Powers vested by this Constitution in the Government of the United States, or in any Department or Officer thereof.

Section 9. The Migration or Importation of such Persons as any of the States now existing shall think proper to admit, shall not be prohibited by the Congress prior to the Year one thousand eight hundred and eight, but a Tax or duty may be imposed on such Importation, not exceeding ten dollars for each Person.

The Privilege of the Writ of Habeas Corpus shall not be suspended, unless when in Cases of Rebellion or Invasion the public Safety may require it.

No Bill of Attainder or ex post facto Law shall be passed.

No Capitation, or other direct, Tax shall be laid, unless in Proportion to the Census or Enumeration herein before directed to be taken.

No Tax or Duty shall be laid on Articles exported from any State.

No Preference shall be given by any Regulation of Commerce or Revenue to the Ports of one State over those of another; nor shall Vessels bound to, or from, one State, be obliged to enter, clear or pay Duties in another.

No Money shall be drawn from the Treasury, but in Consequence of Appropriations made by Law; and a regular Statement and Account of the Receipts and Expenditures of all public Money shall be published from time to time.

No Title of Nobility shall be granted by the United States: And no Person holding any Office or Trust under them, shall, without the Consent of the Congress, accept of any present, Emolument, Office, or Title, of any kind whatever, from any King, Prince or foreign State.

Section 10. No State shall enter into any Treaty, Alliance, or Confederation; grant Letters of Marque and Reprisal, coin Money; emit Bills of Credit, make any Thing but gold and silver Coin a Tender in Payment of Debts; pass any Bill of Attainder, ex post facto Law, or Law impairing the Obligation of Contracts, or grant any Title of Nobility.

No State shall, without the Consent of the Congress, lay any Imposts or Duties on Imports or Exports, except what may be absolutely necessary for executing its inspection Laws: and the net Produce of all Duties and Imposts, laid by any State on Imports or Exports, shall be for the Use of the Treasury of the United States; and all such Laws shall be subject to the Revision and Controul of the Congress.

No State shall, without the Consent of Congress, lay any Duty of Tonnage, keep Troops, or Ships of War in time of Peace, enter into any Agreement or Compact with another State, or with a foreign Power, or engage in War, unless actually invaded, or in such imminent Danger as will not admit of delay.

Article II

Section 1. The executive Power shall be vested in a President of the United States of America. He shall hold his Office during the Term of four Years, and, together with the Vice President, chosen for the same Term, be elected, as follows:

Each State shall appoint, In such Manner as the Legislature thereof may direct, a Number of Electors, equal to the whole Number of Senators and Representatives to which the State may be entitled in the Congress: but no Senator or Representative, or Person holding an Office of Trust or Profit under the United States, shall be appointed an Elector.

The Electors shall meet in their respective States, and vote by Ballot for two Persons, of whom one at least shall not be an Inhabitant of the same State with themselves. And they shall make a List of all the Persons voted for, and of the number of Votes for each; which List they shall sign and certify, and transmit sealed to the Seat of the Government of the United States, directed to the President of the Senate. The President of the Senate shall, in the Presence of the Senate and House of Representatives, open all the Certificates, and the Votes shall then be counted. The Person having the greatest number of Votes shall be the President, if such Number be a Majority of the whole Number of Electors appointed; and if there be more than one who have such Majority, and have an equal Number of Votes, then the House of Representatives shall immediately chuse by Ballot one of them for President; and if no Person have a Majority, then from the five highest on the List the said House shall in like Manner chuse the President. But in chusing the President, the Votes shall be taken by States, the Representation from each State having one Vote; a quorum for this Purpose shall consist of a Member or Members from two thirds of the States, and a Majority of all the States shall be necessary to a Choice. In every Case, after the Choice of the President, the Person having the greatest Number of Votes of the Electors shall be the Vice President. But if there should remain two or more who have equal Votes, the Senate shall chuse from them by Ballot the Vice President.

The Congress may determine the Time of chusing the Electors, and the Day on which they shall give their Votes; which Day shall be the same throughout the United States.

No Person except a natural born Citizen, or a Citizen of the United States at the time of the Adoption of this Constitution, shall be eligible to the Office of President; neither shall any Person be eligible to that Office who shall not have attained to the Age of thirty five Years, and been fourteen Years a Resident within the United States.

In Case of the Removal of the President from Office, or of his Death, Resignation, or Inability to discharge the Powers and Duties of the said Office, the Same shall devolve on the Vice President, and the Congress may by Law provide for the Case of Removal, Death, Resignation or Inability, both of the President and Vice President, declaring what Officer shall then act as President, and such Officer shall act accordingly, until the Disability be removed, or a President shall be elected.

The President shall, at stated Times, receive for his Services, a Compensation, which shall neither be encreased nor diminished during the Period for which he shall have been elected, and he shall not receive within that Period any other emolument from the United States, or any of them.

Before he enter on the Execution of his Office, he shall take the following Oath or Affirmation:—"I do solemnly swear (or affirm) that I will faithfully execute the Office of President of the United States, and will to the best of my Ability, preserve, protect and defend the Constitution of the United States."

Section 2. The President shall be Commander in Chief of the Army and Navy of the United States, and of the Militia of the several States, when called into the actual Service of the United States; he may require the Opinion, in writing, of the principal Officer in each of the executive Departments, upon any Subject relating to the Duties of their respective Offices, and he shall have Power to grant Reprieves and Pardons for Offenses against the United States, except in Cases of Impeachment.

He shall have Power, by and with the Advice and Consent of the Senate, to make Treaties, provided two thirds of the Senators present concur; and he shall nominate, and by and with the Advice and Consent of the Senate, shall appoint Ambassadors, other public Ministers and Consuls, Judges of the supreme Court, and all other Officers of the United States, whose Appointments are not herein otherwise provided for, and which shall be established by Law: but the Congress may by Law vest the Appointment of such inferior Officers, as they think proper, in the President alone, in the Courts of Law, or in the Heads of Departments.

The President shall have Power to fill up all Vacancies that may happen during the Recess of the Senate, by granting Commissions which shall expire at the End of their next Session.

Section 3. He shall from time to time give to the Congress Information of the State of the Union, and recommend to their Consideration such Measures as he shall judge necessary and expedient; he may, on extraordinary Occasions, convene both Houses, or either of them, and in Case of Disagreements between them, with Respect to the Time of Adjournment, he may adjourn them to such Time as he shall think proper; he shall receive Ambassadors and other public Ministers; he shall take Care that the Laws be faithfully executed, and shall Commission all the Officers of the United States.

Section 4. The President, Vice President and all Civil Officers of the United States, shall be removed from Office on Impeachment for, and Conviction of, Treason, Bribery, or other high Crimes and Misdemeanors.

Article III

Section 1. The judicial Power of the United States, shall be vested in one supreme Court, and in such inferior Courts as the Congress may from time to time ordain and establish. The Judges, both of the supreme and inferior Courts, shall hold their Offices during good Behaviour, and shall, at stated Times, receive for their Services, a Compensation, which shall not be diminished during their Continuance in Office.

Section 2. The judicial Power shall extend to all Cases, in Law and Equity, arising under this Constitution, the Laws of the United States, and Treaties made, or which shall be made, under their Authority;—to all Cases affecting Ambassadors, other public Ministers and Consuls;—to all Cases of admiralty and maritime Jurisdiction;—to Controversies to which the United States shall be a Party;—to Controversies between two or more States;—between a State and Citizens of another State;—between Citizens of different States;—between Citizens of the same State claiming Lands under Grants of different States, and between a State, or the Citizens thereof, and foreign States, Citizens or Subjects.

In all Cases affecting Ambassadors, other public Ministers and Consuls, and those in which a State shall be Party, the Supreme Court shall have original Jurisdiction. In all the other Cases before mentioned, the supreme Court shall have appelate Jurisdiction, both as to Law and Fact, with such Exceptions, and under such Regulations as the Congress shall make.

The Trial of all Crimes, except in Cases of Impeachment, shall be by Jury; and such Trial shall be held in the State where the said Crimes shall have been committed; but when not committed within any State, the Trial shall be at such Place or Places as the Congress may by Law have directed.

Section 3. Treason against the United States, shall consist only in levying War against them, or in adhering to their Enemies, giving them Aid and Comfort. No Person shall be convicted of Treason unless on the Testimony of two Witnesses to the same overt Act, or on Confession in open Court.

The Congress shall have Power to declare the Punishment of Treason, but no Attainder of Treason shall work Corruption of Blood, or Forfeiture except during the Life of the Person attainted.

Article IV

Section 1. Full Faith and Credit shall be given in each State to the public Acts, Records, and judicial proceedings of every other State. And the Congress may by general Laws prescribe the Manner in which such Acts, Records and Proceedings shall be proved, and the Effect thereof.

Section 2. The Citizens of each State shall be entitled to all Privileges and Immunities of Citizens in the several States.

A Person charged in any State with Treason, Felony, or other Crime, who shall flee from Justice, and be found in another State, shall on Demand of the executive Authority of the State from which he fled, be delivered up, to be removed to the State having Jurisdiction of the Crime.

No Person held to Service or Labour in one State, under the Laws thereof, escaping into another, shall, in Consequence of any Law or Regulation therein, be discharged from such Service or Labour, but shall be delivered up on Claim of the Party to whom such Service or Labour may be due.

Section 3. New States may be admitted by the Congress into this Union; but no new State shall be formed or erected within the Jurisdiction of any other State; nor any State be formed by the

Junction of two or more States, or Parts of States, without the Consent of the Legislatures of the States concerned as well as of the Congress.

The Congress shall have Power to dispose of and make all needful Rules and Regulations respecting the Territory or other Property belonging to the United States; and nothing in this Constitution shall be so construed as to Prejudice any Claims of the United States, or of any particular State.

Section 4. The United States shall guarantee to every State in this Union a Republican Form of Government, and shall protect each of them against Invasion; and on Application of the Legislature, or of the Executive (when the Legislature cannot be convened) against domestic Violence.

Article V

The Congress, whenever two thirds of both Houses shall deem it necessary, shall propose Amendments to this Constitution, or, on the Application of the Legislatures of two thirds of the several States, shall call a Convention for proposing Amendments, which, in either Case, shall be valid to all Intents and Purposes, as Part of this Constitution, when ratified by the Legislatures of three fourths of the several States, or by Conventions in three fourths thereof, as the one or the other Mode of Ratification may be proposed by the Congress; provided that no Amendment which may be made prior to the Year One thousand eight hundred and eight shall in any Manner affect the first and fourth Clauses in the Ninth Section of the first Article; and that no State, without its Consent, shall be deprived of its equal Suffrage in the Senate.

Article VI

All Debts contracted and Engagements entered into, before the Adoption of this Constitution, shall be as valid against the United States under this Constitution, as under the Confederation.

This Constitution, and the Laws of the United States which shall be made in Pursuance thereof; and all Treaties made, or which shall be made, under the Authority of the United States, shall be the supreme Law of the Land; and the Judges in every State shall be bound thereby, any Thing in the Constitution or Laws of any State to the Contrary notwithstanding.

The Senators and Representatives before mentioned, and the Members of the several State Legislatures, and all executive and judicial Officers, both of the United States and of the several States, shall be bound by Oath or Affirmation, to support this Constitution; but no religious Test shall ever be required as a Qualification to any Office or public Trust under the United States.

Article VII

The Ratification of the Conventions of nine States, shall be sufficient for the Establishment of this Constitution between the States so ratifying the Same.

Done in Convention by the Unanimous Consent of the States present the Seventeenth Day of September in the Year of our Lord one thousand seven hundred and Eighty seven and of the Independence of the United States of America the Twelfth. In witness thereof We have hereunto subscribed our Names,

Articles in Addition to, and Amendment of, the Constitution of the United States of America, Proposed by Congress, and Ratified by the Several States, Pursuant to the Fifth Article of the Original Constitution.

Amendment I

Congress shall make no law respecting an establishment of religion, or prohibiting the free exercise thereof; or abridging the freedom of speech, or of the press; or the right of the people peaceably to assemble, and to petition the Government for a redress of grievances.

Amendment II

A well regulated Militia, being necessary to the security of a free State, the right of the people to keep and bear Arms, shall not be infringed.

Amendment III

No Soldier, in time of peace be quartered in any house, without the consent of the Owner, nor in time of war, but in a manner to be prescribed by law.

Amendment IV

The right of the people to be secure in their persons, houses, papers, and effects, against unreasonable searches and seizures, shall not be violated, and no Warrants shall issue, but upon probable cause, supported by Oath or affirmation, and particularly describing the place to be searched, and the persons or things to be seized.

Amendment V

No Person shall be held to answer for a capital, or otherwise infamous crime, unless on a presentment or indictment of a Grand Jury, except in cases arising in the land or naval forces, or in the Militia, when in actual service in time of War or public danger; nor shall any person be subject for the same offence to be twice put in jeopardy of life or limb; nor shall be compelled in any criminal case to be a witness against himself, nor be deprived of life, liberty, or property, without due process of law; nor shall private property be taken for public use, without just compensation.

Amendment VI

In all criminal prosecutions, the accused shall enjoy the right to a speedy and public trial by an impartial jury of the State and district wherein the crime shall have been committed, which district shall have been previously ascertained by law, and to be informed of the nature and cause of the accusation; to be confronted with the witness against him; to have compulsory process for obtaining Witnesses in his favor, and to have the Assistance of Counsel for his defence.

Amendment VII

In Suits at common law, where the value in controversy shall exceed twenty dollars, the right of trial by jury shall be preserved, and no fact tried by a jury, shall be otherwise re-examined in any Court of the United States, than according to the rules of the common law.

Amendment VIII

Excessive bail shall not be required, nor excessive fines imposed, nor cruel and unusual punishments inflicted.

Amendment IX

The enumeration in the Constitution, of certain rights, shall not be construed to deny or disparage others retained by the people.

Amendment X

The powers not delegated to the United States by the Constitution, nor prohibited by it to the States, are reserved to the States respectively, or to the people.

The first ten amendments were ratified Dec. 15, 1791.

1. How was the slave population counted in determining the number of representatives from a state?

    a. Slaves were not counted.
    b. Each slave counted as one person.
    c. A slave counted as three-fifths of a white person.
    d. A slave family was counted as one person.

2. Which of the following statements about the election of Senators is probably **true**?

    a. One third of the Senate stands for election every two years.
    b. A Senator's term lasts two years.
    c. The number of Senators from each state is determined by population.
    d. A new Senate is elected every six years.

3. The ________ presides over a presidential impeachment trial.

    a. vice-president
    b. Speaker of the House
    c. Chief Justice of the Supreme Court
    d. president pro tempore

4. Which of the following events in the passage of legislation raising revenue happens **second**?

    a. The bill is approved by the House.
    b. The bill is enacted by the relevant agencies.
    c. The bill is signed by the president.
    d. The bill is approved by the Senate.

5. The number of electors representing each state in a presidential election equals the

    a. number of Senators from that state.
    b. total of the Representatives and Senators.
    c. number of representatives.
    d. number of people who voted in the election.

6. Which of the following statements about the election of the vice president as established under the Constitution is probably **true**?

    a. The vice president had to be from the same political party as the president.
    b. The vice president first had to serve as a president of the Senate.
    c. The vice president was the candidate who finished second in the presidential election.
    d. The vice president was appointed by the president.

7. Article Three of the Constitution explains the

   a. makeup of the Judiciary System.
   b. requirement for the State of the Union address.
   c. formation of the states' militias.
   d. presidential electoral system.

8. Which of the following statements about new states according to the Constitution is probably **not** true?

   a. A new state cannot be formed within the boundaries of an established state.
   b. A new state cannot be formed by the combination of two established states.
   c. A new state cannot be formed from lands owned by Native Americans.
   d. A new state can only be admitted by a vote of Congress.

9. How do the age requirements for the House, the Senate, and the presidency indicate the beliefs of the Constitutional Convention about the significance of the presidency?

10. Write a summary of the process for amending the Constitution as it is outlined in the Constitution.

11. Which of the first ten amendments is most important to you personally? Explain your answer.

Farewell Address (1796)
by George Washington

George Washington had been the obvious choice to be the first president of the United States and, indeed, many people had supported ratification of the Constitution on the assumption that Washington would be the head of the new government. By all measures, Washington proved himself a capable, even a great, president, helping to shape the new government and leading the country skillfully through several crises, both foreign and domestic.

Washington, like many of his contemporaries, did not understand or believe in political parties, and saw them as fractious agencies subversive of domestic tranquility. When political parties began forming during his administration, and in direct response to some of his policies, he failed to comprehend that parties would be the chief device through which the American people would debate and resolve major public issues. It was his fear of what parties would do to the nation that led Washington to draft his Farewell Address.

The two parties that developed in the early 1790s were the Federalists, who supported the economic and foreign policies of the Washington administration, and the Jeffersonian Republicans, who in large measure opposed them. The Federalists backed Secretary of the Treasury Alexander Hamilton's plan for a central bank and a tariff and tax policy that would promote domestic manufacturing; the Jeffersonians opposed the strong government inherent in the Hamiltonian plan, and favored farmers as opposed to manufacturers. In foreign affairs, both sides wanted the United States to remain neutral in the growing controversies between Great Britain and France, but the Federalists favored the English and the Jeffersonians the French. The Address derived at least in part from Washington's fear that party factionalism would drag the United States into this fray.

Two-thirds of the Address is devoted to domestic matters and the rise of political parties, and Washington set out his vision of what would make the United States a truly great nation. He called for men to put aside party and unite for the common good, an "American character" wholly free of foreign attachments. The United States must concentrate only on American interests, and while the country ought to be friendly and open its commerce to all nations, it should avoid becoming involved in foreign wars. Contrary to some opinions, Washington did not call for isolation, only the avoidance of entangling alliances. While he called for maintenance of the treaty with France signed during the American Revolution, the problems created by that treaty ought to be clear. The United States must "act for ourselves and not for others."

The Address quickly entered the realm of revealed truth. It was for decades read annually in Congress; it was printed in children's primers, engraved on watches, and woven into tapestries. Many Americans, especially in subsequent generations, accepted Washington's advice as gospel, and in any debate between neutrality and involvement in foreign issues would invoke the message as dispositive of all questions. Not until 1949, in fact, would the United States again sign a treaty of alliance with a foreign nation.

Friends and Fellow-Citizens:

The period for a new election of a citizen to administer the Executive Government of the United States being not far distant, and the time actually arrived when your thoughts must be employed in designating the person who is to be clothed with that important trust, it appears to me proper, especially as it may conduce to a more distinct expression of the public voice, that I should now apprise you of the resolution I have formed to decline being considered among the number of those out of whom a choice is to be made. . . .

The impressions with which I first undertook the arduous trust were explained on the proper occasion. In the discharge of this trust I will only say that I have, with good intentions, contributed toward the organization and administration of the Government the best exertions of which a very fallible judgment was capable. Not unconscious in the outset of the inferiority of my qualifications, experience in my own eyes, perhaps still more in the eyes of others, has strengthened the motives to diffidence of myself; and every day the increasing weight of years admonishes me more and more that the shade of retirement is as necessary to me as it will be welcome. Satisfied that if any circumstances have given peculiar value to my services they were temporary, I have the consolation to believe that, while choice and prudence invite me to quit the political scene, patriotism does not forbid it. . . .

Here, perhaps, I ought to stop. But a solicitude for your welfare which can not end with my life, and the apprehension of danger natural to that solicitude, urge me on an occasion like the present to offer to your solemn contemplation and to recommend to your frequent review some sentiments which are the result of much reflection, of no inconsiderable observation, and which appear to me all important to permanency of your felicity as a people . . .

To the efficacy and permanency of your union a government for the whole is indispensable. No alliances, however strict, between the parts can be an adequate substitute. They must inevitably experience the infractions and interruptions which all alliances in all times have experienced. Sensible of this momentous truth, you have improved upon your first essay by the adoption of a Constitution of Government better calculated than your former for an intimate union and for the efficacious management of your common concerns. This Government, the offspring of our own choice, uninfluenced and unawed, adopted upon full investigation and mature deliberation, completely free in its principles, in the distribution of its powers, uniting security with energy, and containing within itself a provision for its own amendment, has a just claim to your confidence and your support. Respect for its authority, compliance with its laws, acquiescence in its measures, are duties enjoined by the fundamental maxims of true liberty. The basis of our political systems is the right of the people to make and to alter their constitutions of government. But the constitution which at any time exists till changed by an explicit and authentic act of the whole people is sacredly obligatory upon all. The very idea of the power and the right of the people to establish government presupposes the duty of every individual to obey the established government. . . .

Toward the preservation of your Government and the permanency of your present happy state, it is requisite not only that you steadily discountenance irregular oppositions to its acknowledged authority, but also that you resist with care the spirit of innovation upon its principles, however specious the pretexts. One method of assault may be to effect in the forms of the Constitution alterations which will impair the energy of the system, and thus to undermine what can not be directly overthrown. In all the changes to which you may be invited remember that time and habit are at least as necessary to fix the true character of governments as of other human institutions; that experience is the surest standard by which to test the real tendency of the existing constitution of a country; that facility in changes upon the credit of mere hypothesis and opinion exposes to perpetual change, from the endless variety of hypothesis and opinion; and remember especially that for the efficient management of your common interests in a country so extensive as ours a government of as much vigor as is consistent with the perfect security of liberty is indispensable. Liberty itself will find in such a government, with powers properly distributed and adjusted, its surest guardian. It is, indeed, little else than a name where the government is too feeble to withstand the enterprises of faction, to con-fine each member of the society within the limits prescribed by the laws, and to maintain all in the secure and tranquil enjoyment of the rights of person and property.

I have already intimated to you the danger of parties in the State, with particular reference to the founding of them on geographical discriminations. Let me now take a more comprehensive view, and warn you in the most solemn manner against the baneful effects of the spirit of party generally . . .

As a very important source of strength and security, cherish public credit. One method of preserving it is to use it as sparingly as possible, avoiding occasions of expense by cultivating peace, but remembering also that timely disbursements to prepare for danger frequently prevent much greater disbursements to repel it; avoiding likewise the accumulation of debt, not only by shunning occasions of expense, but by vigorous exertions in time of peace to discharge the debts which unavoidable wars have occasioned, not ungenerously throwing upon posterity the burthen which we ourselves ought to bear. . . .

It is our true policy to steer clear of permanent alliances with any portion of the foreign world, so far, I mean, as we are now at liberty to do it, for let me not be understood as capable of patronizing infidelity to existing engagements. I hold the maxim no less applicable to public than to private affairs that honesty is always the best policy. I repeat, therefore, let those engagements be observed in their genuine sense. But in my opinion it is unnecessary and would be unwise to extend them . . .

1. In the opening paragraph of his address, Washington

   a. resigns from office.
   b. declares his candidacy for office.
   c. declines to serve as president again.
   d. nominates the next presidential candidate.

2. Washington goes on to say that the foundation of the American political system is the right to

   a. agree with all laws passed by Congress.
   b. support decisions made by the president.
   c. support a political party.
   d. change the constitution.

3. Washington said that all governments need ________ for success.

   a. a strong president
   b. political parties
   c. time and experience
   d. a strong military

4. When Washington speaks of the "baneful effects" of political parties, he is

   a. warning the nation about the dangers of political parties.
   b. praising the importance of political parties.
   c. encouraging people to join political parties.
   d. asking Congress to ban political parties.

5. Though Washington was duty-bound to lead his country, what is one reason why he finally chose to retire?

   a. His term was finished.
   b. The office was making him feel inferior.
   c. He did not approve of the changes to the Constitution.
   d. He was incapable of leading.

6. According to Washington the one way to keep the country's debt low is to

   a. spend the credit on preparations.
   b. spend the credit on wars.
   c. give the money back to the people.
   d. pass the debt on to future generations.

7. What is the political label that is often associated with Washington's views on foreign policy?

   a. autocratic
   b. democratic
   c. isolationist
   d. bipartisan

8. Though Washington said, "The basis of our political systems is the right of the people to make and to alter their constitutions of government," which part did he warn the people not to change? Why?

Marbury v. *Madison* (1803)

Just as George Washington helped shape the actual form that the executive branch would take, so the third chief justice, John Marshall, shaped the role that the courts would play.

Under the administrations of Washington and his successor, John Adams, only members of the ruling Federalist Party were appointed to the bench, and under the terms of the Constitution, they held office for life during "good behavior." Thus, when the opposing Republicans won the election of 1800, the Jeffersonians found that while they controlled the presidency and Congress, the Federalists still dominated the judiciary. One of the first acts of the new administration was to repeal the Judiciary Act of 1800, which had created a number of new judgeships. Although President Adams had attempted to fill the vacancies prior to the end of his term, a number of commissions had not been delivered, and one of the appointees, William Marbury, sued Secretary of State James Madison to force him to deliver his commission as a justice of the peace.

The new chief justice, John Marshall, understood that if the Court awarded Marbury a writ of mandamus (an order to force Madison to deliver the commission) the Jefferson administration would ignore it, and thus significantly weaken the authority of the courts. On the other hand, if the Court denied the writ, it might well appear that the justices had acted out of fear. Either case would be a denial of the basic principle of the supremacy of the law.

Marshall's decision in this case has been hailed as a judicial tour de force. In essence, he declared that Madison should have delivered the commission to Marbury, but then held that the section of the Judiciary Act of 1789 that gave the Supreme Court the power to issue writs of mandamus exceeded the authority allotted the Court under Article III of the Constitution, and was therefore null and void. Thus he was able to chastise the Jeffersonians and yet not create a situation in which a court order would be flouted.

The critical importance of Marbury is the assumption of several powers by the Supreme Court. One was the authority to declare acts of Congress, and by implication acts of the president, unconstitutional if they exceeded the powers granted by the Constitution. But even more important, the Court became the arbiter of the Constitution, the final authority on what the document meant. As such, the Supreme Court became in fact as well as in theory an equal partner in government, and it has played that role ever since.

The Court would not declare another act of Congress unconstitutional until 1857, and it has used that power sparingly. But through its role as arbiter of the Constitution, it has, especially in the twentieth century, been the chief agency for the expansion of individual rights.

Chief Justice Marshall delivered the opinion of the Court.

At the last term on the affidavits then read and filed with the clerk, a rule was granted in this case, requiring the Secretary of State to show cause why a mandamus should not issue, directing him to deliver to William Marbury his commission as a justice of the peace for the county of Washington, in the district of Columbia.

No cause has been shown, and the present motion is for a mandamus. The peculiar delicacy of this case, the novelty of some of its circumstances, and the real difficulty attending the points which occur in it, require a complete exposition of the principles on which the opinion to be given by the court is founded. . . .

In the order in which the court has viewed this subject, the following questions have been considered and decided:

1st. Has the applicant a right to the commission he demands?

2d. If he has a right, and that right has been violated, do the laws of his country afford him a remedy?

3d. If they do afford him a remedy, is it a mandamus issuing from this court?

The first object of inquiry is—1st. Has the applicant a right to the commission he demands? . . .

It [is] decidedly the opinion of the court, that when a commission has been signed by the president, the appointment is made; and that the commission is complete, when the seal of the United States has been affixed to it by the secretary of state. . . .

To withhold his commission, therefore, is an act deemed by the court not warranted by law, but violative of a vested legal right.

This brings us to the second inquiry; which is 2dly. If he has a right, and that right has been violated, do the laws of his country afford him a remedy?

The very essence of civil liberty certainly consists in the right of every individual to claim the protection of the laws, whenever he receives an injury. One of the first duties of government is to afford that protection. [The] government of the United States has been emphatically termed a government of laws, and not of men. It will certainly cease to deserve this high appellation, if the laws furnish no remedy for the violation of a vested legal right. . . .

By the constitution of the United States, the President is invested with certain important political powers, in the exercise of which he is to use his own discretion, and is accountable only to his country in his political character, and to his own conscience. To aid him in the performance of these duties, he is authorized to appoint certain officers, who act by his authority and in conformity with his orders . . .

It is, then, the opinion of the Court [that Marbury has a] right to the commission; a refusal to deliver which is a plain violation of that right, for which the laws of his country afford him a remedy.

It remains to be enquired whether,

3dly. He is entitled to the remedy for which he applies..;

The act to establish the judicial courts of the United States authorizes the Supreme Court "to issue writs of mandamus in cases warranted by the principles and usages of law, to any courts appointed, or persons holding office, under the authority of the United States."

The Secretary of State, being a person holding an office under the authority of the United States, is precisely within the letter of the description; and if this court is not authorized to issue a writ of mandamus to such an officer, it must be because the law is unconstitutional, and therefore incapable of conferring the authority, and assigning the duties which its words purport to confer and assign.

The constitution vests the whole judicial power of the United States in one Supreme Court, and such inferior courts as congress shall, from time to time, ordain and establish. This power is expressly extended to all cases arising under the laws of the United States; and, consequently, in some form, may be exercised over the present case; because the right claimed is given by a law of the United States.

In the distribution of this power it is declared that "the Supreme Court shall have original jurisdiction in all cases affecting ambassadors, other public ministers and consuls, and those in which a state shall be a party. In all other cases, the Supreme Court shall have appellate jurisdiction."

The judicial power of the United States is extended to all cases arising under the constitution.

Could it be the intention of those who gave this power, to say that in using it the constitution should not be looked into? That a case arising under the constitution should be decided without examining the instrument under which it arises?

This is too extravagant to be maintained.

In some cases, then, the constitution must be looked into by the judges. And if they can open it at all, what part of it are they forbidden to read or to obey?

There are many other parts of the constitution which serve to illustrate this subject.

It is declared that "no tax or duty shall be laid on articles exported from any state." Suppose a duty on the export of cotton, of tobacco, or of flour; and a suit instituted to recover it. Ought judgment to be rendered in such a case? Ought the judges to close their eyes on the constitution, and only see the law?

The constitution declares that "no bill of attainder or ex post facto law shall be passed." If, however, such a bill should be passed, and a person should be prosecuted under it; must the court condemn to death those victims whom the constitution endeavors to preserve?

"No person," says the constitution, "shall be convicted of treason unless on the testimony of two witnesses to the same overt act, or on confession in open court."

Here the language of the constitution is addressed especially to the courts. It prescribes, directly for them, a rule of evidence not to be departed from. If the legislature should change that rule, and declare one witness, or a confession out of court, sufficient for conviction, must the constitutional principle yield to the legislative act?

From these, and many other selections which might be made, it is apparent, that the framers of the constitution contemplated that instrument as a rule for the government of courts, as well as of the legislature. Why otherwise does it direct the judges to take an oath to support it? This oath certainly applies, in an especial manner, to their conduct in their official character. How immoral to impose it on them, if they were to be used as the instruments, and the knowing instruments, for violating what they swear to support!

The oath of office, too, imposed by the legislature, is completely demonstrative of the legislative opinion on this subject. It is in these words: "I do solemnly swear that I will administer justice without respect to persons, and do equal right to the poor and to the rich; and that I will faithfully and impartially discharge all the duties incumbent on me as _____, according to the best of my abilities and understanding, agreeably to the constitution, and laws of the United States." Why does a Judge swear to discharge his duties agreeably the constitution of the United States, if that constitution forms no rule for his government? If it is closed upon him, and cannot be inspected by him?

If such be the real state of things, this is worse than solemn mockery. To prescribe, or to take this oath, becomes equally a crime.

It is also not entirely unworthy of observation that in declaring what shall be the supreme law of the land, the constitution itself is first mentioned; and not the laws of the United States generally, but those only which shall be made in pursuance of the constitution, have that rank.

Thus, the particular phraseology of the constitution of the United States confirms and strengthens the principle, supposed to be essential to all written constitutions, that a law repugnant to the constitution is void; and that courts, as well as other departments, are bound by that instrument.

1. The problem started after the

   a. Federalists left office.
   b. Jeffersonians appointed John Marshall to the Supreme Court.
   c. president vetoed a request.
   d. Supreme Court declared the Judiciary Act of 1800.

2. Marbury sued Madison in the hopes of getting

   a. Madison removed from office.
   b. helping the Federalists get reelected.
   c. a job as a justice of the peace.
   d. monetary rewards.

3. Why didn't the Secretary of State want to help Marbury?

   a. The president vetoed the request.
   b. He did not have the power to appoint Marbury.
   c. He did not like Marbury.
   d. He did not want to help the Federalists.

4. Why did the chief justice avoid supporting Marbury's request?

   a. He knew that the Federalists would retaliate.
   b. He knew that the president would ignore the Supreme Court's ruling.
   c. He suspected that the Jeffersonians would replace Marbury.
   d. He did not believe that the judiciary had power over the executive branch.

5. Why couldn't Marshall simply side with Madison and ignore Marbury's request?

   a. Marshall feared the political ramifications if he angered the Federalists.
   b. He did not want to show favoritism.
   c. It would appear as though the Supreme Court was afraid of the executive.
   d. He was pressured by both the Federalists and the Jeffersonians.

6. Justice Marshall ruled in favor of

   a. Madison.
   b. Marbury.
   c. both Madison and Marbury.
   d. none of the above.

7. How did the Judiciary Act of 1800 help the Federalists?

   a. It allowed them to create judgeships and appoint judges.
   b. It allowed the Federalists to appoint ambassadors and merchants as judges.
   c. It created new jobs for many laborers.
   d. It made it difficult for other parties to appoint judges.

8. John Marshall ruled that the Judiciary Act of 1800 was

   a. unfair.
   b. unconstitutional.
   c. partisan.
   d. constitutional.

9. Why was Marshall's ruling ultimately good for Madison?

   a. The ruling stated that the commission was a reasonable request.
   b. The Federalists were removed from the judiciary system.
   c. The Judiciary Act was unconstitutional; therefore, the commissions were annulled.
   d. The ruling was unconstitutional and favored the Federalists who were later removed from their offices.

10. How was Madison censured?

   a. The court said that Madison should have given Marbury the commission.
   b. He was removed from office.
   c. The court gave Marbury his commission.
   d. The court refused to hear any of Madison's requests.

11. Why is John Marshall's decision in the case considered significant today? How has it shaped the government?

12. Write an essay, on the topic of your choice, in John Marshall's style. Include three specific points and include at least three examples to support your thesis.

Jefferson's Secret Message to Congress Regarding the Lewis & Clark Expedition (1803)

In this secret message of January 18, 1803, President Jefferson asked Congress for $2,500 to explore the west—all the way to the Pacific Ocean. At the time, the territory did not belong to the United States. Congress agreed to fund the expedition that would be led by Meriwether Lewis and William Clark.

The modesty of the request, couched principally in terms of promoting commerce, belied the grandeur of the vision behind it. Jefferson had long been fascinated with the West and dreamed of a United States that would stretch across the entire continent.

Jefferson instructed Meriwether Lewis, who commanded the expedition jointly with William Clark, to seek new trade routes, to befriend the western tribes of Native Americans, and to report on the geography, geology, astronomy, zoology, botany, and climate of the west. The 8,000-mile expedition provided the U.S. Government with its first glimpse of the vast lands that lay west of the Mississippi River.

President Jefferson worked closely with Meriwether Lewis to ensure that he was well prepared—anticipating what the party would need in the way of arms, food, medicines, camping gear, scientific instruments, and presents for the Native Americans. They planned well. While the expedition ran out of such luxuries as whiskey, tobacco, and salt, they never ran out of rifles and powder, needed both for self-defense and food supply—and they never ran out of ink and paper, needed to record their findings.

Gentlemen of the Senate, and of the House of Representatives:

As the continuance of the act for establishing trading houses with the Indian tribes will be under the consideration of the Legislature at its present session, I think it my duty to communicate the views which have guided me in the execution of that act, in order that you may decide on the policy of continuing it, in the present or any other form, or discontinue it altogether, if that shall, on the whole, seem most for the public good.

The Indian tribes residing within the limits of the United States, have, for a considerable time, been growing more and more uneasy at the constant diminution of the territory they occupy, although effected by their own voluntary sales: and the policy has long been gaining strength with them, of refusing absolutely all further sale, on any conditions; insomuch that, at this time, it hazards their friendship, and excites dangerous jealousies and perturbations in their minds to make any overture for the purchase of the smallest portions of their land. A very few tribes only are not yet obstinately in these dispositions. In order peaceably to counteract this policy of theirs, and to provide an extension of territory which the rapid increase of our numbers will call for, two measures are deemed expedient. First: to encourage them to abandon hunting, to apply to the raising stock, to agriculture and domestic manufacture, and thereby prove to themselves that less land and labor will maintain them in this, better than in their former mode of living. The extensive forests necessary in the hunting life, will then become useless, and they will see advantage in exchanging them for the means of improving their farms, and of increasing their domestic comforts. Secondly: to multiply trading houses among them, and place within their reach those things which will contribute more to their domestic comfort, than the possession of extensive, but uncultivated wilds. Experience and reflection will develop to them the wisdom of exchanging what they can spare and we want, for what we can spare and they want. In leading them to agriculture, to manufactures, and civilization; in bringing together their and our settlements, and in preparing them ultimately to participate in the benefits of our governments, I trust and believe we are acting for their greatest good. At these trading houses we have pursued the principles of the act of Congress, which directs that the commerce shall be carried on liberally, and requires only that the capital stock shall not be diminished. We consequently undersell private traders, foreign and domestic, drive them from the competition; and thus, with the good will of the Indians, rid ourselves of a description of men who are constantly endeavoring to excite in the Indian mind suspicions, fears, and irritations towards us. A letter now enclosed, shows the effect of our competition on the operations of the traders, while the Indians, perceiving the advantage of purchasing from us, are soliciting generally, our establishment of trading houses among them. In one quarter this is particularly interesting. The Legislature, reflecting on the late occurrences on the Mississippi, must be sensible how desirable it is to possess a respectable breadth of country on that river, from our Southern limit to the Illinois at least; so that we may present as firm a front on that as on our Eastern border. We possess what is below the Yazoo, and can probably acquire a certain breadth from the Illinois and Wabash to the Ohio; but between the Ohio and Yazoo, the country all belongs to the Chickasaws, the most friendly tribe within our limits, but the most decided against the alienation of lands. The portion of their country most important for us is exactly that which they do not inhabit. Their settlements are not on the Mississippi, but in the interior country. They have lately shown a desire to become agricultural; and this leads to the desire of buying implements and comforts. In the strengthening and gratifying of these wants, I see the only prospect of planting on the Mississippi itself, the means of its own safety. Duty has required me to submit these views to the judgment of the Legislature; but as their disclosure might embarrass and defeat their effect, they are committed to the special confidence of the two Houses.

While the extension of the public commerce among the Indian tribes, may deprive of that source of profit such of our citizens as are engaged in it, it might be worthy the attention of Congress, in their care of individual as well as of the general interest, to point, in another direction, the enterprise of these citizens, as profitably for themselves, and more usefully for the public. The river Missouri, and the Indians inhabiting it, are not as well known as is rendered desirable by their connexion with the Mississippi, and consequently with us. It is, however, understood, that the country on that river is inhabited by numerous tribes, who furnish great supplies of furs and peltry to the trade of another nation, carried on in a high latitude, through an infinite number of portages and lakes, shut up by ice through a long season. The commerce on that line could bear no competition with that of the Missouri, traversing a moderate climate, offering according to the best accounts, a continued navigation from its source, and possibly with a single portage, from the Western Ocean, and finding to the Atlantic a choice of channels through the Illinois or Wabash, the lakes and Hudson, through the Ohio and Susquehanna, or Potomac or James rivers, and through the Tennessee and Savannah, rivers. An intelligent officer, with ten or twelve chosen men, fit for the enterprise, and willing to undertake it, taken from our posts, where they may be spared without inconvenience, might explore the whole line, even to the Western Ocean, have conferences with the natives on the subject of commercial intercourse, get admission among them for our traders, as others are admitted, agree on convenient deposits for an interchange of articles, and return with the information acquired, in the course of two summers. Their arms and accoutrements, some instruments of observation, and light and cheap presents for the Indians, would be all the apparatus they could carry, and with an expectation of a soldier's portion of land on their return, would constitute the whole expense. Their pay would be going on, whether here or there. While other civilized nations have encountered great expense to enlarge the boundaries of knowledge by undertaking voyages of discovery, and for other literary purposes, in various parts and directions, our nation seems to owe to the same object, as well as to its own interests, to explore this, the only line of easy communication across the continent, and so directly traversing our own part of it. The interests of commerce place the principal object within the constitutional powers and care of Congress, and that it should incidentally advance the geographical knowledge of our own continent, cannot be but an additional gratification. The nation claiming the territory, regarding this as a literary pursuit, which is in the habit of permitting within its dominions, would not be disposed to view it with jealousy, even if the expiring state of its interests there did not render it a matter of indifference. The appropriation of two thousand five hundred dollars, "for the purpose of extending the external commerce of the United States," while understood and considered by the Executive as giving the legislative sanction, would cover the undertaking from notice, and prevent the obstructions which interested individuals might otherwise previously prepare in its way.

TH. Jefferson
Jan. 18. 1803

1. Why does Jefferson propose sending an expedition to the Native American tribes?

   a. to ensure peace
   b. to expand territory
   c. to map the different geography of the United States
   d. to learn about the Native Americans and their way of life

2. Why are the Native Americans uneasy toward the U.S. government?

   a. They do not like Americans.
   b. They are an isolated people.
   c. They do not want to sell their land.
   d. They do not want to lose their tribal heritage.

3. How does Jefferson propose to remove the Native Americans from their land?

   a. He proposes instructing the Native Americans to raise livestock.
   b. He proposes forcing them to leave their land
   c. He proposes trading land for gold.
   d. He proposes to make the Native Americans eager for other forms of hunting.

4. Why was it important to Jefferson that the undertaking be covered "from notice"?

   a. He did not want to anger the Native Americans.
   b. He wanted to include Congress in the secret plan.
   c. He was unsure of what the expedition might uncover.
   d. It would be easier for the explorers to discover the geography of the country.

5. Do you agree with Jefferson that an introduction to agriculture would inevitably encourage the Native Americans to abandon hunting and seek out the comforts of domesticity? Why or why not?

6. What, ultimately, do you think was most important to Jefferson? Why did he feel it was necessary to make this plan a secret?

Louisiana Purchase, April 29, 1803

The Louisiana Purchase is considered the greatest real estate deal in history. The United States purchased the Louisiana Territory from France at a price of $15 million, or approximately four cents an acre. The ratification of the Louisiana Purchase treaty by the Senate on October 20, 1803, doubled the size of the United States and opened up the continent to its westward expansion.

TREATY BETWEEN THE UNITED STATES OF AMERICA AND THE FRENCH REPUBLIC

The President of the United States of America and the First Consul of the French Republic in the name of the French People desiring to remove all Source of misunderstanding relative to objects of discussion mentioned in the Second and fifth articles of the Convention of the 8th Vendémiaire on 9/30 September 1800 relative to the rights claimed by the United States in virtue of the Treaty concluded at Madrid the 27 of October 1795, between His Catholic Majesty & the Said United States, & willing to Strengthen the union and friendship which at the time of the Said Convention was happily reestablished between the two nations have respectively named their Plenipotentiaries to wit The President of the United States, by and with the advice and consent of the Senate of the Said States; Robert R. Livingston Minister Plenipotentiary of the United States and James Monroe Minister Plenipotentiary and Envoy extraordinary of the Said States near the Government of the French Republic; And the First Consul in the name of the French people, Citizen Francis Barbé Marbois Minister of the public treasury who after having respectively exchanged their full powers have agreed to the following Articles.

Article I

Whereas by the Article the third of the Treaty concluded . . . on 1st October 1800 between the First Consul of the French Republic and his Catholic Majesty it was agreed as follows.

> "His Catholic Majesty promises and engages on his part to cede to the French Republic six months after the full and entire execution of the conditions and Stipulations herein relative to his Royal Highness the Duke of Parma, the Colony or Province of Louisiana with the Same extent that it now has in the hand of Spain, & that it had when France possessed it; and Such as it Should be after the Treaties subsequently entered into between Spain and other States."

And whereas in pursuance of the Treaty and particularly of the third article the French Republic has an incontestable title to the domain and to the possession of the said Territory. The First Consul of the French Republic desiring to give to the United States a strong proof of his friendship doth hereby cede to the United States in the name of the French Republic for ever and in full Sovereignty the said territory with all its rights and appurtenances as fully and in the Same manner as they have been acquired by the French Republic in virtue of the above mentioned Treaty concluded with his Catholic Majesty.

Article II

In the cession made by the preceding article are included the adjacent Islands belonging to Louisiana all public lots and Squares, vacant lands and all public buildings, fortifications, barracks and other edifices which are not private property. The Archives, papers & documents relative to the domain and Sovereignty of Louisiana and its dependences will be left in the possession of the Commissaries of the United States, and copies will be afterwards given in due form to the Magistrates and Municipal officers of such of the said papers and documents as may be necessary to them.

Article III

The inhabitants of the ceded territory shall be incorporated in the Union of the United States and admitted as soon as possible according to the principles of the federal Constitution to the enjoyment of all these rights, advantages and immunities of citizens of the United States, and in the mean time they shall be maintained and protected in the free enjoyment of their liberty, property and the Religion which they profess . . .

Article V

Immediately after the ratification of the present Treaty by the President of the United States and in case that of the first Consul's shall have been previously obtained, the commissary of the French Republic shall remit all military posts of New Orleans and other parts of the ceded territory to the Commissary or Commissaries named by the President to take possession—the troops whether of France or Spain who may be there shall cease to occupy any military post from the time of taking possession and shall be embarked as soon as possible in the course of three months after the ratification of this treaty.

Article VI

The United States promise to execute Such treaties and articles as may have been agreed between Spain and the tribes and nations of Indians until by mutual consent of the United States and the said tribes or nations other Suitable articles Shall have been agreed upon.

Article VII

As it is reciprocally advantageous to the commerce of France and the United States to encourage the communication of both nations for a limited time in the country ceded by the present treaty until general arrangements relative to commerce of both nations may be agreed on; it has been agreed between the contracting parties that the French Ships coming directly from France or any of her colonies loaded only with the produce and manufactures of France or her Said Colonies; and the Ships of Spain coming directly from Spain or any of her colonies loaded only with the produce or manufactures of Spain or her Colonies shall be admitted during the Space of twelve years in the Port of New-Orleans and in all other legal ports-of-entry within the ceded territory in the Same manner as the Ships of the United States coming directly from France or Spain or any of their Colonies without being Subject to any other or greater duty on merchandize or other or greater tonnage than that paid by the citizens of the United. States.

During that Space of time above mentioned no other nation Shall have a right to the Same privileges in the Ports of the ceded territory—the twelve years Shall commence three months after the exchange of ratifications if it Shall take place in France or three months after it Shall have been notified at Paris to the French Government if it Shall take place in the United States; It is however well understood that the object of the above article is to favour the manufactures, Commerce, freight and navigation of France and of Spain So far as relates to the importations that the French and Spanish Shall make into the Said Ports of the United States without in any Sort affecting the regulations that the United States may make concerning the exportation of the produce and merchandize of the United States, or any right they may have to make Such regulations.

Article VIII

In future and for ever after the expiration of the twelve years, the Ships of France shall be treated upon the footing of the most favoured nations in the ports above mentioned.

1. The Louisiana Purchase Treaty implies that the French Republic was eager to

   a. trade with the United States.
   b. start a war with the United States.
   c. eliminate any misunderstanding between the two powers.
   d. reduce Spanish control in the region of Louisiana.

2. In the treaty, what did the French Republic give the U.S.?

   a. authority over the inhabitants of Louisiana
   b. ownership over the adjacent islands of Louisiana
   c. ownership of towns, barracks, and public documents of Louisiana
   d. all of the above

3. Why are the inhabitants of the ceded territory given rights "in the mean time"?

   a. France and America were unsure who had authority over them.
   b. The inhabitants had a right to leave the Louisiana.
   c. The inhabitants have rights during the period of exchange.
   d. The inhabitants did not have rights under the French Republic.

4. Why does France want a period of 12 years during which its ships can enter the New Orleans port?

   a. in order to ensure continuing commerce between the countries
   b. in order to protect the inhabitants of Louisiana
   c. in order to help the United States gain authority in Louisiana
   d. in order to remove its military from New Orleans

5. In the treaty, what did the United States promise France?

   a. 10 years of free commerce in the port of New Orleans
   b. to honor the treaties between the Native Americans and the Spanish
   c. to declare war on any country that was in conflict with France
   d. to remove all of its military bases in Louisiana

6. Why was the Louisiana Purchase so important to the United States? How does the treaty contribute to the idea that the United States was destined to expand?

____

____

____

____

____

The Treaty of Ghent, December 24, 1814

The Treaty of Ghent ended the War of 1812 between the United States and Great Britain. Peace negotiations began in Ghent, Belgium, starting in August of 1814. After four months of talks, the treaty was signed on December 24, 1814. The Senate unanimously ratified the Treaty of Ghent on February 16, 1815.

Treaty of Peace and Amity between His Britannic Majesty and the United States of America.

His Britannic Majesty and the United States of America desirous of terminating the war which has unhappily subsisted between the two Countries, and of restoring upon principles of perfect reciprocity, Peace, Friendship, and good Understanding between them, have for that purpose appointed their respective Plenipotentiaries, that is to say, His Britannic Majesty on His part has appointed the Right Honourable James Lord Gambier, late Admiral of the White now Admiral of the Red Squadron of His Majesty's Fleet; Henry Goulburn Esquire, a Member of the Imperial Parliament and Under Secretary of State; and William Adams Esquire, Doctor of Civil Laws: And the President of the United States, by and with the advice and consent of the Senate thereof, has appointed John Quincy Adams, James A. Bayard, Henry Clay, Jonathan Russell, and Albert Gallatin, Citizens of the United States; who, after a reciprocal communication of their respective Full Powers, have agreed upon the following Articles.

ARTICLE THE FIRST

There shall be a firm and universal Peace between His Britannic Majesty and the United States, and between their respective Countries, Territories, Cities, Towns, and People of every degree without exception of places or persons. All hostilities both by sea and land shall cease as soon as this Treaty shall have been ratified by both parties as hereinafter mentioned. All territory, places, and possessions whatsoever taken by either party from the other during the war, or which may be taken after the signing of this Treaty, excepting only the Islands hereinafter mentioned, shall be restored without delay and without causing any destruction or carrying away any of the Artillery or other public property originally captured in the said forts or places, and which shall remain therein upon the Exchange of the Ratifications of this Treaty, or any Slaves or other private property; And all Archives, Records, Deeds, and Papers, either of a public nature or belonging to private persons, which in the course of the war may have fallen into the hands of the Officers of either party, shall be, as far as may be practicable, forthwith restored and delivered to the proper authorities and persons to whom they respectively belong. Such of the Islands in the Bay of Passamaquoddy as are claimed by both parties shall remain in the possession of the party in whose occupation they may be at the time of the Exchange of the Ratifications of this Treaty until the decision respecting the title to the said Islands shall have been made in conformity with the fourth Article of this Treaty. No disposition made by this Treaty as to such possession of the Islands and territories claimed by both parties shall in any manner whatever be construed to affect the right of either.

ARTICLE THE SECOND

Immediately after the ratifications of this Treaty by both parties as hereinafter mentioned, orders shall be sent to the Armies, Squadrons, Officers, Subjects, and Citizens of the two Powers to cease from all hostilities: and to prevent all causes of complaint which might arise on account of the prizes which may be taken at sea after the said Ratifications of this Treaty, it is reciprocally agreed that all vessels and effects which may be taken after the space of twelve days from the said Ratifications upon all parts of the Coast of North America from the Latitude of twenty three degrees North to the Latitude of fifty degrees North, and as far Eastward in the Atlantic Ocean as the thirty sixth degree of West Longitude from the Meridian of Greenwich, shall be restored on each side:—that the time shall be thirty days in all other parts of the Atlantic Ocean North of the Equinoctial Line or Equator:—and the same time for the British and Irish Channels, for the Gulf of Mexico, and all parts of the West Indies:—forty days for the North Seas for the Baltic, and for all parts of the Mediterranean—sixty days for the Atlantic Ocean South of the Equator as far as the Latitude of the Cape of Good Hope.—ninety days for every other part of the world South of the Equator, and one hundred and twenty days for all other parts of the world without exception.

ARTICLE THE THIRD

All Prisoners of war taken on either side as well by land as by sea shall be restored as soon as practicable after the Ratifications of this Treaty as hereinafter mentioned on their paying the debts which they may have contracted during their captivity. The two Contracting Parties respectively engage to discharge in specie the advances which may have been made by the other for the sustenance and maintenance of such prisoners.

1. From this treaty, you can ascertain that the War of 1812 ended in a

    a. victory for the United States.
    b. victory for Great Britain.
    c. stalemate.
    d. none of the above.

2. Concerning the articles taken during war, the treaty specifies what?

    a. The islands are the rightful property of Britain and Canada.
    b. All articles, except the islands, shall be returned to their rightful owners.
    c. All articles should be returned to the their rightful owners.
    d. Most articles should be kept as spoils of war.

3. If a person in the North Seas wishes to return an item to his enemy, how many days does he have to do so?

    a. 12 days
    b. 30 days
    c. 40 days
    d. 60 days

4. Why is it important that both the United States and Great Britain do their best to ensure that all objects and persons taken during the war are returned? How would it appear if they did not return the "spoils of war" with all due alacrity?

McCulloch v. Maryland (1819)

In many ways, the opinion in this case represents a final step in the creation of the federal government. The issue involved, the power of Congress to charter a bank, seems insignificant, but the larger questions go to the very heart of constitutional interpretation, and are still debated today.

In 1791, as part of his financial plan, Secretary of the Treasury Alexander Hamilton proposed that Congress charter a Bank of the United States, to serve as a central bank for the country. Secretary of State Thomas Jefferson opposed the notion, on the grounds that the Constitution did not specifically give Congress such a power, and that under a limited government, Congress had no powers other than those explicitly given to it. Hamilton responded by arguing that Congress had all powers except those specifically denied to it in the Constitution, and that moreover, the "necessary and proper" clause of Article I required a broad reading of the designated powers. President Washington backed Hamilton, and the bank was given a twenty-year charter. The charter expired in 1811, and the Jeffersonians had not renewed it.

Then came the War of 1812, and President Madison realized that the government needed the services of a central bank. In 1816, at his recommendation, Congress chartered a second Bank of the United States (BUS), which quickly established branches throughout the Union. Many local, state-chartered banks, eager to follow speculative policies, resented the cautious fiscal policy of the BUS, and looked to state legislatures to restrict the BUS operations. Maryland imposed a tax on the bank's operations, and when James McCulloch, the cashier of the Baltimore branch of the BUS, refused to pay the tax, the issue went to court.

Few people expected the court to hold the charter establishing the bank unconstitutional; what was at issue was the extent of state power vis-a-vis federal authority. In what has justly been termed a state paper, Chief Justice Marshall not only endorsed the constitutionality of the bank, but went on to uphold a broad interpretation of the federal government's powers under the Constitution, and thus pave the way for the modern national state that would emerge after the Civil War. Although there have been some people who have disagreed and continue to disagree with the Marshall opinion, it has for the most part won the approval not only of subsequent courts but of the American people as well.

Chief Justice Marshall delivered the opinion of the Court.

In the case now to be determined, the defendant, a sovereign State, denies the obligation of a law enacted by the legislature of the Union, and the plaintiff, on his part, contests the validity of an act which has been passed by the legislature of that State. The constitution of our country, in its most interesting and vital parts, is to be considered; the conflicting powers of the government of the Union and of its members, as marked in that constitution, are to be discussed; and an opinion given, which may essentially influence the great operations of the government. No tribunal can approach such a question without a deep sense of its importance, and of the awful responsibility involved in its decision. But it must be decided peacefully, or remain a source of hostile legislation, perhaps of hostility of a still more serious nature; and if it is to be so decided, by this tribunal alone can the decision be made. On the Supreme Court of the United States has the constitution of our country devolved this important duty.

The first question made in the cause is, has Congress power to incorporate a bank?

It has been truly said that this can scarcely be considered as an open question, entirely unprejudiced by the former proceedings of the nation respecting it. The principle now contested was introduced at a very early period of our history, has been recognized by many successive legislatures, and has been acted upon by the judicial department, in cases of peculiar delicacy, as a law of undoubted obligation. . . .

The power now contested was exercised by the first Congress elected under the present constitution. The bill for incorporating the bank of the United States did not steal upon an unsuspecting legislature, and pass unobserved. Its principle was completely understood, and was opposed with equal zeal and ability. After being resisted, first in the fair and open field of debate, and afterwards in the executive cabinet, with as much persevering talent as any measure has ever experienced, and being supported by arguments which convinced minds as pure and as intelligent as this country can boast, it became a law. The original act was permitted to expire; but a short experience of the embarrassments to which the refusal to revive it exposed the government, convinced those who were most prejudiced against the measure of its necessity, and induced the passage of the present law. It would require no ordinary share of intrepidity to assert that a measure adopted under these circumstances was a bold and plain usurpation, to which the constitution gave no countenance.

These observations belong to the cause; but they are not made under the impression that, were the question entirely new, the law would be found irreconcilable with the constitution.

In discussing this question, the counsel for the State of Maryland have deemed it of some importance, in the construction of the constitution, to consider that instrument not as emanating from the people, but as the act of sovereign and independent States. The powers of the general government, it has been said, are delegated by the States, who alone are truly sovereign; and must be exercised in subordination to the States, who alone possess supreme dominion.

It would be difficult to sustain this proposition. The Convention which framed the constitution was indeed elected by the State legislatures. But the instrument, when it came from their hands, was a mere proposal, without obligation, or pretensions to it. It was reported to the then existing Congress of the United States, with a request that it might "be submitted to a convention of delegates, chosen in each State by the people thereof, under the recommendation of its legislature, for their assent and ratification." This mode of proceeding was adopted; and by the convention, by Congress, and by the State legislatures, the instrument was submitted to the people. They acted upon it in the only manner in which they can act safely, effectively, and wisely, on such a subject, by assembling in convention. It is true, they assembled in their several States—and where else should they have assembled? No political dreamer was ever wild enough to think of breaking down the lines which separate the States, and of compounding the American people into one common mass. Of consequence, when they act, they act in their States. But the measures they adopt do not, on that account, cease to be the measures of the people themselves, or become the measures of the State governments.

From these conventions the constitution derives its whole authority. The government proceeds directly from the people; is "ordained and established" in the name of the people; and is declared to be ordained, "in order to form a more perfect union, establish justice, ensure domestic tranquility, and secure the blessings of liberty to themselves and to their posterity." The assent of the States, in their sovereign capacity, is implied in calling a convention, and thus submitting that instrument to the people. But the people were at perfect liberty to accept or reject it; and their act was final . . .

Among the enumerated powers, we do not find that of establishing a bank or creating a corporation. But there is no phrase in the instrument which, like the articles of confederation, excludes incidental or implied powers; and which requires that everything granted shall be expressly and minutely described. Even the 10th amendment, which was framed for the purpose of quieting the excessive jealousies which had been excited, omits the word "expressly," and declares only that the powers "not delegated to the United States, nor prohibited to the States, are reserved to the States or to the people"; thus leaving the question, whether the particular power which may become the subject of contest has been delegated to the one government, or prohibited to the other, to depend on a fair construction of the whole instrument. The men who drew and adopted this amendment had experienced the embarrassments resulting from the insertion of this word in the articles of confederation, and probably omitted it to avoid those embarrassments. A constitution, to contain an accurate detail of all the subdivisions of which its great powers will admit, and of all the means by which they may be carried into execution, would partake of the prolixity of a legal code, and could scarcely be embraced by the human mind. It would probably never be understood by the public. Its nature, therefore, requires, that only its great outlines should be marked, its important objects designated, and the minor ingredients which compose those objects be deduced from the nature of the objects themselves . . .

Although, among the enumerated powers of government, we do not find the word "bank," or "incorporation," we find the great powers to lay and collect taxes; to borrow money; to regulate commerce; to declare and conduct a war; and to raise and support armies and navies. The sword and the purse, all the external relations, and no inconsiderable portion of the industry of the nation, are entrusted to its government. It can never be pretended that these vast powers draw after them others of inferior importance, merely because they are inferior. Such an idea can never be advanced. But it may with great reason be contended, that a government, entrusted with such ample powers, on the due execution of which the happiness and prosperity of the nation so vitally depends, must also be entrusted with ample means for their execution. The power being given, it is the interest of the nation to facilitate its execution . . .

It is not denied, that the powers given to the government imply the ordinary means of execution. That, for example, of raising revenue, and applying it to national purposes, is admitted to imply the power of conveying money from place to place, as the exigencies of the nation may require, and of employing the usual means of conveyance. But it is denied that the government has its choice of means; or, that it may employ the most convenient means, if, to employ them, it be necessary to erect a corporation. . . .

The government which has a right to do an act, and has imposed on it the duty of performing that act, must, according to the dictates of reason, be allowed to select the means; and those who contend that it may not select any appropriate means, that one particular mode of effecting the object is excepted, take upon themselves the burden of establishing that exception. . . . The power of creating a corporation, though appertaining to sovereignty, is not like the power of making war, or levying taxes, or of regulating commerce, a great substantive and independent power, which cannot be implied as incidental to other powers, or used as a means of executing them. It is never the end for which other powers are exercised, but a means by which other objects are accomplished. . .

But the constitution of the United States has not left the right of Congress to employ the necessary means, for the execution of the powers conferred on the government, to general reasoning. To its enumeration of powers is added that of making "all laws which shall be necessary and proper for carrying into execution the foregoing powers, and all other powers vested by this constitution, in the government of the United States, or in any department thereof . . . "

After the most deliberate consideration, it is the unanimous and decided opinion of this Court, that the act to incorporate the Bank of the United States is a law made in pursuance of the constitution, and is a part of the supreme law of the land. . . .

It being the opinion of the Court, that the act incorporating the bank is constitutional; and that the power of establishing a branch in the State of Maryland might be properly exercised by the bank itself, we proceed to inquire—

2. Whether the State of Maryland may, without violating the constitution, tax that branch? . . .

(T)he power of taxing by the States may be exercised so as to destroy.

We are unanimously of opinion, that the law passed by the legislature of Maryland, imposing a tax on the Bank of the United States, is unconstitutional and void.

This opinion does not deprive the States of any resources which they originally possessed. It does not extend to a tax paid by the real property of the bank, in common with the other real property within the State, nor to a tax imposed on the interest which the citizens of Maryland may hold in this institution, in common with other property of the same description throughout the State. But this is a tax on the operations of the bank, and is, consequently, a tax on the operation of an instrument employed by the government of the Union to carry its powers into execution. Such a tax must be unconstitutional.

1. Why did Hamilton feel it was necessary to create a central bank?

    a. to stabilize the currency
    b. to renew the charter
    c. to anger the Jeffersonians
    d. all of the above

2. How did the state of Maryland respond to the central bank?

    a. It approved and added taxes for government bonds.
    b. It opposed the bank and taxed the branch.
    c. It did not care either way.
    d. It believed that the bank was corrupt.

3. Why did McCulloch refuse to issue the Maryland State tax?

    a. He did not believe that the state tax was fair.
    b. He did not believe that the federal government could levy a tax.
    c. He disagreed with the constitution.
    d. He knew that the state would not enforce the tax.

4. McCulloch believed that his protest against the legislative act was

    a. Maryland state law.
    b. unconstitutional.
    c. part of the federal government's mandate.
    d. his right as a citizen.

5. What was Chief Justice Marshall's answer to the question, "Has Congress power to incorporate a bank?"

   a. It can only if the executive branch approves of Congress's decision.
   b. It does not because the government is subordinate to the sovereign states.
   c. It does because the sovereign states have agreed to a constitution.
   d. It does not have the power to do so because the people assembled and voted in their states, not as a single mass.

6. Does the Constitution specify that the Congress has the right to open a national bank?

   a. Yes, it does in the 10th Amendment to the Constitution.
   b. No, it does not give any specific powers in that area.
   c. Yes, it does only if the states ratify the bill.
   d. only during a national crisis

7. Formulate an argument against Chief Justice Marshall's decision. Use at least two points in Marshall's opinion and argue against them.

8. Essentially *McCulloch* v. *Maryland* is a debate about the distinction between implied and enumerated constitutional powers. Please define those two terms in your own words and explain how Chief Justice Marshall used implied powers to rule in favor of the federal government.

Missouri Compromise (1820)

The Senate debated the admission of Maine and Missouri from February 8–17, 1820. On February 16th, the Senate agreed to unite the Maine and Missouri bills into one bill. The following day the Senate agreed to an amendment that prohibited slavery in the Louisiana Territory north of the 36° 30′ latitude line, except for Missouri, and then agreed to the final version of the bill by a vote of 24 to 20. After rejecting the Senate's version of the bill, the House of Representatives passed a bill on March 1st, that admitted Missouri without slavery. On March 2nd, after a House-Senate conference agreed to the Senate's version, the House voted 90 to 87 to allow slavery in Missouri and then voted 134 to 42 to prohibit slavery in the Louisiana Territory north of the 36° 30′ latitude.

In an effort to preserve the balance of power in Congress between slave and free states, the Missouri Compromise was passed in 1820, admitting Missouri as a slave state and Maine as a free state. Furthermore, with the exception of Missouri, this law prohibited slavery in the Louisiana Territory north of the 36° 30′ latitude line. In 1854, the Missouri Compromise was repealed by the Kansas-Nebraska Act. Three years later the Missouri Compromise was declared unconstitutional by the Supreme Court in the Dred Scott decision. It ruled that Congress did not have the authority to prohibit slavery in the territories.

An Act to authorize the people of the Missouri territory to form a constitution and state government, and for the admission of such state into the Union on an equal footing with the original states, and to prohibit slavery in certain territories.

Be it enacted by the Senate and House of Representatives of the United States of America, in Congress assembled, That the inhabitants of that portion of the Missouri territory included within the boundaries herein after designated, be, and they are hereby, authorized to form for themselves a constitution and state government, and to assume such name as they shall deem proper; and the said state, when formed, shall be admitted into the Union, upon an equal footing with the original states, in all respects whatsoever.

SEC.2. And be it further enacted, That the said state shall consist of all the territory included within the following boundaries, to wit: Beginning in the middle of the Mississippi river, on the parallel of thirty-six degrees of north latitude; thence west, along that parallel of latitude, to the St. Francois river; thence up, and following the course of that river, in the middle of the main channel thereof, to the parallel of latitude of thirty-six degrees and thirty minutes; thence west, along the same, to a point where the said parallel is intersected by a meridian line passing through the middle of the mouth of the Kansas river, where the same empties into the Missouri river, thence, from the point aforesaid north, along the said meridian line, to the intersection of the parallel of latitude which passes through the rapids of the river Des Moines, making the said line to correspond with the Indian boundary line; thence east, from the point of intersection last aforesaid, along the said parallel of latitude, to the middle of the channel of the main fork of the said river Des Moines; thence down arid along the middle of the main channel of the said river Des Moines, to the mouth of the same, where it empties into the Mississippi river; thence, due east, to the middle of the main channel of the Mississippi river; thence down, and following the course of the Mississippi river, in the middle of the main channel thereof, to the place of beginning: Provided, The said state shall ratify the boundaries aforesaid. And provided also, That the said state shall have concurrent jurisdiction on the river Mississippi, and every other river bordering on the said state so far as the said rivers shall form a common boundary to the said state; and any other state or states, now or hereafter to be formed and bounded by the same, such rivers to be common to both; and that the river Mississippi, and the navigable rivers and waters leading into the same, shall be common highways, and for ever free, as well to the inhabitants of the said state as to other citizens of the United States, without any tax, duty impost, or toll, therefor, imposed by the said state.

SEC. 3. And be it further enacted, That all free white male citizens of the United States, who shall have arrived at the age of twenty-one years, and have resided in said territory: three months previous to the day of election, and all other persons qualified to vote for representatives to the general assembly of the said territory, shall be qualified to be elected and they are hereby qualified and authorized to vote, and choose representatives to form a convention, who shall be apportioned amongst the several counties as follows:

From the county of Howard, five representatives. From the county of Cooper, three representatives. From the county of Montgomery, two representatives. From the county of Pike, one representative. From the county of Lincoln, one representative. From the county of St. Charles, three representatives. From the county of Franklin, one representative. From the county of St. Louis, eight representatives. From the county of Jefferson, one representative. From the county of Washington, three representatives. From the county of St. Genevieve, four representatives. From the county of Madison, one representative. From the county of Cape Girardeau, five representatives. From the county of New Madrid, two representatives. From the county of Wayne, and that portion of the county of Lawrence which falls within the boundaries herein designated, one representative.

And the election for the representatives aforesaid shall be holden on the first Monday, and two succeeding days of May next, throughout the several counties aforesaid in the said territory, and shall be, in every respect, held and conducted in the same manner, and under the same regulations as is prescribed by the laws of the said territory regulating elections therein for members of the general assembly, except that the returns of the election in that portion of Lawrence county included in the boundaries aforesaid, shall be made to the county of Wayne, as is provided in other cases under the laws of said territory.

SEC. 4. And be it further enacted, That the members of the conven tion thus duly elected, shall be, and they are hereby authorized to meet at the seat of government of said territory on the second Monday of the month of June next; and the said convention, when so assembled, shall have power and authority to adjourn to any other place in the said territory, which to them shall seem best for the convenient transaction of their business; and which convention, when so met, shall first determine by a majority of the whole number elected, whether it be, or be not, expedient at that time to form a constitution and state government for the people within the said territory, as included within the boundaries above designated; and if it be deemed expedient, the convention shall be, and hereby is, authorized to form a constitution and state government; or, if it be deemed more expedient, the said convention shall provide by ordinance for electing representatives to form a constitution or frame of government; which said representatives shall be chosen in such manner, and in such proportion as they shall designate; and shall meet at such time and place as shall be prescribed by the said ordinance; and shall then form for the people of said territory, within the boundaries aforesaid, a constitution and state government: Provided, That the same, whenever formed, shall be republican, and not repugnant to the constitution of the United States; and that the legislature of said state shall never interfere with the primary disposal of the soil by the United States, nor with any regulations Congress may find necessary for securing the title in such soil to the bona fide purchasers ; and that no tax shall be imposed on lands the property of the United States; and in no case shall non-resident proprietors be taxed higher than residents.

SEC. 5. And be it further enacted, That until the next general census shall be taken, the said state shall be entitled to one representative in the House of Representatives of the United States.

SEC. 6. And be it further enacted, That the following propositions be, and the same are hereby, offered to the convention of the said territory of Missouri, when formed, for their free acceptance or rejection, which, if accepted by the convention, shall be obligatory upon the United States:

First. That section numbered sixteen in every township, and when such section has been sold, or otherwise disposed of, other lands equivalent thereto, and as contiguous as may be, shall be granted to the state for the use of the inhabitants of such township, for the use of schools.

Second. That all salt springs, not exceeding twelve in number, with six sections of land adjoining to each, shall be granted to the said state for the use of said state, the same to be selected by the legislature of the said state, on or before the first day of January, in the year one thousand eight hundred and twenty-five ; and the same, when so selected, to be used under such terms, conditions, and regulations, as the legislature of said state shall direct: Provided, That no salt spring, the right whereof now is, or hereafter shall be, confirmed or adjudged to any individual or individuals, shall, by this section, be granted to the said state: And provided also, That the legislature shall never sell or lease the same, at anyone time, for a longer period than ten years, without the consent of Congress.

Third. That five per cent. of the net proceeds of the sale of lands lying within the said territory or state, and which shall be sold by Congress, from and after the first day of January next, after deducting all expenses incident to the same, shall be reserved for making public roads and canals, of which three fifths shall be applied to those objects within the state, under the direction of the legislature thereof; and the other two fifths in defraying, under the direction of Congress, the expenses to be incurred in making of a road or roads, canal or canals, leading to the said state.

Fourth. That four entire sections of land be, and the same are hereby, granted to the said state, for the purpose of fixing their seat of government thereon; which said sections shall, under the direction of the legislature of said state, be located, as near as may be, in one body, at any time, in such townships and ranges as the legislature aforesaid may select, on any of the public lands of the United States: Provided, That such locations shall be made prior to the public sale of the lands of the United States surrounding such location.

Fifth. That thirty-six sections, or one entire township, which shall be designated by the President of the United States, together with the other lands heretofore reserved for that purpose, shall be reserved for the use of a seminary of learning, and vested in the legislature of said state, to be appropriated solely to the use of such seminary by the said legislature: Provided, That the five foregoing propositions herein offered, are on the condition that the convention of the said state shall provide, by an ordinance, irrevocable without the consent or the United States, that every and each tract of land sold by the United States, from and after the firsl day of January next, shall remain exempt from any tax laid by order or under the authority of the state, whether for state, county, or township, or any other purpose whatever, for the term of five years from and after the day of sale; And further, That the bounty lands granted, or hereafter to be granted, for military services during the late war, shall, while they continue to be held by the patentees, or their heirs remain exempt as aforesaid from taxation for the term of three year; from and after the date of the patents respectively.

SEC. 7. And be it further enacted, That in case a constitution and state government shall be formed for the people of the said territory of Missouri, the said convention or representatives, as soon thereafter as may be, shall cause a true and attested copy of such constitution or frame of state government, as shall be formed or provided, to be transmitted to Congress.

SEC. 8. And be it further enacted. That in all that territory ceded by France to the United States, under the name of Louisiana, which lies north of thirty-six degrees and thirty minutes north latitude, not included within the limits of the state, contemplated by this act, slavery and involuntary servitude, otherwise than in the punishment of crimes, whereof the parties shall have been duly convicted, shall be, and is hereby, forever prohibited: Provided always, That any person escaping into the same, from whom labour or service is lawfully claimed, in any state or territory of the United States, such fugitive may be lawfully reclaimed and conveyed to the person claiming his or her labour or service as aforesaid.

APPROVED, March 6, 1820.

1. The act authorizes that inhabitants of Missouri have a right to

   a. migrate to other states.
   b. establish a constitution and state government.
   c. secede from the Union and create a separate nation.
   d. free the slaves in the territory and surrounding territories.

2. Why does the compromise specify that the Mississippi River and other rivers bordering Missouri are common highways?

   a. The Congress fears that the Missouri legislature will neglect the upkeep of the waterways and canals.
   b. The Congress wants to set up a military branch in the area.
   c. The Congress does not want each state to set up tariffs on the rivers in their territories.
   d. The Congress wants to levy taxes on the rivers.

3. To whom was the right to vote given?

   a. free white male citizens of the U.S.
   b. all citizens of the U.S.
   c. citizens who serve in the House of Representatives
   d. all of the above

4. What county in Missouri qualified for the highest number of representatives?

   a. Cape Girardeau
   b. Cooper
   c. St. Louis
   d. Howard

5. Why did the Congress specify that five percent of the proceeds made from the sale of land in Missouri be reserved for public roads?

   a. The Congress wanted to have control over Missouri.
   b. The Congress did not trust Missouri to do the right thing.
   c. The Congress believed that the upkeep of roads was extremely important.
   d. The Congress needed to ensure that roads were well kept for commerce and communication.

6. Congress stated that slavery in the territories was abolished **except**

   a. if Missouri chose to veto the compromise.
   b. when it was used as a punishment for a crime.
   c. if neighboring states chose to disregard the compromise.
   d. if a slave owner argued against the prohibition.

7. If Missouri decided to create a constitution immediately it would have had to

   a. expand its territory and pay a heavy tax to the Union.
   b. elect representatives to meet with the president.
   c. first divest itself of all involuntary servants.
   d. elect members of the convention, meet, and vote.

8. Though the compromise is remembered largely for section 8, which discusses slavery, other sections discuss ways in which Missouri should develop as a state. Choose two significant aspects of the compromise that do not include section 8 and explain their importance in your own words.

The Monroe Doctrine (1823)

President James Monroe's 1823 annual message to Congress contained the Monroe Doctrine, which warned European powers not to interfere in the affairs of the Western Hemisphere.

Understandably, the United States has always taken a particular interest in its closest neighbors—the nations of the Western Hemisphere. Equally understandably, expressions of this concern have not always been favorably regarded by other American nations.

The Monroe Doctrine is the best known U.S. policy toward the Western Hemisphere. Buried in a routine annual message delivered to Congress by President James Monroe in December 1823, the doctrine warns European nations that the United States would not tolerate further colonization or puppet monarchs. The doctrine was conceived to meet major concerns of the moment, but it soon became a watchword of U.S. policy in the Western Hemisphere.

The end of the Napoleonic Wars in 1815 marked the breakup of the Spanish empire in the New World. Between 1815 and 1822, Jose de San Martin led Argentina to independence, while Bernardo O'Higgins in Chile and Simon Bolivar in Venezuela guided their countries out of colonialism. The new republics sought—and expected—recognition by the United States, and many Americans endorsed that idea.

But President James Monroe and his secretary of state, John Quincy Adams, were not willing to risk war for nations they did not know would survive. From their point of view, as long as the other European powers did not intervene, the government of the United States could just let Spain and her rebellious colonies fight it out.

Great Britain was torn between monarchical principle and a desire for new markets; South America as a whole constituted, at the time, a much larger market for English goods than the United States. When Russia and France proposed that England join in helping Spain regain her New World colonies, Great Britain vetoed the idea.

The United States was also negotiating with Spain to purchase the Floridas and, once that treaty had been ratified, the Monroe administration began to extend recognition to the new Latin American republics. Argentina, Chile, Peru, Colombia and Mexico were all recognized in 1822.

In 1823, France invited Spain to restore the Bourbon power, and there was talk of France and Spain warring upon the new republics with the backing of the Holy Alliance (Russia, Prussia and Austria). This news appalled the British government. All the work of Wolfe, Chatham, and other eighteenth-century British statesmen to get France out of the New World would be undone, and France would again be a power in the Americas.

George Canning, the British foreign minister, proposed that the United States and Great Britain join to warn France and Spain from trying to intervene. Both Jefferson and Madison urged Monroe to accept the offer, but John Quincy Adams was more suspicious. Adams also was quite concerned about Russia's efforts to extend its influence down the Pacific coast from Alaska south to California, then owned by Mexico.

At the Cabinet meeting of November 7, 1823, Adams argued against Canning's offer, and declared, "It would be more candid, as well as more dignified, to avow our principles explicitly to Russia and France, than to come in as a cockboat in the wake of the British man-of-war."

Adams argued and finally won the Cabinet over to an independent policy. In Monroe's message to Congress on December 2, 1823, he delivered what we have always called the Monroe Doctrine, although in truth it should have been called the Adams Doctrine. Essentially, the United States was informing the powers of the Old World that the American continents were no longer open to European colonization, and that any effort to extend European political influence into the New World would be considered by the United States "as dangerous to our peace and safety." The United States would not interfere in European wars or internal affairs, and expected Europe to stay out of American affairs.

Although it would take decades to coalesce into an identifiable policy, John Quincy Adams did raise a standard of an independent American foreign policy so strongly that future administrations could not ignore it. One should note, however, that the policy succeeded because it met British interests as well as American, and for the next 100 years was secured by the backing of the British fleet.

The Monroe Doctrine was invoked in 1865 when the U.S. government exerted diplomatic and military pressure in support of the Mexican President Benito Juárez. This support enabled Juárez to lead a successful revolt against the Emperor Maximilian, who had been placed on the throne by the French government.

Almost forty years later, in 1904, European creditors of a number of Latin American countries threatened armed intervention to collect debts. President Theodore Roosevelt promptly proclaimed the right of the United States to exercise an "international police power" to curb such "chronic wrongdoing." As a result, U. S. Marines were sent into Santo Domingo in 1904, Nicaragua in 1911, and Haiti in 1915, ostensibly to keep the Europeans out. Other Latin American nations viewed these interventions with misgiving, and relations between the "great Colossus of the North" and its southern neighbors remained strained for many years.

In 1962, the Monroe Doctrine was invoked symbolically when the Soviet Union began to build missile-launching sites in Cuba. With the support of the Organization of American States, President John F. Kennedy threw a naval and air quarantine around the island. After several tense days, the Soviet Union agreed to withdraw the missiles and dismantle the sites. Subsequently, the United States dismantled several of its obsolete air and missile bases in Turkey.

. . . At the proposal of the Russian Imperial Government, made through the minister of the Emperor residing here, a full power and instructions have been transmitted to the minister of the United States at St. Petersburg to arrange by amicable negotiation the respective rights and interests of the two nations on the northwest coast of this continent. A similar proposal had been made by His Imperial Majesty to the Government of Great Britain, which has likewise been acceded to. The Government of the United States has been desirous by this friendly proceeding of manifesting the great value which they have invariably attached to the friendship of the Emperor and their solicitude to cultivate the best understanding with his Government. In the discussions to which this interest has given rise and in the arrangements by which they may terminate the occasion has been judged proper for asserting, as a principle in which the rights and interests of the United States are involved, that the American continents, by the free and independent condition which they have assumed and maintain, are henceforth not to be considered as subjects for future colonization by any European powers. . . .

It was stated at the commencement of the last session that a great effort was then making in Spain and Portugal to improve the condition of the people of those countries, and that it appeared to be conducted with extraordinary moderation. It need scarcely be remarked that the result has been so far very different from what was then anticipated. Of events in that quarter of the globe, with which we have so much intercourse and from which we derive our origin, we have always been anxious and interested spectators. The citizens of the United States cherish sentiments the most friendly in favor of the liberty and happiness of their fellowmen on that side of the Atlantic. In the wars of the European powers in matters relating to themselves we have never taken any part, nor does it comport with our policy so to do. It is only when our rights are invaded or seriously menaced that we resent injuries or make preparation for our defense. With the movements in this hemisphere we are of necessity more immediately connected, and by causes which must be obvious to all enlightened and impartial observers. The political system of the allied powers is essentially different in this respect from that of America. This difference proceeds from that which exists in their respective Governments; and to the defense of our own, which has been achieved by the loss of so much blood and treasure, and matured by the wisdom of their most enlightened citizens, and under which we have enjoyed unexampled felicity, this whole nation is devoted. We owe it, therefore, to candor and to the amicable relations existing between the United States and those powers to declare that we should consider any attempt on their part to extend their system to any portion of this hemisphere as dangerous to our peace and safety. With the existing colonies or dependencies of any European power we have not interfered and shall not interfere. But with the Governments who have declared their independence and maintained it, and whose independence we have, on great consideration and on just principles, acknowledged, we could not view any interposition for the purpose of oppressing them, or controlling in any other manner their destiny, by any European power in any other light than as the manifestation of an unfriendly disposition toward the United States. In the war between those new Governments and Spain we declared our neutrality at the time of their recognition, and to this we have adhered, and shall continue to adhere, provided no change shall occur which, in the judgment of the competent authorities of this Government, shall make a corresponding change on the part of the United States indispensable to their security.

The late events in Spain and Portugal show that Europe is still unsettled. Of this important fact no stronger proof can be adduced than that the allied powers should have thought it proper, on any principle satisfactory to themselves, to have interposed by force in the internal concerns of Spain. To what extent such interposition may be carried, on the same principle, is a question in which all independent powers whose governments differ from theirs are interested, even those most remote, and surely none more so than the United States. Our policy in regard to Europe, which was adopted at an early stage of the wars which have so long agitated that quarter of the globe, nevertheless remains the same, which is, not to interfere in the internal concerns of any of its powers; to consider the government de facto as the legitimate government for us; to cultivate friendly relations with it, and to preserve those relations by a frank, firm, and manly policy, meeting in all instances the just claims of every power, submitting to injuries from none. But in regard to those continents circumstances are eminently and conspicuously different. It is impossible that the allied powers should extend their political system to any portion of either continent without endangering our peace and happiness; nor can anyone believe that our southern brethren, if left to themselves, would adopt it of their own accord. It is equally impossible, therefore, that we should behold such interposition in any form with indifference. If we look to the comparative strength and resources of Spain and those new Governments, and their distance from each other, it must be obvious that she can never subdue them. It is still the true policy of the United States to leave the parties to themselves, in the hope that other powers will pursue the same course. . . .

1. The Monroe Doctrine was actually the brain child of

   a. James Monroe.
   b. Thomas Jefferson.
   c. John Quincy Adams.
   d. George Canning.

2. Why is the Monroe Doctrine a symbol of United States' isolation?

   a. It states that the U.S. will declare war if its rights are violated.
   b. It states that Britain, Prussia and France are forbidden to colonize on U.S. borders.
   c. It states that it will not trade with foreign powers outside of the Western Hemisphere.
   d. It states that the United States will avoid European concerns as long as Europe bypasses the U.S.

3. Why did some Americans believe that the Doctrine was necessary at the time of its inception?

   a. The independent countries on U.S. borders were asking for aid.
   b. An alliance was made by Prussia and France that forced the United States to join Great Britain.
   c. European powers were looking to build colonies in the New World.
   d. The U.S. wanted to show the Old World that it would control trade agreements and foreign colonies.

4. How did the Monroe Doctrine characterize the type of relations it wanted to have with foreign powers?

   a. friendly
   b. antagonistic
   c. indifferent
   d. none of the above

5. Why were foreign colonies in America considered to be "dangerous to our peace and safety"?

   a. They would force Americans to work with foreigners.
   b. They would give the foreign powers a foothold in the Americas.
   c. They would make it difficult for Americans to form a unified culture.
   d. They would bring in trade and force a tax on the United States.

6. How do you think the statement of the Monroe Doctrine affected the opinions of foreign powers? Do you think it had a good or bad reception? Why do you think it had that response?

7. If the United States had not declared the Monroe Doctrine what could have happened? Do you think that foreign powers would have created colonies in the Americas? Do you think that the United States would have entered into a war against Russia and France? Why or why not? Please use specific examples from the text to support your answer.

President Andrew Jackson's Message to Congress, "On Indian Removal" (1830)

With the onset of westward expansion and increased contact with Native American tribes, President Jackson set the tone for his position on Native American affairs in his message to Congress on December 6, 1830. Jackson's message justified the removal policy already established by the Indian Removal Act of May 28, 1830.

The Indian Removal Act was passed to open up for settlement those lands still held by Native Americans in states east of the Mississippi River, primarily Georgia, Tennessee, Alabama, Mississippi, North Carolina, and others. Jackson declared that removal would "incalculably strengthen the southwestern frontier." Clearing Alabama and Mississippi of their Native American populations, he said, would "enable those states to advance rapidly in population, wealth, and power."

White inhabitants of Georgia were particularly anxious to have the Cherokee removed from the state because gold had been discovered on tribal lands. Violence was commonplace in Georgia, and in all likelihood, a portion of the tribe would have been decimated if they had not been removed.

Removal of the Native American tribes continued beyond Jackson's tenure as president. The most infamous of the removals took place in 1838, two years after the end of Jackson's final term, when the Cherokee were forcibly removed by the military. Their journey west became known as the "Trail of Tears" because of the thousands of deaths along the way.

It gives me pleasure to announce to Congress that the benevolent policy of the Government, steadily pursued for nearly thirty years, in relation to the removal of the Indians beyond the white settlements is approaching to a happy consummation. Two important tribes have accepted the provision made for their removal at the last session of Congress, and it is believed that their example will induce the remaining tribes also to seek the same obvious advantages.

The consequences of a speedy removal will be important to the United States, to individual States, and to the Indians themselves. The pecuniary advantages which it promises to the Government are the least of its recommendations. It puts an end to all possible danger of collision between the authorities of the General and State Governments on account of the Indians. It will place a dense and civilized population in large tracts of country now occupied by a few savage hunters. By opening the whole territory between Tennessee on the north and Louisiana on the south to the settlement of the whites it will incalculably strengthen the southwestern frontier and render the adjacent States strong enough to repel future invasions without remote aid. It will relieve the whole State of Mississippi and the western part of Alabama of Indian occupancy, and enable those States to advance rapidly in population, wealth, and power. It will separate the Indians from immediate contact with settlements of whites; free them from the power of the States; enable them to pursue happiness in their own way and under their own rude institutions; will retard the progress of decay, which is lessening their numbers, and perhaps cause them gradually, under the protection of the Government and through the influence of good counsels, to cast off their savage habits and become an interesting, civilized, and Christian community.

What good man would prefer a country covered with forests and ranged by a few thousand savages to our extensive Republic, studded with cities, towns, and prosperous farms embellished with all the improvements which art can devise or industry execute, occupied by more than 12,000,000 happy people, and filled with all the blessings of liberty, civilization and religion?

The present policy of the Government is but a continuation of the same progressive change by a milder process. The tribes which occupied the countries now constituting the Eastern States were annihilated or have melted away to make room for the whites. The waves of population and civilization are rolling to the westward, and we now propose to acquire the countries occupied by the red men of the South and West by a fair exchange, and, at the expense of the United States, to send them to land where their existence may be prolonged and perhaps made perpetual. Doubtless it will be painful to leave the graves of their fathers; but what do they [do] more than our ancestors did or than our children are now doing? To better their condition in an unknown land our forefathers left all that was dear in earthly objects. Our children by thousands yearly leave the land of their birth to seek new homes in distant regions. Does Humanity weep at these painful separations from everything, animate and inanimate, with which the young heart has become entwined? Far from it. It is rather a source of joy that our country affords scope where our young population may range unconstrained in body or in mind, developing the power and facilities of man in their highest perfection. These remove hundreds and almost thousands of miles at their own expense, purchase the lands they occupy, and support themselves at their new homes from the moment of their arrival. Can it be cruel in this Government when, by events which it can not control, the Indian is made discontented in his ancient home to purchase his lands, to give him a new and extensive territory, to pay the expense of his removal, and support him a year in his new abode? How many thousands of our own people would gladly embrace the opportunity of removing to the West on such conditions! If the offers made to the Indians were extended to them, they would be hailed with gratitude and joy.

And is it supposed that the wandering savage has a stronger attachment to his home than the settled, civilized Christian? Is it more afflicting to him to leave the graves of his fathers than it is to our brothers and children? Rightly considered, the policy of the General Government toward the red man is not only liberal, but generous. He is unwilling to submit to the laws of the States and mingle with their population. To save him from this alternative, or perhaps utter annihilation, the General Government kindly offers him a new home, and proposes to pay the whole expense of his removal and settlement.

1. How would you describe the tone of the Jackson's message to Congress?

   a. arrogant
   b. humble
   c. angry
   d. uncertain

2. Why did Jackson believe that Indian Removal would help the Native Americans?

   a. It would make the Native Americans civilized.
   b. He did not say that the removal would help the Native Americans.
   c. It would humiliate the white Americans.
   d. It would make the Native Americans more prosperous.

3. Why would the state government protest against the Native Americans?

   a. The Native Americans did not trade with the government.
   b. The state wanted to tax the Native Americans.
   c. The state did not want to share the land with the Native Americans.
   d. The state feared the wrath of the Native Americans.

4. According to Jackson, both the Native Americans and the white Americans share a

   a. civilization based on religious freedom.
   b. rebellious history.
   c. belief in freedom.
   d. connection to their homelands.

5. How did Jackson attempt to make the removal of the Native Americans sound more compassionate to Congress? Please give at least two examples from the text and explain.

Proclamation to the People of South Carolina, December 10, 1832

The nullification controversy of 1832–1833 confronted Andrew Jackson (1767–1845) with the greatest crisis of his presidency—the defiance of the federal government by South Carolina. The doctrine of nullification, which asserted that a state could on its own authority declare a federal law unconstitutional, had manifested itself in American life before, but never to such a dangerous degree. The passage of tariff bills in 1828 and 1832, favoring northern manufacturing over southern agriculture, had been the immediate cause of the crisis leading to South Carolina's Ordinance of Nullification of 24 November 1832, declaring the tariff acts null, void, and not binding upon her. Jackson's swift response, his Proclamation to the People of South Carolina, 10 December 1832, considered the greatest state paper of the era, made it clear that any action taken to uphold nullification by armed force was treason.

President Jackson's Proclamation Regarding Nullification, December 10, 1832

Whereas a convention, assembled in the State of South Carolina, have passed an ordinance, by which they declare that the several acts and parts of acts of the Congress of the United States, purporting to be laws for the imposing of duties and imposts on the importation of foreign commodities, and now having actual operation and effect within the United States, and more especially "two acts for the same purposes, passed on the 29th of May, 1828, and on the 14th of July, 1832, are unauthorized by the Constitution of the United States, and violate the true meaning and intent thereof, and are null and void, and no law," nor binding on the citizens of that State or its officers, and by the said ordinance it is further declared to he unlawful for any of the constituted authorities of the State, or of the United States, to enforce the payment of the duties imposed by the said acts within the same State, and that it is the duty of the legislature to pass such laws as may be necessary to give full effect to the said ordinances:

And whereas, by the said ordinance it is further ordained, that, in no case of law or equity, decided in the courts of said State, wherein shall be drawn in question the validity of the said ordinance, or of the acts of the legislature that may be passed to give it effect, or of the said laws of the United States, no appeal shall be allowed to the Supreme Court of the United States, nor shall any copy of the record be permitted or allowed for that purpose; and that any person attempting to take such appeal, shall be punished as for a contempt of court:

And, finally, the said ordinance declares that the people of South Carolina will maintain the said ordinance at every hazard, and that they will consider the passage of any act by Congress abolishing or closing the ports of the said State, or otherwise obstructing the free ingress or egress of vessels to and from the said ports, or any other act of the Federal Government to coerce the State, shut up her ports, destroy or harass her commerce, or to enforce the said acts otherwise than through the civil tribunals of the country, as inconsistent with the longer continuance of South Carolina in the Union; and that the people of the said State will thenceforth hold themselves absolved from all further obligation to maintain or preserve their political connection with the people of the other States, and will forthwith proceed to organize a separate government, and do all other acts and things which sovereign and independent States may of right do.

And whereas the said ordinance prescribes to the people of South Carolina a course of conduct in direct violation of their duty as citizens of the United States, contrary to the laws of their country, subversive of its Constitution, and having for its object the instruction of the Union—that Union, which, coeval with our political existence, led our fathers, without any other ties to unite them than those of patriotism and common cause, through the sanguinary struggle to a glorious independence—that sacred Union, hitherto inviolate, which, perfected by our happy Constitution, has brought us, by the favor of Heaven, to a state of prosperity at home, and high consideration abroad, rarely, if ever, equaled in the history of nations; to preserve this bond of our political existence from destruction, to maintain inviolate this state of national honor and prosperity, and to justify the confidence my fellow-citizens have reposed in me, I, Andrew Jackson, President of the United States, have thought proper to issue this my PROCLAMATION, stating my views of the Constitution and laws applicable to the measures adopted by the Convention of South Carolina, and to the reasons they have put forth to sustain them, declaring the course which duty will require me to pursue, and, appealing to the understanding and patriotism of the people, warn them of the consequences that must inevitably result from an observance of the dictates of the Convention.

Strict duty would require of me nothing more than the exercise of those powers with which I am now, or may hereafter be, invested, for preserving the Union, and for the execution of the laws. But the imposing aspect which opposition has assumed in this case, by clothing itself with State authority, and the deep interest which the people of the United States must all feel in preventing a resort to stronger measures, while there is a hope that anything will be yielded to reasoning and remonstrances, perhaps demand, and will certainly justify, a full exposition to South Carolina and the nation of the views I entertain of this important question, as well as a distinct enunciation of the course which my sense of duty will require me to pursue.

The ordinance is founded, not on the indefeasible right of resisting acts which are plainly unconstitutional, and too oppressive to be endured, but on the strange position that any one State may not only declare an act of Congress void, but prohibit its execution—that they may do this consistently with the Constitution—that the true construction of that instrument permits a State to retain its place in the Union, and yet be bound by no other of its laws than those it may choose to consider as constitutional. It is true they add, that to justify this abrogation of a law, it must be palpably contrary to the Constitution, but it is evident, that to give the right of resisting laws of that description, coupled with the uncontrolled right to decide what laws deserve that character, is to give the power of resisting all laws. For, as by the theory, there is no appeal, the reasons alleged by the State, good or bad, must prevail. If it should be said that public opinion is a sufficient check against the abuse of this power, it may be asked why it is not deemed a sufficient guard against the passage of an unconstitutional act by Congress. There is, however, a restraint in this last case, which makes the assumed power of a State more indefensible, and which does not exist in the other. There are two appeals from an unconstitutional act passed by Congress—one to the judiciary, the other to the people and the States. There is no appeal from the State decision in theory; and the practical illustration shows that the courts are closed against an application to review it, both judges and jurors being sworn to decide in its favor. But reasoning on this subject is superfluous, when our social compact in express terms declares, that the laws of the United States, its Constitution, and treaties made under it, are the supreme law of the land; and for greater caution adds, "that the judges in every State shall be bound thereby, anything in the Constitution or laws of any State to the contrary notwithstanding." And it may be asserted, without fear of refutation, that no federative government could exist without a similar provision. Look, for a moment, to the consequence. If South Carolina considers the revenue laws unconstitutional, and has a right to prevent their execution in the port of Charleston, there would be a clear constitutional objection to their collection in every other port, and no revenue could be collected anywhere; for all imposts must be equal. It is no answer to repeat that an unconstitutional law is no law, so long as the question of its legality is to be decided by the State itself, for every law operating injuriously upon any local interest will be perhaps thought, and certainly represented, as unconstitutional, and, as has been shown, there is no appeal.

If this doctrine had been established at an earlier day, the Union would have been dissolved in its infancy. The excise law in Pennsylvania, the embargo and non-intercourse law in the Eastern States, the carriage tax in Virginia, were all deemed unconstitutional, and were more unequal in their operation than any of the laws now complained of; but, fortunately, none of those States discovered that they had the right now claimed by South Carolina. The war into which we were forced, to support the dignity of the nation and the rights of our citizens, might have ended in defeat and disgrace instead of victory and honor, if the States, who supposed it a ruinous and unconstitutional measure, had thought they possessed the right of nullifying the act by which it was declared, and denying supplies for its prosecution. Hardly and unequally as those measures bore upon several members of the Union, to the legislatures of none did this efficient and peaceable remedy, as it is called, suggest itself. The discovery of this important feature in our Constitution was reserved to the present day. To the statesmen of South Carolina belongs the invention, and upon the citizens of that State will, unfortunately, fall the evils of reducing it to practice.

If the doctrine of a State veto upon the laws of the Union carries with it internal evidence of its impracticable absurdity, our constitutional history will also afford abundant proof that it would have been repudiated with indignation had it been proposed to form a feature in our Government.

In our colonial state, although dependent on another power, we very early considered ourselves as connected by common interest with each other. Leagues were formed for common defense, and before the Declaration of Independence, we were known in our aggregate character as the United Colonies of America. That decisive and important step was taken jointly. We declared ourselves a nation by a joint, not by several acts; and when the terms of our confederation were reduced to form, it was in that of a solemn league of several States, by which they agreed that they would, collectively, form one nation, for the purpose of conducting some certain domestic concerns, and all foreign relations. In the instrument forming that Union, is found an article which declares that "every State shall abide by the determinations of Congress on all questions which by that Confederation should be submitted to them."

Under the Confederation, then, no State could legally annul a decision of the Congress, or refuse to submit to its execution, but no provision was made to enforce these decisions. Congress made requisitions, but they were not complied with. The Government could not operate on individuals. They had no judiciary, no means of collecting revenue.

But the defects of the Confederation need not be detailed. Under its operation we could scarcely be called a nation. We had neither prosperity at home nor consideration abroad. This state of things could not be endured, and our present happy Constitution was formed, but formed in vain, if this fatal doctrine prevails. It was formed for important objects that are announced in the preamble made in the name and by the authority of the people of the United States, whose delegates framed, and whose conventions approved it.

The most important among these objects, that which is placed first in rank, on which all the others rest, is "to form a more perfect Union." Now, is it possible that, even if there were no express provision giving supremacy to the Constitution and laws of the United States over those of the States, it can be conceived that an Instrument made for the purpose of "forming; a more perfect Union" than that of the confederation, could be so constructed by the assembled wisdom of our country as to substitute for that confederation a form of government, dependent for its existence on the local interest, the party spirit of a State, or of a prevailing faction in a State? Every man, of plain, unsophisticated understanding, who hears the question, will give such an answer as will preserve the Union. Metaphysical subtlety, in pursuit of an impracticable theory, could alone have devised one that is calculated to destroy it.

I consider, then, the power to annul a law of the United States, assumed by one State, incompatible with the existence of the Union, contradicted expressly by the letter of the Constitution, unauthorized by its spirit, inconsistent with every principle on which It was founded, and destructive of the great object for which it was formed . . .

. . . Done at the City of Washington, this 10th day of December, in the year of our Lord one thousand eight hundred and thirty-two, and of the independence of the United States the fifty-seventh.

ANDREW JACKSON.

By the President

EDW. LIVINGSTON, Secretary of State.

1. Why did South Carolina create the Ordinance of Nullification in 1832?

   a. to boost revenue for agricultural enterprise
   b. to thwart federal tariff acts
   c. to encourage northern business in the south
   d. to offer farmers a voice in the growing economic state

2. How does the ordinance also protect against anyone who would call its actions into question?

   a. An appeal is forbidden.
   b. The federal government has no jurisdiction in the state.
   c. The state has declared the ordinance a law.
   d. The Constitution is unlawful and holds no power in South Carolina.

3. Why would South Carolina's Ordinance of Nullification be construed as a declaration of its independence from the Union?

   a. It states that the federal tariffs are unconstitutional.
   b. It states that it can close ports and create military bases.
   c. It states that South Carolina can organize a separate government.
   d. It states that South Carolina can form its own political party.

4. Why does Jackson declare South Carolina's ordinance a violation of the laws of the U.S.?

   a. It misinterprets the rights in the Constitution.
   b. It says that Congress is the only body that can declare an act unconstitutional.
   c. It says that South Carolina did not use appropriate methods to advocate its purpose.
   d. It stats that tariffs were part of the economic balance of the Union.

5. According to Jackson, can a state be a member of the Union and yet neglect certain laws?

   a. yes
   b. no
   c. only if those laws are unconstitutional
   d. none of the above

6. South Carolina's ordinance was expressly against the notion that the United States was created to

   a. bring prosperity to the colonies.
   b. form a union.
   c. make the Constitution binding.
   d. form a solemn league.

7. Why does the right of a state to pick and choose what laws it wishes to follow lead to a breakdown of the Union?

8. Do you agree with Jackson's argument? Do you think that the ordinance was unconstitutional? Why or why not?

Henry David Thoreau, *Civil Disobedience* (1846)

The Mexican War was not popular in much of the North. Abraham Lincoln, then a young congressman from Illinois, spoke out against it in the House of Representatives. And in New England, Henry David Thoreau refused to pay a poll tax as a symbol of his opposition to the war, and spent a night in jail as a result. The next day a friend paid the fee, much to Thoreau's regret, and he was released.

Thoreau is best remembered for his superb essays on nature, especially the classic Walden *(1854). But the essay in which he explored what he considered the honest citizen's options when facing immoral acts of government became a landmark in political thought. From his idea of civil disobedience grew the theory and practice of passive resistance advocated by Gandhi and Martin Luther King, Jr. In the essay one finds not only the philosophy of a man determined to live an honest life, but also the revulsion that many less eloquent Americans were beginning to feel toward slavery.*

I heartily accept the motto,—"That government is best which governs least"; and I should like to see it acted up to more readily and systematically. Carried out, it finally amounts to this, which also I believe,—"That government is best which governs not at all"; and when men are prepared for it, that will be the kind of government which they will have. Government is at best but an expedient; but most governments are usually, and all governments are sometimes, inexpedient. The objections which have been brought against a standing army, and they are many and weighty, and deserve to prevail, may also at last be brought against a standing government. The standing army is only an arm of the standing government. The government itself, which is only the mode which the people have chosen to execute their will, is equally liable to be abused and perverted before the people can act through it. Witness the present Mexican war, the work of comparatively a few individuals using the standing government as their tool; for, in the outset, the people would not have consented to this measure . . .

But, to speak practically and as a citizen, unlike those who call themselves no-government men, I ask for, not at once no government, but at once a better government. Let every man make known what kind of government would command his respect, and that will be one step toward obtaining it.

After all, the practical reason why, when the power is once in the hands of the people, a majority are permitted, and for a long period continue, to rule, is not because they are most likely to be in the right, nor because this seems fairest to the minority, but because they are physically the strongest. But a government in which the majority rule in all cases cannot be based on justice, even as far as men understand it. Can there not be a government in which majorities do not virtually decide right and wrong, but conscience?—in which majorities decide only those questions to which the rule of expediency is applicable? Must the citizen ever for a moment, or in the least degree, resign his conscience to the legislator? Why has every man a conscience, then? I think that we should be men first, and subjects afterward. It is not desirable to cultivate a respect for the law, so much as for the right. The only obligation which I have a right to assume, is to do at any time what I think right. It is truly enough said, that a corporation has no conscience; but a corporation of conscientious men is a corporation with a conscience. Law never made men a whit more just; and, by means of their respect for it, even the well-disposed are daily made the agents of injustice. A common and natural result of an undue respect for law is, that you may see a file of soldiers, colonel, captain, corporal, privates, powder-monkeys and all, marching in admirable order over hill and dale to the wars, against their wills, aye, against their common sense and consciences, which makes it very steep marching indeed, and produces a palpitation of the heart. They have no doubt that it is a damnable business in which they are concerned; they are all peaceably inclined. Now, what are they? Men at all? or small moveable forts and magazines, at the service of some unscrupulous man in power? . . .

The mass of men serve the State thus, not as men mainly, but as machines, with their bodies . . . Others, as most legislators, politicians, lawyers, ministers, and officeholders, serve the State chiefly with their heads; and, as they rarely make any moral distinctions, they are as likely to serve the devil, without intending it, as God. A very few, as heroes, patriots, martyrs, reformers in the great sense, and men, serve the State with their consciences also, and so necessarily resist it for the most part; and they are commonly treated by it as enemies . . . .

How does it become a man to behave toward this American government to-day? I answer that he cannot without disgrace be associated with it. I cannot for an instant recognize that political organization as my government which is the slave's government also.

All men recognize the right of revolution; that is, the right to refuse allegiance to and to resist the government, when its tyranny or its inefficiency are great and unendurable. But almost all say that such is not the case now. But such was the case, they think, in the Revolution of '75. If one were to tell me that this was a bad government because it taxed certain foreign commodities brought to its ports, it is most probable that I should not make an ado about it, for I can do without them . . .

(W)hen a sixth of the population of a nation which has undertaken to be the refuge of liberty are slaves, and a whole country is unjustly overrun and conquered by a foreign army, and subjected to military law, I think that it is not too soon for honest men to rebel and revolutionize. What makes this duty the more urgent is the fact, that the country so overrun is not our own, but ours is the invading army.

1. According to Thoreau, what is a typical characteristic of a government?

   a. inexperience
   b. evil
   c. strength
   d. lack of wisdom

2. Why does Thoreau call for citizens to be men first, and then subjects?

   a. He wants people to be individuals and then members of a majority.
   b. He wants people to be strong so as to enhance the government machine.
   c. He wants the subjects of government to mainly be men.
   d. He wants the best men to rule as subjects of government.

3. According to the document, how does the government reduce men to machines?

   a. It starts wars.
   b. It forces men to follow orders against their wills.
   c. It tells men to be strong and powerful.
   d. It is made up of corporations.

4. How should a conscientious person respond to a government that he violently disagrees with?

   a. He should leave his country.
   b. He should join the government and try to change it.
   c. He should start a revolution.
   d. none of the above

5. Pick your favorite sentence from Thoreau's essay and explain what it means in its context. Then, please explain why it stood out and what it means to you.

TREATY OF GUADALUPE HIDALGO, FEBRUARY 2, 1848

The Treaty of Guadalupe Hidalgo, which brought an official end to the Mexican-American War (1846–1848), was signed on February 2, 1848, at Guadalupe Hidalgo, a city to which the Mexican government had fled with the advance of U.S. forces.

With the defeat of its army and the fall of the capital, Mexico City, in September 1847, the Mexican government surrendered to the United States and entered into negotiations to end the war. The peace talks were negotiated by Nicholas Trist, chief clerk of the State Department, who had accompanied General Winfield Scott as a diplomat and President Polk's representative. Trist and General Scott, after two previous unsuccessful attempts to negotiate a treaty with President Santa Anna, determined that the only way to deal with Mexico was as a conquered enemy. Nicholas Trist negotiated with a special commission representing the collapsed government led by Don Bernardo Couto, Don Miguel Atristain, and Don Luis Gonzaga Cuevas.

President Polk had recalled Trist under the belief that negotiations would be carried out with a Mexican delegation in Washington. In the six weeks it took to deliver Polk's message, Trist had received word that the Mexican government had named its special commission to negotiate. Trist determined that Washington did not understand the situation in Mexico and negotiated the peace treaty in defiance of the president.

In a December 4, 1847, letter to his wife, he wrote, "Knowing it to be the very last chance and impressed with the dreadful consequences to our country which cannot fail to attend the loss of that chance, I decided today at noon to attempt to make a treaty; the decision is altogether my own."

TREATY OF PEACE, FRIENDSHIP, LIMITS, AND SETTLEMENT BETWEEN THE UNITED STATES OF AMERICA AND THE UNITED MEXICAN STATES CONCLUDED AT GUADALUPE HIDALGO, FEBRUARY 2, 1848; RATIFICATION ADVISED BY SENATE, WITH AMENDMENTS, MARCH 10, 1848; RATIFIED BY PRESIDENT, MARCH 16, 1848; RATIFICATIONS EXCHANGED AT QUERETARO, MAY 30, 1848; PROCLAIMED, JULY 4, 1848.

IN THE NAME OF ALMIGHTY GOD

The United States of America and the United Mexican States animated by a sincere desire to put an end to the calamities of the war which unhappily exists between the two Republics and to establish Upon a solid basis relations of peace and friendship, which shall confer reciprocal benefits upon the citizens of both, and assure the concord, harmony, and mutual confidence wherein the two people should live, as good neighbors have for that purpose appointed their respective plenipotentiaries, that is to say: The President of the United States has appointed Nicholas P. Trist, a citizen of the United States, and the President of the Mexican Republic has appointed Don Luis Gonzaga Cuevas, Don Bernardo Couto, and Don Miguel Atristain, citizens of the said Republic; Who, after a reciprocal communication of their respective full powers, have, under the protection of Almighty God, the author of peace, arranged, agreed upon, and signed the following: Treaty of Peace, Friendship, Limits, and Settlement between the United States of America and the Mexican Republic.

ARTICLE I

There shall be firm and universal peace between the United States of America and the Mexican Republic, and between their respective countries, territories, cities, towns, and people, without exception of places or persons.

ARTICLE II

Immediately upon the signature of this treaty, a convention shall be entered into between a commissioner or commissioners appointed by the General-in-chief of the forces of the United States, and such as may be appointed by the Mexican Government, to the end that a provisional suspension of hostilities shall take place, and that, in the places occupied by the said forces, constitutional order may be reestablished, as regards the political, administrative, and judicial branches, so far as this shall be permitted by the circumstances of military occupation.

ARTICLE III

Immediately upon the ratification of the present treaty by the Government of the United States, orders shall be transmitted to the commanders of their land and naval forces, requiring the latter (provided this treaty shall then have been ratified by the Government of the Mexican Republic, and the ratifications exchanged) immediately to desist from blockading any Mexican ports and requiring the former (under the same condition) to commence, at the earliest moment practicable, withdrawing all troops of the United States then in the interior of the Mexican Republic, to points that shall be selected by common agreement, at a distance from the seaports not exceeding thirty leagues; and such evacuation of the interior of the Republic shall be completed with the least possible delay; the Mexican Government hereby binding itself to afford every facility in its power for rendering the same convenient to the troops, on their march and in their new positions, and for promoting a good understanding between them and the inhabitants. In like manner orders shall be despatched to the persons in charge of the custom houses at all ports occupied by the forces of the United States, requiring them (under the same condition) immediately to deliver possession of the same to the persons authorized by the Mexican Government to receive it, together with all bonds and evidences of debt for duties on importations and on exportations, not yet fallen due. Moreover, a faithful and exact account shall be made out, showing the entire amount of all duties on imports and on exports, collected at such custom-houses, or elsewhere in Mexico, by authority of the United States, from and after the day of ratification of this treaty by the Government of the Mexican Republic; and also an account of the cost of collection; and such entire amount, deducting only the cost of collection, shall be delivered to the Mexican Government, at the city of Mexico, within three months after the exchange of ratifications.

The evacuation of the capital of the Mexican Republic by the troops of the United States, in virtue of the above stipulation, shall be completed in one month after the orders there stipulated for shall have been received by the commander of said troops, or sooner if possible.

ARTICLE IV

Immediately after the exchange of ratifications of the present treaty all castles, forts, territories, places, and possessions, which have been taken or occupied by the forces of the United States during the present war, within the limits of the Mexican Republic, as about to be established by the following article, shall be definitely restored to the said Republic, together with all the artillery, arms, apparatus of war, munitions, and other public property, which were in the said castles and forts when captured, and which shall remain there at the time when this treaty shall be duly ratified by the Government of the Mexican Republic. To this end, immediately upon the signature of this treaty, orders shall be despatched to the American officers commanding such castles and forts, securing against the removal or destruction of any such artillery, arms, apparatus of war, munitions, or other public property. The city of Mexico, within the inner line of intrenchments surrounding the said city, is comprehended in the above stipulation, as regards the restoration of artillery, apparatus of war, & c.

The final evacuation of the territory of the Mexican Republic, by the forces of the United States, shall be completed in three months from the said exchange of ratifications, or sooner if possible; the Mexican Government hereby engaging, as in the foregoing article to use all means in its power for facilitating such evacuation, and rendering it convenient to the troops, and for promoting a good understanding between them and the inhabitants.

If, however, the ratification of this treaty by both parties should not take place in time to allow the embarcation of the troops of the United States to be completed before the commencement of the sickly season, at the Mexican ports on the Gulf of Mexico, in such case a friendly arrangement shall be entered into between the General-in-Chief of the said troops and the Mexican Government, whereby healthy and otherwise suitable places, at a distance from the ports not exceeding thirty leagues, shall be designated for the residence of such troops as may not yet have embarked, until the return of the healthy season. And the space of time here referred to as, comprehending the sickly season shall be understood to extend from the first day of May to the first day of November.

All prisoners of war taken on either side, on land or on sea, shall be restored as soon as practicable after the exchange of ratifications of this treaty. It is also agreed that if any Mexicans should now be held as captives by any savage tribe within the limits of the United States, as about to be established by the following article, the Government of the said United States will exact the release of such captives and cause them to be restored to their country.

ARTICLE V

The boundary line between the two Republics shall commence in the Gulf of Mexico, three leagues from land, opposite the mouth of the Rio Grande, otherwise called Rio Bravo del Norte, or Opposite the mouth of its deepest branch, if it should have more than one branch emptying directly into the sea; from thence up the middle of that river, following the deepest channel, where it has more than one, to the point where it strikes the southern boundary of New Mexico; thence, westwardly, along the whole southern boundary of New Mexico (which runs north of the town called Paso) to its western termination; thence, northward, along the western line of New Mexico, until it intersects the first branch of the river Gila; (or if it should not intersect any branch of that river, then to the point on the said line nearest to such branch, and thence in a direct line to the same); thence down the middle of the said branch and of the said river, until it empties into the Rio Colorado; thence across the Rio Colorado, following the division line between Upper and Lower California, to the Pacific Ocean . . .

1. What did the treaty between Mexico and the United States establish?

   a. commerce
   b. peace
   c. rights
   d. laws

2. In reading the treaty, what did the United States most likely use against Mexico during the war?

   a. an atomic bomb
   b. submarines
   c. biological weapons
   d. blockades

3. The United States, upon the ratification of the treaty, will

   a. declare Mexico a territory.
   b. take control of all ports within 30 leagues of Mexico City.
   c. remove all troops.
   d. require a tariff on all imports received after three months of the ratification of the treaty.

4. When is the "sickly season"?

   a. June to November
   b. January to July
   c. May to November
   d. December to May

5. Throughout the treaty, mention is made of "promoting a good understanding between the [evacuating troops] and the inhabitants." Why is this important? Please give at least two examples of how a government might a accomplish this.

Seneca Falls Declaration (1848)

One of the reform movements that arose during "freedom's ferment" of the early nineteenth century was a drive for greater rights for women, especially in the political area. Women were heavily involved in many of the reform movements of this time, but they discovered that, while they did much of the drudge work, with few exceptions (such as Dorothea Dix) they could not take leadership roles or lobby openly for their goals. Politically, women were to be neither seen nor heard. The drudgery of daily housework and its deadening impact on the mind also struck some women as unfair.

The convention at Seneca Falls, New York, in July 1848, was organized by Lucretia Mott and Elizabeth Cady Stanton, two Quakers whose concern for women's rights was aroused when Mott, as a woman, was denied a seat at an international antislavery meeting in London. The Seneca Falls meeting attracted 240 sympathizers, including forty men, among them the famed former slave and abolitionist leader, Frederick Douglass. The delegates adopted a statement, deliberately modeled on the Declaration of Independence, as well as a series of resolutions calling for women's suffrage and the reform of marital and property laws that kept women in an inferior status.

Very little in the way of progress came from the Seneca Falls Declaration, although it would serve for the next seventy years as the goal for which the suffrage movement strove. Women's suffrage and nearly all of the other reforms of this era were swallowed up by the single issue of slavery and its abolition, and women did not receive the right to vote until the adoption of the Nineteenth Amendment to the Constitution in 1920.

When, in the course of human events, it becomes necessary for one portion of the family of man to assume among the people of the earth a position different from that which they have hitherto occupied, but one to which the laws of nature and of nature's God entitle them, a decent respect to the opinions of mankind requires that they should declare the causes that impel them to such a course.

We hold these truths to be self-evident: that all men and women are created equal; that they are endowed by their Creator with certain inalienable rights; that among these are life, liberty, and the pursuit of happiness; that to secure these rights governments are instituted, deriving their just powers from the consent of the governed. Whenever any form of government becomes destructive of these ends, it is the right of those who suffer from it to refuse allegiance to it, and to insist upon the institution of a new government, laying its foundation on such principles, and organizing its powers in such form, as to them shall seem most likely to effect their safety and happiness. Prudence, indeed, will dictate that governments long established should not be changed for light and transient causes; and accordingly all experience hath shown that mankind are more disposed to suffer, while evils are sufferable, than to right themselves by abolishing the forms to which they were accustomed. But when a long train of abuses and usurpations, pursuing invariably the same object, evinces a design to reduce them under absolute despotism, it is their duty to throw off such government, and to provide new guards for their future security. Such has been the patient sufferance of the women under this government, and such is now the necessity which constrains them to demand the equal station to which they are entitled.

The history of mankind is a history of repeated injuries and usurpations on the part of man toward woman, having in direct object the establishment of an absolute tyranny over her. To prove this, let facts be submitted to a candid world.

He has never permitted her to exercise her inalienable right to the elective franchise.

He has compelled her to submit to laws, in the formation of which she had no voice.

He has withheld from her rights which are given to the most ignorant and degraded men—both natives and foreigners.

Having deprived her of this first right of a citizen, the elective franchise, thereby leaving her without representation in the halls of legislation, he has oppressed her on all sides.

He has made her, if married, in the eye of the law, civilly dead.

He has taken from her all right in property, even to the wages she earns.

He has made her, morally, an irresponsible being, as she can commit many crimes with impunity, provided they be done in the presence of her husband. In the covenant of marriage, she is compelled to promise obedience to her husband, he becoming to all intents and purposes, her master—the law giving him power to deprive her of her liberty, and to administer chastisement.

He has so framed the laws of divorce, as to what shall be the proper causes, and in case of separation, to whom the guardianship of the children shall be given, as to be wholly regardless of the happiness of women—the law, in all cases, going upon a false supposition of the supremacy of man, and giving all power into his hands.

After depriving her of all rights as a married woman, if single, and the owner of property, he has taxed her to support a government which recognizes her only when her property can be made profitable to it.

He has monopolized nearly all the profitable employments, and from those she is permitted to follow, she receives but a scanty remuneration. He closes against her all the avenues to wealth and distinction which he considers most honorable to himself. As a teacher of theology, medicine, or law, she is not known.

He has denied her the facilities for obtaining a thorough education, all colleges being closed against her.

He allows her in Church, as well as State, but a subordinate position, claiming Apostolic authority for her exclusion from the ministry, and, with some exceptions, from any public participation in the affairs of the Church.

He has created a false public sentiment by giving to the world a different code of morals for men and women, by which moral delinquencies which exclude women from society, are not only tolerated, but deemed of little account in man.

He has usurped the prerogative of Jehovah himself, claiming it as his right to assign for her a sphere of action, when that belongs to her conscience and to her God.

He has endeavored, in every way that he could, to destroy her confidence in her own powers, to lessen her self-respect, and to make her willing to lead a dependent and abject life.

Now, in view of this entire disfranchisement of one-half the people of this country, their social and religious degradation—in view of the unjust laws above mentioned, and because women do feel themselves aggrieved, oppressed, and fraudulently deprived of their most sacred rights, we insist that they have immediate admission to all the rights and privileges which belong to them as citizens of the United States.

In entering upon the great work before us, we anticipate no small amount of misconception, misrepresentation, and ridicule; but we shall use every instrumentality within our power to effect our object. We shall employ agents, circulate tracts, petition the State and National legislatures, and endeavor to enlist the pulpit and the press in our behalf. We hope this Convention will be followed by a series of Conventions embracing every part of the country.

1. What is the position "different from that which they have hitherto occupied"?

   a. a position as a housewife
   b. a position of equality
   c. a position in government
   d. a position as a leader

2. According to the declaration for what reason do those who are governed have a right to refuse allegiance to their government?

   a. if they feel that their government is not honoring them
   b. if they do not agree with government
   c. if their inalienable rights are violated
   d. if the government does not support them

3. A despot is someone who

   a. works for the government.
   b. launders money.
   c. is a misogynist.
   d. abuses power.

4. What is one reason why it was important for women to have the vote?

   a. Women wanted to have representation in the laws created.
   b. Women wanted have an equal education.
   c. Women wanted the right to earn equal pay.
   d. all of the above

5. What is one reason why a woman would be considered "civilly dead" once she was married?

   a. She could see her family.
   b. She could not own property.
   c. She could not go out alone.
   d. She could not use money.

6. If a woman committed a crime in front of her husband, who would have taken responsibility for that crime?

   a. her husband
   b. herself
   c. both parties
   d. none of the above

7. How did modeling the Seneca Falls Declaration after the Declaration of Independence affect its tone? Why would the tone be important? Do you think this was a good idea? Why or why not?

8. In the list of injuries submitted, what do you think is the most important right that a woman should have? Why do you think so? Please explain thoroughly.

Compromise of 1850

By 1850, sectional disagreements centering on slavery were straining the bonds of union between the North and South. These tensions became especially acute when Congress began to consider whether western lands acquired after the Mexican War would permit slavery. In 1849, California requested permission to enter the Union as a free state. Adding more free state senators to Congress would destroy the balance between slave and free states that had existed since the Missouri Compromise of 1820.

Because everyone looked to the Senate to defuse the growing crisis, Senator Henry Clay of Kentucky proposed a series of resolutions designed to "Adjust amicably all existing questions of controversy . . . arising out of the institution of slavery." Clay attempted to frame his compromise so that nationally-minded senators would vote for legislation in the interest of the Union.

In one of the most famous congressional debates in American history, the Senate discussed Clay's solution for seven months. It initially voted down his legislative package, but Senator Stephen A. Douglas of Illinois stepped forward with substitute bills, which passed both Houses. With the Compromise of 1850, Congress had addressed the immediate crisis created by territorial expansion. However, one aspect of the compromise—a strengthened fugitive slave act—soon began to tear at sectional peace.

The Compromise of 1850 is composed of five statues enacted in September of 1850. The acts called for the admission of California as a "free state," provided for a territorial government for Utah and New Mexico, established a boundary between Texas and the United States, called for the abolition of slave trade in Washington, D.C., and amended the Fugitive Slave Act.

CLAY'S RESOLUTIONS January 29, 1850

It being desirable, for the peace, concord, and harmony of the Union of these States, to settle and adjust amicably all existing questions of controversy between them arising out of the institution of slavery upon a fair, equitable and just basis: therefore,

1. Resolved, That California, with suitable boundaries, ought, upon her application to be admitted as one of the States of this Union, without the imposition by Congress of any restriction in respect to the exclusion or in- troduction of slavery within those boundaries.

2. Resolved, That as slavery does not exist by law, and is not likely to be introduced into any of the territory acquired by the United States from the republic of Mexico, it is inexpedient for Congress to provide by law either for its introduction into, or exclusion from, any part of the said territory; and that appropriate territorial governments ought to be established by Congress in all of the said territory, not assigned as the boundaries of the proposed State of California, without the adoption of any restriction or condition on the subject of slavery.

3. Resolved, That the western boundary of the State of Texas ought to be fixed on the Rio del Norte, commencing one marine league from its mouth, and running up that river to the southern line of New Mexico; thence with that line eastwardly, and so continuing in the same direction to the line as established between the United States and Spain, excluding any portion of New Mexico, whether lying on the east or west of that river.

4. Resolved, That it be proposed to the State of Texas, that the United States will provide for the payment of all that portion of the legitimate and bona fide public debt of that State contracted prior to its annexation to the United States, and for which the duties on foreign imports were pledged by the said State to its creditors, not exceeding the sum of dollars, in consideration of the said duties so pledged having been no longer applicable to that object after the said annexa- tion, but having thenceforward become payable to the United States; and upon the condition, also, that the said State of Texas shall, by some solemn and authentic act of her legislature or of a convention, relinquish to the United States any claim which it has to any part of New Mexico.

5. Resolved, That it is inexpedient to abolish slavery in the District of Columbia whilst that institution continues to exist in the State of Maryland, without the consent of that State, without the consent of the people of the District, and without just compensation to the owners of slaves within the District.

6. But, resolved, That it is expedient to prohibit, within the District, the slave trade in slaves brought into it from States or places beyond the limits of the District, either to be sold therein as merchandise, or to be transported to other markets without the District of Columbia.

7. Resolved, That more effectual provision ought to be made by law, according to the requirement of the constitution, for the restitution and delivery of persons bound to service or labor in any State, who may escape into any other State or Territory in the Union. And,

8. Resolved, That Congress has no power to promote or obstruct the trade in slaves between the slaveholding States; but that the admission or exclusion of slaves brought from one into another of them, depends exclusively upon their own particular laws.

1. Because slavery ________ Congress decided to allow territorial governments to uphold it.

   a. is not a crime,
   b. does not exist as a law,
   c. is part of the Constitution,
   d. is restricted in the state of California,

2. The United States agreed to

   a. transport goods to the state of California.
   b. free the slaves in California.
   c. pay the public debts accrued by Texas before it became a state.
   d. force the District of Columbia to abolish slavery as part of the compromise.

3. Why did the compromise state that it was inexpedient to abolish slavery in the District of Columbia? Please explain using quotations from the text to help support your argument.

Massachusetts Personal Liberty Act (1855)

Article IV, Section 2 of the Constitution called for the states to surrender escaped slaves to their owners, but as abolition sentiment had grown, northern states not only refused to extradite runaway slaves but protected them from their owners and hired slave-catchers. Since part of the Compromise of 1850 designed to reduce tensions between the North and the South, Congress passed a new and tougher Fugitive Slave Act that so one-sidedly favored slave owners that it became a major propaganda weapon of the abolitionists.

Several northern states responded to the new law by passing so-called "personal liberty" laws aimed at thwarting the federal requirements. Among other things, the laws guaranteed the writ of habeas corpus, the right to a jury trial and other procedural devices that not only protected the runaways, but made it difficult for slave owners to prove their cases in court, and also made it costly for them to do so.

The Massachusetts Personal Liberty Act resulted from the uproar over the capture and extradition of a slave named Anthony Burns in 1854. A hostile mob attempted a rescue, a guard was killed in the uproar, and Burns was marched back to Virginia under massive federal and state escort. At about the same time Congress passed the Kansas-Nebraska Act, which seemed an open invitation for southerners to bring slaves into that part of the Louisiana Purchase hitherto considered free.

The Massachusetts legislature passed the 1855 law with the defiant title, "An Act to Protect the Rights and Liberties of the People of the Commonwealth of Massachusetts." A key provision was the section calling for the removal of any state official who aided in the return of runaway slaves. The personal liberty laws, while anathema in the South, reflected the growing opposition of mainstream northern society to the "peculiar institution" of slavery.

Revised Statutes is hereby declared to be, that every person imprisoned or restrained of his liberty is entitled, as of right and of course, to the writ of habeas corpus, except in the cases mentioned in the second section of that chapter.

Sec. 3. The writ of habeas corpus may be issued by the supreme judicial court, the court of common pleas, by any justice's court or police court of any town or city, by any court of record, or by any justice of either of said courts, or by any judge of probate; and it may be issued by any justice of the peace, if no magistrate above named is known to said justice of the peace to be within five miles of the place where the party is imprisoned or restrained, and it shall be returnable before the supreme judicial court, or any one of the justices thereof, whether the court may be in session or not, and in term time or vacation . . .

Sec. 6. If any claimant shall appear to demand the custody or possession of the person for whose benefit such writ is sued out, such claimant shall state in writing the facts on which he relies, with precision and certainty; and neither the claimant of the alleged fugitive, nor any person interested in his alleged obligation to service or labor, nor the alleged fugitive, shall be permitted to testify at the trial of the issue; and no confessions, admissions or declarations of the alleged fugitive against himself shall be given in evidence. Upon every question of fact involved in the issue, the burden of proof shall be on the claimant, and the facts alleged and necessary to be established, must be proved by the testimony of at least two credible witnesses, or other legal evidence equivalent thereto, and by the rules of evidence known and secured by the common law; and no ex parte deposition or affidavit shall be received in proof in behalf of the claimant, and no presumption shall arise in favor of the claimant from any proof that the alleged fugitive or any of his ancestors had actually been held as a slave, without proof that such holding was legal.

Sec. 7. If any person shall remove from the limits of this Commonwealth, or shall assist in removing therefrom, or shall come into the Commonwealth with the intention of removing or of assisting in the removing therefrom, or shall procure or assist in procuring to be so removed, any person being in the peace thereof who is not "held to service or labor" by the "party" making "claim," or who has not "escaped" from the "party" making "claim," within the meaning of those words in the constitution of the United States, on the pretence that such person is so held or has so escaped, or that his "service or labor" is so "due," or with the intent to subject him to such "service or labor," he shall be punished by a fine of not less than one thousand, nor more than five thousand dollars, and by imprisonment in the State Prison not less than one, nor more than five years . . .

Sec. 9. No person, while holding any office of honor, trust, or emolument, under the laws of this Commonwealth, shall, in any capacity, issue any warrant or other process, or grant any certificate, under or by virtue of an act of congress . . . or shall in any capacity, serve any such warrant or other process.

Sec. 10. Any person who shall grant any certificate under or by virtue of the acts of congress, mentioned in the preceding section, shall be deemed to have resigned any commission from the Commonwealth which he may possess, his office shall be deemed vacant, and he shall be forever thereafter ineligible to any office of trust, honor or emolument under the laws of this Commonwealth.

Sec. 11. Any person who shall act as counsel or attorney for any claimant of any alleged fugitive from service or labor, under or by virtue of the acts of congress mentioned in the ninth section of this act, shall be deemed to have resigned any commission from the Commonwealth that he may possess, and he shall be thereafter incapacitated from appearing as counsel or attorney in the courts of this Commonwealth . . .

Sec. 14. Any person holding any judicial office under the constitution or laws of this Commonwealth, who shall continue, for ten days after the passage of this act, to hold the office of United States commissioner, or any office . . . which qualifies him to issue any warrant or other process . . . under the [Fugitive Slave Acts] shall be deemed to have violated good behavior, to have given reason for the loss of public confidence, and furnished sufficient ground either for impeachment or for removal by address.

Sec. 15. Any sheriff, deputy sheriff, jailer, coroner, constable, or other officer of this Commonwealth, or the police of any city or town, or any district, county, city or town officer, or any officer or other member of the volunteer militia of this Commonwealth, who shall hereafter arrest . . . any person for the reason that he is claimed or adjudged to be a fugitive from service or labor, shall be punished by fine . . . and by imprisonment . . .

Sec. 16. The volunteer militia of the Commonwealth shall not act in any manner in the seizure . . . of any person for the reason that he is claimed or adjudged to be a fugitive from service or labor . . .

Sec. 19. No jail, prison, or other place of confinement belonging to, or used by, either the Commonwealth of Massachusetts or any county therein, shall be used for the detention or imprisonment of any person accused or convicted of any offence created by [the Federal Fugitive

Slave Acts] . . . or accused or convicted of obstructing or resisting any process, warrant, or order issued under either of said acts, or of rescuing, or attempting to rescue, any person arrested or detained under any of the provisions of either of the said acts.

1. The writ of habeas corpus gives an individual the right to bear witness in court. Why did the state of Massachusetts allow this writ to be issued by many different courts?

   a. Many of these writs would anger southern states.
   b. The writs would give the prisoners a chance to escape while they crossed state lines.
   c. More writs issued meant that a greater number of slaves could remain in northern states.
   d. The writs would make it easier for prosecutors to gather information and witnesses.

2. How did the Personal Liberty Act make it difficult for claimants to issue their case?

   a. They had to provide documents proving that the slave had been aided when he escaped.
   b. They had to write down the facts.
   c. They had to force the fugitive slave to confess.
   d. They had to show that the fugitive had family in the south.

3. If a person removes a slave from the state, what is one part of the punishment?

   a. 3–6 months in jail
   b. 2–4 months in jail
   c. $500–1,000 fine
   d. $1,000–5,000 fine

4. Why was Section 19 of the act important?

   a. It showed that the fugitives were political criminals.
   b. It showed that the militia had no place in these debates.
   c. It showed that the fugitives were not criminals in Massachusetts.
   d. It showed that commissioners were held liable for their actions.

5. How did the Massachusetts Personal Liberty Act make it nearly impossible for any attorney in Massachusetts to argue against a fugitive? Do you think this was fair? Why or why not?

6. Do you think that these laws were helpful? Do you think that they aided the fugitives or made it more difficult for them? Which section do you think was most helpful in Liberty Act and why?

DRED SCOTT V. SANDFORD (1857)

Dred Scott's case holds a unique place in American constitutional history as an example of the Supreme Court trying to impose a judicial solution on a political problem. It called down enormous criticism on the court and on Chief Justice Roger Brooke Taney; a later chief justice, Charles Evans Hughes, described it as a great "self-inflicted wound."

Scott, born a slave, had been taken by his master, an army surgeon, into the free portion of the Louisiana territory. Upon his master's death, Scott sued for his freedom, on the grounds that since slavery was outlawed in the free territory, he had become a free man there, and "once free, always free." The argument was rejected by a Missouri court, but Scott and his white supporters managed to get the case into federal court, where the issue was simply whether or not a slave had standing—that is, the legal right—to sue in a federal court. So the first question the Supreme Court had to decide was whether it had jurisdiction. If Scott had standing, then the court had jurisdiction, and the justices could go on to decide the merits of his claim. But if, as a slave, Scott did not have standing, then the court could dismiss the suit for lack of jurisdiction.

The court ruled that Scott, as a slave, could not exercise the prerogative of a free citizen to sue in federal court. That should have been the end of the case, but Chief Justice Taney and the other southern sympathizers on the Court hoped that a definitive ruling would settle the issue of slavery in the territories once and for all. So they went on to rule that the Missouri Compromise of 1820 was unconstitutional since Congress could not forbid citizens from taking their property, i.e., slaves, into any territory owned by the United States. A slave, Taney ruled, was property, nothing more, and could never be a citizen.

The South, of course, welcomed the ruling, but in the North it raised a storm of protest and scorn. It helped create the Republican Party, and disgust at the decision may have played a role in the election of Abraham Lincoln in 1860.

Chief Justice Taney delivered the opinion of the Court.

The question is simply this: Can a negro, whose ancestors were imported into this country, and sold as slaves, become a member of the political community formed and brought into existence by the Constitution of the United States, and as such become entitled to all the rights, and privileges, and immunities, guarantied by that instrument to the citizen? One of which rights is the privilege of suing in a court of the United States in the cases specified in the constitution . . .

The words "people of the United States" and "citizens" are synonymous terms, and mean the same thing. They both describe the political body who, according to our republican institutions, form the sovereignty, and who hold the power and conduct the government through their representatives. They are what we familiarly call the "sovereign people," and every citizen is one of this people, and a constituent member of this sovereignty. The question before us is, whether the class of persons described in the plea in abatement compose a portion of this people, and are constituent members of this sovereignty? We think they are not, and that they are not included, and were not intended to be included, under the word "citizens" in the constitution, and can therefore claim none of the rights and privileges which that instrument provides for and secures to citizens of the United

States. On the contrary, they were at that time considered as a subordinate and inferior class of beings, who had been subjugated by the dominant race, and, whether emancipated or not, yet remained subject to their authority, and had no rights or privileges but such as those who held the power and the government might choose to grant them.

It is not the province of the court to decide upon the justice or injustice, the policy or impolicy, of these laws. The decision of that question belonged to the political or law-making power; to those who formed the sovereignty and framed the constitution. The duty of the court is, to interpret the instrument they have framed, with the best lights we can obtain on the subject, and to administer it as we find it, according to its true intent and meaning when it was adopted.

In discussing this question, we must not confound the rights of citizenship which a State may confer within its own limits, and the rights of citizenship as a member of the Union. It does not by any means follow, because he has all the rights and privileges of a citizen of a State, that he must be a citizen of the United States. He may have all of the rights and privileges of the citizen of a State, and yet not be entitled to the rights and privileges of a citizen in any other State. For, previous to the adoption of the constitution of the United States, every State had the undoubted right to confer on whomsoever it pleased the character of citizen, and to endow him with all its rights. But this character of course was confirmed to the boundaries of the State, and gave him no rights or privileges in other States beyond those secured to him by the laws of nations and the comity of States. Nor have the several States surrendered the power of conferring these rights and privileges by adopting the constitution of the United States . . .

It is very clear, therefore, that no State can, by any act or law of its own, passed since the adoption of the constitution, introduce a new member into the political community created by the constitution of the United States. It cannot make him a member of this community by making him a member of its own. And for the same reason it cannot introduce any person, or description of persons, who were not intended to be embraced in this new political family, which the constitution brought into existence, but were intended to be excluded from it.

The question then arises, whether the provisions of the constitution, in relation to the personal rights and privileges to which the citizen of a State should be entitled, embraced the negro African race, at that time in this country, or who might afterwards be imported, who had then or should afterwards be made free in any State; and to put it in the power of a single State to make him a citizen of the United States, and endue him with the full rights of citizenship in every other State without their consent? Does the constitution of the United States act upon him whenever he shall be made free under the laws of a State, and raised there to the rank of a citizen, and immediately clothe him with all the privileges of a citizen in every other State, and in its own courts?

The court think the affirmative of these propositions cannot be maintained. And if it cannot, the plaintiff in error could not be a citizen of the State of Missouri, within the meaning of the constitution of the United States, and, consequently, was not entitled to sue in its courts.

It is true, every person, and every class and description of persons, who were at the time of the adoption of the constitution recognized as citizens in the several States, became also citizens of this new political body; but none other; it was formed by them, and for them and their posterity, but for no one else. And the personal rights and privileges guaranteed to citizens of this new sovereignty were intended to embrace those only who were then members of the several State communities, or who should afterwards by birthright or otherwise become members, according to the provisions of the constitution and the principles on which it was founded. It was the union of those who were at that time members of distinct and separate political communities into one political family, whose power, for certain specified purposes, was to extend over the whole territory of the United States.

And it gave to each citizen rights and privileges outside of his State which he did not before possess, and placed him in every other State upon a perfect equality with its own citizens as to rights of person and rights of property; it made him a citizen of the United States . . .

In the opinion of the court, the legislation and histories of the times, and the language used in the declaration of independence, show, that neither the class of persons who had been imported as slaves, nor their descendants, whether they had become free or not, were then acknowledged as a part of the people, nor intended to be included in the general words used in that memorable instrument . . .

It is too clear for dispute, that the enslaved African race were not intended to be included, and formed no part of the people who framed and adopted this declaration; for if the language, as understood in that day, would embrace them, the conduct of the distinguished men who framed the declaration of independence would have been utterly and flagrantly inconsistent with the principles they asserted; and instead of the sympathy of mankind, to which they so confidently appealed, they would have deserved and received universal rebuke and reprobation . . .

But there are two clauses in the constitution which point directly and specifically to the negro race as a separate class of persons, and show clearly that they were not regarded as a portion of the people or citizens of the government then formed.

One of these clauses reserves to each of the thirteen States the right to import slaves until the year 1808, if it thinks proper . . . And by the other provision the States pledge themselves to each other to maintain the right of property of the master, by delivering up to him any slave who may have escaped from his service, and be found within their respective territories . . .

The only two provisions which point to them and include them, treat them as property, and make it the duty of the government to protect it; no other power, in relation to this race, is to be found in the constitution; and as it is a government of special, delegated powers, no authority beyond these two provisions can be constitutionally exercised. The government of the United States had no right to interfere for any other purpose but that of protecting the rights of the owner, leaving it altogether with the several States to deal with this race, whether emancipated or not, as each State may think justice, humanity, and the interests and safety of society, require. The States evidently intended to reserve this power exclusively to themselves . . .

Upon a full and careful consideration of the subject, the court is of opinion, that, upon the facts stated . . . Dred Scott was not a citizen of Missouri within the meaning of the constitution of the United States, and not entitled as such to sue in its courts; and, consequently, that the circuit court had no jurisdiction of the case, and that the judgment on the plea in abatement is erroneous . . .

We proceed . . . to inquire whether the facts relied on by the plaintiff entitled him to his freedom . . .

The act of Congress, upon which the plaintiff relies, declares that slavery and involuntary servitude, except as a punishment for crime, shall be forever prohibited in all that part of the territory ceded by France, under the name of Louisiana, which lies north of thirty-six degrees thirty minutes north latitude and not included within the limits of Missouri. And the difficulty which meets us at the threshold of this part of the inquiry is whether Congress was authorized to pass this law under any of the powers granted to it by the Constitution; for, if the authority is not given by that instrument, it is the duty of this Court to declare it void and inoperative and incapable of conferring freedom upon anyone who is held as a slave under the laws of any one of the states.

The counsel for the plaintiff has laid much stress upon that article in the Constitution which confers on Congress the power "to dispose of and make all needful rules and regulations respecting the territory or other property belonging to the United States"; but, in the judgment of the Court, that provision has no bearing on the present controversy, and the power there given, whatever it may be, is confined, and was intended to be confined, to the territory which at that time belonged to, or was claimed by, the United States and was within their boundaries as settled by the treaty with Great Britain and can have no influence upon a territory afterward acquired from a foreign government. It was a special provision for a known and particular territory, and to meet a present emergency, and nothing more . . .

We do not mean, however, to question the power of Congress in this respect. The power to expand the territory of the United States by the admission of new states is plainly given; and in the construction of this power by all the departments of the government, it has been held to authorize the acquisition of territory, not fit for admission at the time, but to be admitted as soon as its population and situation would entitle it to admission . . .

It may be safely assumed that citizens of the United States who migrate to a territory belonging to the people of the United States cannot be ruled as mere colonists, dependent upon the will of the general government, and to be governed by any laws it may think proper to impose. The principle upon which our governments rest, and upon which alone they continue to exist, is the union of states, sovereign and independent within their own limits in their internal and domestic concerns, and bound together as one people by a general government, possessing certain enumerated and restricted powers, delegated to it by the people of the several states, and exercising supreme authority within the scope of the powers granted to it, throughout the dominion of the United States. A power, therefore, in the general government to obtain and hold colonies and dependent territories, over which they might legislate without restriction, would be inconsistent with its own existence in its present form. Whatever it acquires, it acquires for the benefit of the people of the several states who created it. It is their trustee acting for them and charged with the duty of promoting the interests of the whole people of the Union in the exercise of the powers specifically granted . . .

But the power of Congress over the person or property of a citizen can never be a mere discretionary power under our Constitution and form of government. The powers of the government and the rights and privileges of the citizen are regulated and plainly defined by the Constitution itself. And, when the territory becomes a part of the United States, the federal government enters into possession in the character impressed upon it by those who created it. It enters upon it with its powers over the citizen strictly defined and limited by the Constitution, from which it derives its own existence, and by virtue of which alone it continues to exist and act as a government and sovereignty. It has no power of any kind beyond it; and it cannot, when it enters a territory of the United States, put off its character and assume discretionary or despotic powers which the Constitution has denied to it. It cannot create for itself a new character separated from the citizens of the United States and the duties it owes them under the provisions of the Constitution. The territory, being a part of the United States, the government and the citizen both enter it under the authority of the Constitution, with their respective rights defined and marked out; and the federal government can exercise no power over his person or property, beyond what that instrument confers, nor lawfully deny any right which it has reserved . . .

These powers, and others, in relation to rights of person, which it is not necessary here to enumerate, are, in express and positive terms, denied to the general government; and the rights of private property have been guarded with equal care. Thus the rights of property are united with the rights of person and placed on the same ground by the Fifth Amendment to the Constitution, which provides that no person shall be deprived of life, liberty, and property without due process of law.

And an act of Congress which deprives a citizen of the United States of his liberty or property, without due process of law, merely because he came himself or brought his property into a particular territory of the United States, and who had committed no offense against the laws, could hardly be dignified with the name of due process of law . . .

It seems, however, to be supposed that there is a difference between property in a slave and other property and that different rules may be applied to it in expounding the Constitution of the United States. And the laws and usages of nations, and the writings of eminent jurists upon the relation of master and slave and their mutual rights and duties, and the powers which governments may exercise over it, have been dwelt upon in the argument.

But, in considering the question before us, it must be borne in mind that there is no law of nations standing between the people of the United States and their government and interfering with their relation to each other. The powers of the government and the rights of the citizen under it are positive and practical regulations plainly written down. The people of the United States have delegated to it certain enumerated powers and forbidden it to exercise others. It has no power over the person or property of a citizen but what the citizens of the United States have granted. And no laws or usages of other nations, or reasoning of statesmen or jurists upon the relations of master and slave, can enlarge the powers of the government or take from the citizens the rights they have reserved. And if the Constitution recognizes the right of property of the master in a slave, and makes no distinction between that description of property and other property owned by a citizen, no tribunal, acting under the authority of the United States, whether it be legislative, executive, or judicial, has a right to draw such a distinction or deny to it the benefit of the provisions and guaranties which have been provided for the protection of private property against the encroachments of the government.

Now, as we have already said in an earlier part of this opinion, upon a different point, the right of property in a slave is distinctly and expressly affirmed in the Constitution. The right to traffic in it, like an ordinary article of merchandise and property, was guaranteed to the citizens of the United States, in every state that might desire it, for twenty years. And the government in express terms is pledged to protect it in all future time if the slave escapes from his owner. That is done in plain words—too plain to be misunderstood. And no word can be found in the Constitution which gives Congress a greater power over slave property or which entitles property of that kind to less protection than property of any other description. The only power conferred is the power coupled with the duty of guarding and protecting the owner in his rights.

Upon these considerations it is the opinion of the Court that the act of Congress which prohibited a citizen from holding and owning property of this kind in the territory of the United States north of the line therein mentioned is not warranted by the Constitution and is therefore void; and that neither Dred Scott himself, nor any of his family, were made free by being carried into this territory; even if they had been carried there by the owner with the intention of becoming a permanent resident.

1. Why did Chief Justice Taney rule that Dred Scott did not have the right in the constitution to sue?

   a. The court did not want to enter into a political battle.
   b. The court was in favor of slavery.
   c. The court did not think that Dred Scott had a reasonable case.
   d. The court did not consider slaves to be citizens.

2. Why does the court rule that only the Constitution can recognize citizens?

   a. The Constitution stated that slaves were not citizens.
   b. The Constitution was created for those who were there at the time.
   c. The Constitution is the only document that all of the states adhere to.
   d. The Constitution does not specify who qualifies as a citizen.

3. How do the sections from the Constitution that Taney quotes support his point?

   a. They show that states have sovereign rights.
   b. They show that the Constitution is irrefutable.
   c. They show that slaves are property and not free citizens.
   d. They show that slaves are imported and traded across state lines.

4. Why was the Missouri Compromise ruled unconstitutional?

   a. The House of Representatives vetoed the treaty.
   b. The government can only protect slaves; it does not have the power to abolish slavery.
   c. The government can import and export slaves, however, it does not have the power to prosecute fugitives.
   d. The Constitution does not specify whether or not slave states can export slaves across free-state borders.

5. The case ruled in favor of

   a. Dred Scott.
   b. Sanford.
   c. southern states.
   d. northern states.

6. According to Taney, Congress does not have power

   a. over a territory's private property.
   b. to expand the territory of the United States.
   c. to declare a political war on the territories.
   d. to trade land with foreign powers.

7. Why could a territory, according to Taney, enter the union as a slave territory and remain so?

   a. The Union can change only those powers specified in the territory's constitution.
   b. The territory has the authority to veto Congress.
   c. The territory has a clause in its constitution that argues against the Constitution of the United States.
   d. The Union must accept slavery as an expression of the people's will.

8. According to Taney, the reason that the debates about the differences in typical property and slave property are moot points is because

   a. they do not come to any decisive conclusions.
   b. the debates are not practical.
   c. they favor abolition.
   d. the Constitution does not give the government power over property.

9. Ultimately, why did Dred Scott and the Missouri Compromise “lose” in Taney’s opinion?

   a. The Constitution could not free slaves.
   b. The Constitution allowed slavery and protected owner’s rights.
   c. The Constitution did not have the power to change state law.
   d. none of the above

10. Do you agree with this statement: “It is true, every person, and every class and description of persons, who were at the time of the adoption of the constitution recognized as citizens in the several States, became also citizens of this new political body; but none other; it was formed by them, and for them and their posterity, but for no one else”? Why or why not?

11. How do you think that Chief Justice Taney was able to keep an unbiased opinion? Please support your answer with relevant quotations from the text.

Abraham Lincoln's Speech, "A House Divided" (1858)

The Dred Scott decision came just three years after Senator Stephen Douglas of Illinois had engineered the Kansas-Nebraska bill through Congress. Pressure to build a transcontinental railroad had been intensifying, but southerners declared they would continue to block the necessary legislation unless they were allowed additional territory to which to take their slaves. Douglas had come up with a proposal to allow slavery in the northern part of the Louisiana Purchase, but only if it received the blessing of the settlers in the territory. The formula, known as popular sovereignty, temporarily satisfied both southerners and some northerners, since it appeared democratic; as Douglas pointed out, unless a majority of people in a territory supported slavery, it could not take hold. In Dred Scott, the Supreme Court had held that Congress had no power to keep slavery out of the territories, a decision that seemingly nullified the popular sovereignty proposal.

Increasingly, northerners came to the conclusion that opposition to the expansion of slavery in the territories was not enough, that the real evil was the peculiar institution itself. But this commitment to total abolition scared many moderates, who believed that if they attacked slavery in the South, it could spell the end of the Union. Abraham Lincoln was among these moderates. He opposed the expansion of slavery, but believed it had to be left in place where it existed, and he hoped that by so containing it, it would eventually die a natural death. In 1858 the new Republican Party named Lincoln its candidate for the U.S. Senate seat then held by Stephen Douglas, author of the doctrine of popular sovereignty. The debates Lincoln and Douglas held that fall would receive national attention, and turn Lincoln into a serious contender for the Republican Party's 1860 presidential election.

In a speech delivered on June 17, 1858, at the close of the Republican State Convention, Lincoln caught the mood of many in the North who were increasingly concerned about the morality of slavery on the one hand, and the need to preserve the Union on the other. Though the "house divided" phrase had been used frequently before, it was this speech of Lincoln's that gave currency and familiarity to the phrase and the idea.

Mr. President and Gentlemen of the Convention:

If we could first know where we are, and whither we are tending, we could better judge what to do, and how to do it. We are now far into the fifth year since apolicy was initiated with the avowed object and confident promise of putting an end to slavery agitation. Under the operation of that policy, that agitation has not only not ceased, but has constantly augmented. In my opinion, it will not cease until a crisis shall have been reached and passed. "A house divided against itself cannot stand." I believe this government cannot endure permanently half slave and half free. I do not expect the Union to be dissolved; I do not expect the house to fall; but I do expect it will cease to be divided. It will become all one thing, or all the other. Either the opponents of slavery will arrest the further spread of it, and place it where the public mind shall rest in the belief that it is in the course of ultimate extinction, or its advocates will push it forward till it shall become alike lawful in all the States, old as well as new, North as well as South.

Have we no tendency to the latter condition?

Let any one who doubts, carefully contemplate that now almost complete legal combination—pieces of machinery, so to speak—compounded of the Nebraska doctrine and the Dred Scott decision. Let him consider, not only what work the machinery is adapted to do, and how well adapted, but also let him study the history of its construction, and trace, if he can, or rather fail, if he can, to trace the evidence of design, and concert of action, among its chief architects, from the beginning.

The new year of 1854 found slavery excluded from more that half the States by State Constitutions, and from most of the National territory by Congressional prohibition. Four days later, commenced the struggle which ended in repealing that Congressional prohibition. This opened all the National territory to slavery, and was the first point gained . . .

While the Nebraska Bill was passing through Congress, a law case, involving the question of a negro's freedom by reason of his owner having voluntarily taken him first into a free State, and then into a territory covered by the Congressional prohibition, and held him as a slave for a long time in each, was passing through the United States Circuit Court for the District of Missouri; and both Nebraska Bill and lawsuit were brought to a decision in the same month of May, 1854. The negro's name was "Dred Scott," which name now designates the decision finally made in the case. Before the then next Presidential election, the law case came to, and was argued in, the Supreme Court of the United States; but the decision of it was deferred until after the election. Still, before the election, Senator Trumbull, on the floor of the Senate, requested the leading advocate of the Nebraska Bill to state his opinion whether the people of a Territory can constitutionally exclude slavery from their limits; and the latter answers: "That is a question for the Supreme Court."

The election came. Mr. Buchanan was elected, and the indorsement, such as it was, secured. That was the second point gained . . . The Presidential inauguration came, and still no decision of the court; but the incoming President, in his inaugural address, fervently exhorted the people to abide by the forthcoming decision, whatever it might be. Then, in a few days, came the decision.

The reputed author of the Nebraska Bill finds an early occasion to make a speech at this capital indorsing the Dred Scott decision, and vehemently denouncing all opposition to it. The new President, too, seizes the early occasion of the Silliman letter to indorse and strongly construe that decision, and to express his astonishment that any different view had ever been entertained!

At length a squabble springs up between the President and the author of the Nebraska Bill, on the mere question of fact, whether the Lecompton Constitution was or was not in any just sense made by the people of Kansas; and in that quarrel the latter declares that all he wants is a fair vote for the people, and that he cares not whether slavery be voted down or voted up. I do not understand his declaration, that he cares not whether slavery be voted down or voted up, to be intended by him other than as an apt definition of the policy he would impress upon the public mind . . . That principle is the only shred left of his original Nebraska doctrine. Under the Dred Scott decision "squatter sovereignty" squatted out of existence, tumbled down like temporary scaffolding; like the mould at the foundry, served through one blast, and fell back into loose sand; helped to carry an election, and then was kicked to the winds. His late joint struggle with the Republicans, against the Lecompton Constitution, involves nothing of the original Nebraska doctrine. That struggle was made on a point—the right of a people to make their own constitution—upon which he and the Republicans have never differed.

The several points of the Dred Scott decision, in connection with Senator Douglas's "care not" policy, constitute the piece of machinery, in its present state of advancement. This was the third point gained. The working points of that machinery are:

Firstly, That no negro slave imported as such from Africa, and descendant of such slave, can ever be a citizen of any State, in the sense of that term as used in the Constitution of the United States. This point is made in order to deprive the negro, in every possible event, of the benefit of the provision of the United States Constitution which declares that "The citizens of each State shall be entitled to all privileges and immunities of citizens in the several States."

Secondly, That, "subject to the Constitution of the United States," neither Congress nor a Territorial Legislature can exclude slavery from any United States Territory. This point is made in order that individual men fill up the Territories with slaves, without danger of losing them as property, and thus to enhance the chances of permanency to the institution through all the future.

Thirdly, That whether the holding a negro in actual slavery in a free State makes him free, as against the holder, the United States courts will not decide, but will leave to be decided by the courts of any slave state the negro may be forced into by the master. This point is made, not to be pressed immediately; but, if acquiesced in for a while, and apparently indorsed by the people at an election, then to sustain the logical conclusion that what Dred Scott's master might lawfully do with Dred Scott, in the free State of Illinois, every other master may lawfully do with any other one, or one thousand slaves, in Illinois, or in any other free State.

Auxiliary to all this, and working hand in hand with it, the Nebraska doctrine, or what is left of it, is to educate and mould public opinion, at least Northern public opinion, not to care whether slavery is voted down or voted up. This shows exactly where we now are; and partially, also, whither we are tending . . .

Why was the amendment, expressly declaring the right of the people, voted down? Plainly enough now,—the speaking out then would have damaged the "perfectly free" argument upon which the election was to be carried. Why the outgoing President's felicitation on the indorsement? Why the delay of a reargument? Why the incoming President's advance exhortation in favor of the decision? These things look like the cautious patting and petting of a spirited horse preparatory to mounting him, when it is dreaded that he may give the rider a fall. And why the hasty after-indorsement of the decision by the President and others?

We cannot absolutely know that all these exact adaptations are the result of preconcert. But when we see a lot of framed timbers, different portions of which we know have been gotten out at different times and places and by different workmen,—Stephen, Franklin, Roger, and James, for instance,—and when we see these timbers joined together, and see they exactly make the frame of a house or a mill, all the tenons and mortises exactly fitting, and all the lengths and proportions of the different pieces exactly adapted to their respective places, and not a piece too many or too few,—not omitting even scaffolding,—or, if a single piece be lacking, we see the place in the frame exactly fitted and prepared yet to bring such piece in,—in such a case, we find it impossible not to believe that Stephen and Franklin and Roger and James all understood one another from the beginning, and all worked upon a common plan or draft drawn up before the first blow was struck . . .

1. Why do you think Lincoln began the "House Divided" speech with questions about where we are, where we are tending, what to do, and how to do it?

   a. He was uncertain of his position.
   b. He wanted to show the opposition that he could solve the problem.
   c. He wanted to indicate the political puzzle that was taking shape.
   d. He wanted to refute the opposition one point at a time.

2. Lincoln first explains how the United States could become a

    a. free country for all citizens.
    b. stable democracy.
    c. part slave, part free country.
    d. country that endorses slavery.

3. What is "the machinery" that Lincoln refers to?

    a. politics
    b. slavery
    c. industry
    d. territory

4. Why was it important to Lincoln that both President Buchanan and the incoming president indorsed the Supreme Court's decision in the Dred Scott case?

    a. It showed a united front in a conflicted country.
    b. The case would have the support of the executive for years to come.
    c. Lincoln wanted to draw attention to the government's fear.
    d. none of the above

5. Why did "popular sovereignty" make the public indifferent to slavery?

    a. They could not understand the complicated policy.
    b. It was democratic and, therefore, the public thought it was a good compromise.
    c. The policy made the southern states happy.
    d. The policy showed that the slaves were satisfied with their rights.

6. Why does Lincoln conclude his speech with the image of a house?

    a. He wanted to show that politicians could be brought to justice.
    b. He was illustrating how the Constitution works for the people.
    c. He wanted to show the strength and flexibility of the Constitution.
    d. He was trying to explain that the "machinery" of slavery would create a fortress.

7. The "House Divided" speech mentions that some politicians did not care whether or not slavery was voted down or up. How do you think Lincoln felt about that opinion? Support your essay with quotations. How do you feel about that opinion?

Homestead Act, May 20, 1862

The Homestead Act, enacted during the Civil War in 1862, provided that any adult citizen, or intended citizen, who had never borne arms against the U.S. government could claim 160 acres of surveyed government land. Claimants were required to "improve" the plot by building a dwelling and cultivating the land. After five years on the land, the original filer was entitled to the property, free and clear, except for a small registration fee. Title could also be acquired after only a six-month residency and trivial improvements, provided the claimant paid the government $1.25 per acre. After the Civil War, Union soldiers could deduct the time they had served from the residency requirements.

Although this act was included in the Republican party platform of 1860, support for the idea began decades earlier. Even under the Articles of Confederation, before 1787, the distribution of government lands generated much interest and discussion.

The act, however, proved to be no panacea for poverty. Comparatively few laborers and farmers could afford to build a farm or acquire the necessary tools, seed, and livestock. In the end, most of those who purchased land under the act came from areas quite close to their new homesteads (Iowans moved to Nebraska, Minnesotans to South Dakota, and so on). Unfortunately, the act was framed so ambiguously that it seemed to invite fraud, and early modifications by Congress only compounded the problem. Most of the land went to speculators, cattlemen, miners, lumbermen, and railroads. Of some 500 million acres dispersed by the General Land Office between 1862 and 1904, only 80 million acres went to homesteaders. Indeed, small farmers acquired more land under the Homestead Act in the 20th century than in the 19th.

CHAP. LXXV. —An Act to secure Homesteads to actual Settlers on the Public Domain.

Be it enacted by the Senate and House of Representatives of the United States of America in Congress assembled, That any person who is the head of a family, or who has arrived at the age of twenty-one years, and is a citizen of the United States, or who shall have filed his declaration of intention to become such, as required by the naturalization laws of the United States, and who has never borne arms against the United States Government or given aid and comfort to its enemies, shall, from and after the first January, eighteen hundred and. sixty-three, be entitled to enter one quarter section or a less quantity of unappropriated public lands, upon which said person may have filed a preemption claim, or which may, at the time the application is made, be subject to preemption at one dollar and twenty-five cents, or less, per acre; or eighty acres or less of such unappropriated lands, at two dollars and fifty cents per acre, to be located in a body, in conformity to the legal subdivisions of the public lands, and after the same shall have been surveyed: Provided, That any person owning and residing on land may, under the provisions of this act, enter other land lying contiguous to his or her said land, which shall not, with the land so already owned and occupied, exceed in the aggregate one hundred and sixty acres.

SEC. 2. And be it further enacted, That the person applying for the benefit of this act shall, upon application to the register of the land office in which he or she is about to make such entry, make affidavit before the said register or receiver that he or she is the head of a family, or is twenty-one years or more of age, or shall have performed service in the army or navy of the United States, and that he has never borne arms against the Government of the United States or given aid and comfort to its enemies, and that such application is made for his or her exclusive use and benefit, and that said entry is made for the purpose of actual settlement and cultivation, and not either directly or indirectly for the use or benefit of any other person or persons whomsoever; and upon filing the said affidavit with the register or receiver, and on payment of ten dollars, he or she shall thereupon be permitted to enter the quantity of land specified: Provided, however, That no certificate shall be given or patent issued therefor until the expiration of five years from the date of such entry; and if, at the expiration of such time, or at any time within two years thereafter, the person making such entry; or, if he be dead, his widow; or in case of her death, his heirs or devisee; or in case of a widow making such entry, her heirs or devisee, in case of her death; shall prove by two credible witnesses that he, she, or they have resided upon or cultivated the same for the term of five years immediately succeeding the time of filing the affidavit aforesaid, and shall make affidavit that no part of said land has been alienated, and that he has borne true allegiance to the Government of the United States; then, in such case, he, she, or they, if at that time a citizen of the United States, shall be entitled to a patent, as in other cases provided for by law: And provided, further, That in case of the death of both father and mother, leaving an Infant child, or children, under twenty-one years of age, the right and fee shall ensure to the benefit of said infant child or children; and the executor, administrator, or guardian may, at any time within two years after the death of the surviving parent, and in accordance with the laws of the State in which such children for the time being have their domicil, sell said land for the benefit of said infants, but for no other purpose; and the purchaser shall acquire the absolute title by the purchase, and be entitled to a patent from the United States, on payment of the office fees and sum of money herein specified.

SEC. 3. And be it further enacted, That the register of the land office shall note all such applications on the tract books and plats of, his office, and keep a register of all such entries, and make return thereof to the General Land Office, together with the proof upon which they have been founded.

SEC. 4. And be it further enacted, That no lands acquired under the provisions of this act shall in any event become liable to the satisfaction of any debt or debts contracted prior to the issuing of the patent therefor . . .

1. Why was the Homestead Act, in theory, a good idea?

   a. It gave people an opportunity to make a home.
   b. It gave farmers more land.
   c. It gave poor people a chance to create a sustainable farm.
   d. It opened up the north.

2. Why were two credible witnesses necessary at the end of the term?

   a. in order to prove that the landowners were sustaining the farm and selling the goods
   b. in order to prove that the land was fertile
   c. in order to prove that the homeowners did not lie or cheat
   d. in order to prove that the person or people lived on and cultivated the land

3. How old did a person have to be to acquire the land?

   a. 16
   b. 18
   c. 21
   d. 23

4. Would you have taken this land? Why or why not?

THE MORRILL ACT (1862)

Once the South had left the Union, the remaining northern states began passing a number of measures which the South had blocked prior to 1860. Many of these laws, such as the authorization of the transcontinental railroads, helped to spur on economic growth and expansion in the western territories.

In 1862, Congress passed two such measures. The Homestead Act permitted any citizen, or any person who intended to become a citizen, to receive 160 acres of public land, and then to purchase it at a nominal fee after living on the land for five years. The Homestead Act provided the most generous terms of any land act in American history to enable people to settle and own their own farms.

Just as important was the Morrill Act of that year, which made it possible for the new western states to establish colleges for their citizens. Ever since colonial times, basic education had been a central tenet of American democratic thought. By the 1860s, higher education was becoming more accessible, and many politicians and educators wanted to make it possible for all young Americans to receive some sort of advanced education.

Sponsored by Congressman Justin Morrill of Vermont, who had been pressing for it since 1857, the act gave to every state that had remained in the Union a grant of 30,000 acres of public land for every member of its congressional delegation. Since under the Constitution every state had at least two senators and one representative, even the smallest state received 90,000 acres. The states were to sell this land and use the proceeds to establish colleges in engineering, agriculture and military science. Over seventy "land grant" colleges, as they came to be known, were established under the original Morrill Act; a second act in 1890 extended the land grant provisions to the sixteen southern states.

The importance of the land grant colleges cannot be exaggerated. Although originally started as agricultural and technical schools, many of them grew, with additional state aid, into large public universities which over the years have educated millions of U.S. citizens who otherwise might not have been able to afford college.

An Act donating Public Lands to the several States and Territories which may provide Colleges for the Benefit of Agriculture and the Mechanic Arts.

Be it enacted by the Senate and House of Representatives of the United States of America in Congress assembled, That there be granted to the several States, for the purposes hereinafter mentioned, an amount of public land, to be apportioned to each State a quantity equal to thirty thousand acres for each senator and representative in Congress to which the States are respectively entitled by the apportionment under the census of eighteen hundred and sixty: Provided, That no mineral lands shall be selected or purchased under the provisions of this act.

Sec. 2. And be it further enacted, That the land aforesaid, after being surveyed, shall be apportioned to the several States in sections or subdivisions of sections, not less than one quarter of a section; and whenever there are public lands in a State subject to sale at private entry at one dollar and twenty five cents per acre, the quantity to which said State shall be entitled shall be selected from such lands within the limits of such State, and the Secretary of the Interior is hereby directed to issue to each of the States in which there is not the quantity of public lands subject to sale at private entry at one dollar and twenty-five cents per acre, to which said State may be entitled under the provisions of this act, land scrip to the amount in acres for the deficiency of its distributive share: said scrip to be sold by said States and the proceeds thereof applied to the uses and purposes prescribed in this act, and for no other use or purpose whatsoever . . .

Sec. 4. And be it further enacted, That all moneys derived from the sale of the lands aforesaid by the States to which the lands are apportioned, and from the sale of land scrip hereinbefore provided for, shall be invested in stocks of the United States, or of the States, or some other safe stocks, yielding not less than five per centum upon the par value of the said stocks; and that the moneys so invested shall constitute a perpetual fund, the capital of which shall remain forever undiminished, (except so far as may be provided in section fifth of this act,) and the interest of which shall be inviolably appropriated, by each State which may take and claim the benefits of this act, to the endowment, support, and maintenance of at least one college where the leading object shall be, without excluding other scientific and classical studies, and including military tactics, to teach such branches of learning as are related to agriculture and mechanic arts, in such manner as the legislatures of the State may respectively prescribe, in order to promote the liberal and practical education of the industrial classes in the several pursuits and professions in life . . .

Sixth. No State while in a condition of rebellion or insurrection against the government of the United States shall be entitled to the benefit of this Act . . .

1. If a state has two senators and three representatives, how much land would it be allotted according to the Morrill Act?

   a. 90,000 acres
   b. 120,000 acres
   c. 150,000 acres
   d. 170,000 acres

2. The money accrued from the interest of the funds made from each state's sale of the land grant goes to

   a. a college.
   b. the state.
   c. the government.
   d. none of the above.

3. What is one condition of the Morrill Act?

   a. The land must be used to create agricultural colleges only.
   b. The state cannot rebel against the government.
   c. The land must remain the property of the government.
   d. The state can remove the funding if its debt exceeds the investment.

4. Do you think the Morrill Act was a good decision? Do you think that it benefited society in any meaningful way? Why or why not?

Abraham Lincoln's Emancipation Proclamation (1863)

Lincoln and the North had entered the war to preserve the Union rather than to free the slaves, but within a relatively short time emancipation became an accepted war aim. Neither Congress nor the president knew exactly what constitutional powers they had in this area; according to the Dred Scott decision, they had none. However, Lincoln believed that the Constitution gave the Union whatever powers it needed to preserve itself, and that he, as commander-in-chief, had the authority to use those powers.

In the fall of 1862, after the Union army victory at Antietam, Lincoln issued a preliminary proclamation, warning that on January 1, 1863, he would free all the slaves in those states still in rebellion. Intended as a war and propaganda measure, the Emancipation Proclamation had far more symbolic than real impact, because the federal government had no means to enforce it at the time. However, the document clearly and irrevocably notified the South and the world that the war was being fought not just to preserve the Union, but to put an end to the peculiar institution. Eventually, as Union armies occupied more and more southern territory, the Proclamation turned into reality, as thousands of slaves were actually set free by the advancing federal troops.

Whereas, on the twenty-second day of September, in the year of our Lord one thousand eight hundred and sixty-two, a proclamation was issued by the President of the United States, containing, among other things, the following, to wit:

"That on the first day of January, in the year of our Lord one thousand eight hundred and sixty-three, all persons held as slaves within any State, or designated part of a State, the people whereof shall then be in rebellion against the United States, shall be then, thenceforward, and forever free; and the Executive Government of the United States, including the military and naval authority thereof, will recognize and maintain the freedom of such persons, and will do no act or acts to repress such persons, or any of them, in any efforts they may make for their actual freedom."

"That the Executive will, on the first day of January aforesaid, by proclamation, designate the States and parts of States, if any, in which the people thereof respectively shall then be in rebellion against the United States; and the fact that any State, or the people thereof, shall on that day be in good faith represented in the Congress of the United States by members chosen thereto at elections wherein a majority of the qualified voters of such State shall have participated, shall in the absence of strong countervailing testimony be deemed conclusive evidence that such State and the people thereof are not then in rebellion against the United States."

Now, therefore, I, Abraham Lincoln, President of the United States, by virtue of the power in me vested as commander-in-chief of the army and navy of the United States, in time of actual armed rebellion against the authority and government of the United States, and as a fit and necessary war measure for suppressing said rebellion, do, on this first day of January, in the year of our Lord one thousand eight hundred and sixty-three, and in accordance with my purpose so to do, publicly proclaimed for the full period of 100 days from the day first above mentioned, order and designate as the States and parts of States wherein the people thereof, respectively, are this day in rebellion against the United States, the following, to wit:

Arkansas, Texas, Louisiana (except the parishes of St. Bernard, Plaquemines, Jefferson, St. John, St. Charles, St. James, Ascension, Assumption, Terre Bonne, Lafourche, St. Mary, St. Martin, and Orleans, including the city of New Orleans), Mississippi, Alabama, Florida, Georgia, South Carolina, North Carolina, and Virginia (except the forty-eight counties designated as West Virginia, and also the counties of Berkeley, Accomac, Northampton, Elizabeth City, York, Princess Anne, and Norfolk, including the cities of Norfolk and Portsmouth), and which excepted parts are for the present left precisely as if this proclamation were not issued.

And by virtue of the power and for the purpose aforesaid, I do order and declare that all persons held as slaves within said designated States and parts of States are, and henceforward shall be, free; and that the Executive Government of the United States, including the military and naval authorities thereof, will recognize and maintain the freedom of said persons.

And I hereby enjoin upon the people so declared to be free to abstain from all violence, unless in necessary self-defense; and I recommend to them that, in all cases where allowed, they labor faithfully for reasonable wages.

And I further declare and make known that such persons of suitable condition will be received into the armed service of the United States to garrison forts, positions, stations, and other places, and to man vessels of all sorts in said service.

And upon this act, sincerely believed to be an act of justice, warranted by the Constitution upon military necessity, I invoke the considerate judgment of mankind and the gracious favor of Almighty God.

In witness whereof, I have hereunto set my hand and caused the seal of the United States to be affixed.

Done at the city of Washington, this first day of January, in the year of our Lord one thousand eight hundred and sixty-three, and of the independence of the United States of America the eighty-seventh.

Abraham Lincoln

1. The Emancipation Proclamation states that

   a. the United States has declared war on Arkansas, Texas, and Louisiana.
   b. all the slaves are free.
   c. slaves are free in the northern states.
   d. Congress does not have the power to free the slaves.

2. Why does the proclamation ask that the freed slaves "abstain from all violence"?

   a. The president was uncertain how the slaves would react to their newfound freedom.
   b. The president wanted the slaves to be treated fairly.
   c. The president was merely giving advice.
   d. The president did not want uprisings to occur.

3. Any state that does not follow the proclamation is considered to be

   a. in rebellion.
   b. uncertain of its position.
   c. annexed from the Union.
   d. its own separate government.

4. How do you think this proclamation was received in the south? How was it received in the north? Please explain.

War Department General Order 143: Creation of the U.S. Colored Troops (1863)

The issues of emancipation and military service were intertwined from the onset of the Civil War. News from Fort Sumter set off a rush by free black men to enlist in U.S. military units. They were turned away, however, because a Federal law dating from 1792 barred Negroes from bearing arms for the U.S. Army. In Boston disappointed would-be volunteers met and passed a resolution requesting that the Government modify its laws to permit their enlistment.

The Lincoln administration wrestled with the idea of authorizing the recruitment of black troops, concerned that such a move would prompt the border states to secede. When Gen. John C. Frémont in Missouri and Gen. David Hunter in South Carolina issued proclamations that emancipated slaves in their military regions and permitted them to enlist, their superiors sternly revoked their orders. By mid-1862, however, the escalating number of former slaves (contrabands), the declining number of white volunteers, and the pressing personnel needs of the Union Army pushed the Government into reconsidering the ban.

As a result, on July 17, 1862, Congress passed the Second Confiscation and Militia Act, freeing slaves who had masters in the Confederate Army. Two days later, slavery was abolished in the territories of the United States, and on July 22nd President Lincoln presented the preliminary draft of the Emancipation Proclamation to his Cabinet. After the Union Army turned back Lee's first invasion of the North at Antietam, Maryland, and the Emancipation Proclamation was subsequently announced, black recruitment was pursued in earnest. Volunteers from South Carolina, Tennessee, and Massachusetts filled the first authorized black regiments. Recruitment was slow until black leaders such as Frederick Douglass encouraged black men to become soldiers to ensure eventual full citizenship. (Two of Douglass's own sons contributed to the war effort.) Volunteers began to respond, and in May 1863 the Government established the Bureau of Colored Troops to manage the burgeoning numbers of black soldiers.

Nearly 40,000 black soldiers died over the course of the war—30,000 of infection or disease. Black soldiers served in artillery and infantry and performed all noncombat support functions that sustain an army as well. Black carpenters, chaplains, cooks, guards, laborers, nurses, scouts, spies, steamboat pilots, surgeons, and teamsters also contributed to the war cause. There were nearly eighty black commissioned officers. Black women, who could not formally join the Army, nonetheless served as nurses, spies, and scouts, the most famous being Harriet Tubman, who scouted for the 2nd South Carolina Volunteers.

GENERAL ORDERS,
No. 143
WAR DEPARTMENT,
ADJUTANT GENERAL'S OFFICE,
Washington, May 22, 1863.

I—A Bureau is established in the Adjutant General's Office for the record of all matters relating to the organization of Colored Troops, An officer, will be assigned to the charge of the Bureau, with such number of clerks as may be designated by the Adjutant General.

II—Three or more field officers will be detailed as Inspectors to supervise the organization of colored troops at such points as may be indicated by the War Department in the Northern and Western States.

III—Boards will be convened at such posts as may be decided upon by the War Department to examine applicants for commissions to command colored troops, who, on Application to the Adjutant General, may receive authority to present themselves to the board for examination.

IV—No persons shall be allowed to recruit for colored troops except specially authorized by the War Department; and no such authority will be given to persons who have not been examined and passed by a board; nor will such authority be given any one person to raise more than one regiment.

V—The reports of Boards will specify the grade of commission for which each candidate is fit, and authority to recruit will be given in accordance. Commissions will be issued from the Adjutant General's Office when the prescribed number of men is ready for muster into service.

VI—Colored troops maybe accepted by companies, to be afterward consolidated in battalions and regiments by the Adjutant General. The regiments will be numbered seriatim, in the order in which they are raised, the numbers to be determined by the Adjutant General. They will be designated: "— —Regiment of U. S. Colored Troops."

VII—Recruiting stations and depots will be established by the Adjutant General as circumstances shall require, and officers will be detailed to muster and inspect the troops.

VIII—The non-commissioned officers of colored troops may be selected and appointed from the best men of their number in the usual mode of appointing non-commissioned officers. Meritorious commissioned officers will be entitled to promotion to higher rank if they prove themselves equal to it.

IX—All personal applications for appointments in colored regiments, or for information concerning them, must be made to the Chief of the Bureau; all written communications should be addressed to the Chief of the Bureau, to the care of the Adjutant General,

BY ORDER OF THE SECRETARY OF WAR:

E. D. TOWNSEND,

Assistant Adjutant General.

1. Ultimately, why did the Congress pass the Second Confiscation and Militia Act?

    a. Congress bowed under the pressure from northern states.
    b. Lincoln demanded that the act pass.
    c. The army needed more men.
    d. The southern states would lose military personnel.

2. Though the freed slaves entered the forces, they were

    a. not given important jobs.
    b. not allowed to carry weapons.
    c. separated from white troops.
    d. forced to work for white commissioned officers.

3. Do you think that the right to fight in the war won the slaves a greater equality? Though the enlisting was partially motivated by necessity, how do you think the "colored" troops affected the opinions of white soldiers? Explain.

Abraham Lincoln's Gettysburg Address (1863)

Few documents in the growth of American democracy are as well known or as beloved as the prose poem Abraham Lincoln delivered at the dedication of the military cemetery in Gettysburg, Pennsylvania.

In June 1863 Confederate forces under Robert E. Lee moved north in an effort to win a dramatic victory that would reverse the South's declining fortunes. On July 1–3, Lee's forces fought the Union army under the command of George C. Meade and, before the fighting ended, the two sides suffered more than 45,000 casualties. Lee, having lost more than a third of his men, retreated, and the Battle of Gettysburg is considered a turning point in the American Civil War.

At the end of the Battle of Gettysburg, more than 51,000 Confederate and Union soldiers were wounded, missing, or dead. Many of those who died were laid in makeshift graves along the battlefield. Pennsylvania Governor Andrew Curtin commissioned David Wills, an attorney, to purchase land for a proper burial site for the deceased Union soldiers. Wills acquired seventeen acres for the cemetery, which was planned and designed by landscape architect William Saunders.

The cemetery was dedicated on November 19, 1863. The main speaker for the event was Edward Everett, one of the nation's foremost orators. President Lincoln was also invited to speak "as Chief Executive of the nation, formally [to] set apart these grounds to their sacred use by a few appropriate remarks." At the ceremony, Everett spoke for more than two hours; Lincoln spoke for two minutes.

The dedication of the battlefield and cemetery had provided Lincoln with an opportunity for a major address, but he disappointed many of his supporters when he gave this short talk. In fact, many of the spectators did not even know that the president had started speaking when he finished.

President Lincoln had given his brief speech a lot of thought. He saw meaning in the fact that the Union victory at Gettysburg coincided with the nation's birthday; rather than focus on the specific battle in his remarks, he wanted to present a broad statement about the larger significance of the war. He invoked the Declaration of Independence, and its principles of liberty and equality, and he spoke of "a new birth of freedom" for the nation. In his brief address, he continued to reshape the aims of the war for the American people—transforming it from a war for Union to a war for Union and freedom. Although Lincoln expressed disappointment in the speech initially, it has come to be regarded as one of the most elegant and eloquent speeches in U.S. history.

Fourscore and seven years ago our fathers brought forth on this continent a new nation, conceived in liberty, and dedicated to the proposition that all men are created equal.

Now we are engaged in a great civil war, testing whether that nation, or any nation so conceived and so dedicated, can long endure. We are met on a great battlefield of that war. We have come to dedicate a portion of that field as a final resting-place for those who here gave their lives that this nation might live. It is altogether fitting and proper that we should do this.

But, in a larger sense, we cannot dedicate—we cannot consecrate—we cannot hallow this ground. The brave men, living and dead, who struggled here, have consecrated it, far above our poor power to add or detract. The world will little note nor long remember what we say here, but it can never forget what they did here. It is for us, the living, rather, to be dedicated here to the unfinished work which they who fought here have thus far so nobly advanced. It is rather for us to be here dedicated to the great task remaining before us—that from these honored dead we take increased devotion to that cause for which they gave the last full measure of devotion; that we here highly resolve that these dead shall not have died in vain; that this nation, under God, shall have a new birth of freedom; and that government of the people, by the people, for the people, shall not perish from the earth.

November 19, 1863

1. What does this phrase mean: "The brave men, living and dead, who struggled here, have consecrated it far above our poor power to add or detract"?

   a. Only those who fought and died can contribute.
   b. No one living has the right words to properly consecrate the ground.
   c. The men who fought and died gave so much, while the living can only give words.
   d. No one can accurately testify to the amount of pain waged on the battlefield.

2. What, according to Lincoln, is the duty of the living?

   a. to consecrate the ground
   b. to free the slaves
   c. to make a better nation
   d. to fight for the living

3. Why do you think this speech has remained a key part of American history? Are there any specific lines that reflect our modern times? If so, which ones and why?

Wade-Davis Bill (1864)

In late 1863, President Abraham Lincoln and the Congress began to consider the question of how the Union would be reunited if the North won the Civil War. In December President Lincoln proposed a reconstruction program that would allow Confederate states to establish new state governments after 10 percent of their male population took loyalty oaths and the states recognized the "permanent freedom of slaves."

Several congressional Republicans thought Lincoln's 10 Percent Plan was too mild. A more stringent plan was proposed by Senator Benjamin F. Wade and Representative Henry Winter Davis in February 1864. The Wade-Davis Bill required that 50 percent of a state's white males take a loyalty oath to be readmitted to the Union. In addition, states were required to give blacks the right to vote.

Congress passed the Wade-Davis Bill, but President Lincoln chose not to sign it, killing the bill with a pocket veto. Lincoln continued to advocate tolerance and speed in plans for the reconstruction of the Union in opposition to the Congress. After Lincoln's assassination in April 1865, however, the Congress had the upper hand in shaping Federal policy toward the defeated South and imposed the harsher reconstruction requirements first advocated in the Wade-Davis Bill.

A Bill to guarantee to certain States whose Governments have been usurped or overthrown a Republican Form of Government.

Be it enacted by the Senate and House of Representatives of the United States of America in Congress assembled, That in the states declared in rebellion against the United States, the President shall, by and with the advice and consent of the Senate, appoint for each a provisional governor, whose pay and emoluments shall not exceed that of a brigadier-general of volunteers, who shall be charged with the civil administration of such state until a state government therein shall be recognized as hereinafter provided.

SEC. 2. And be it further enacted, That so soon as the military resistance to the United States shall have been suppressed in any such state, and the people thereof shall have sufficiently returned to their obedience to the constitution and the laws of the United States, the provisional governor shall direct the marshal of the United States, as speedily as may be, to name a sufficient number of deputies, and to enroll all white male citizens of the United States, resident in the state in their respective counties, and to request each one to take the oath to support the constitution of the United States, and in his enrolment to designate those who take and those who refuse to take that oath, which rolls shall be forthwith returned to the provisional governor; and if the persons taking that oath shall amount to a majority of the persons enrolled in the state, he shall, by proclamation, invite the loyal people of the state to elect delegates to a convention charged to declare the will of the people of the state relative to the reestablishment of a state government subject to, and in conformity with, the constitution of the United States.

SEC. 3. And be it further enacted, That the convention shall consist of as many members as both houses of the last constitutional state legislature, apportioned by the provisional governor among the counties, parishes, or districts of the state, in proportion to the white population, returned as electors, by the marshal, in compliance with the provisions of this act. The provisional governor shall, by proclamation, declare the number of delegates to be elected by each county, parish, or election district; name a day of election not less than thirty days thereafter; designate the places of voting in each county, parish, or district, conforming as nearly as may be convenient to the places used in the state elec- tions next preceding the rebellion; appoint one or more commissioners to hold the election at each place of voting, and provide an adequate force to keep the peace during the election.

SEC.4. And be it further enacted, That the delegates shall be elected by the loyal white male citizens of the United States of the age of twenty-one years, and resident at the time in the county, parish, or district in which they shall offer to vote, and enrolled as aforesaid, or absent in the military service of the United States, and who shal1 take and subscribe the oath of allegiance to the United States in the form contained in the act of congress of July two, eighteen hundred and sixty-two; and all such citizens of the United States who are in the military service of the United States shall vote at the head-quarters of their respective commands, under such regulations as may be prescribed by the pro-visional governor for the taking and return of their votes; but no person who has held or exercised any office, civil or military, state or confederate, under the rebel usurpation, or who has voluntarily borne arms against the United States, shall vote, or be eligible to be elected as delegate, at such election.

SEC.5. And be it further enacted, That the said commissioners, or either of them, shall hold the election in conformity with this act, and, so far as may be consistent therewith, shall proceed in the manner used in the state prior to the rebellion. The oath of allegiance shall be taken and subscribed on thc poll-book by every voter in the form above prescribed, but every person known by or proved to, the commissioners to have held or exercised any office, civil or military, state or confederate, under the rebel usurpation, or to have voluntarily borne arms against the United States, shall be excluded, though he offer to take the oath ; and in case any person who shall have borne arms against the United States shall offer to vote he shall be deemed to have borne arms voluntarily unless he shall prove the contrary by the testimony of a qualified voter. The poll-book, showing the name and oath of each voter, shall be returned to the provisional governor by the commissioners of election or the one acting, and the provisional governor shall canvass such returns, and declare the person having the highest number of votes elected.

SEC. 6. And be it further enacted, That the provisional governor shall, by proclamation, convene the delegates elected as aforesaid, at the capital of the state, on a day not more than three months after the election, giving at least thirty days' notice of such day. In case the said capital shall in his judgment be unfit, he shall in his proclamation appoint another place. He shall preside over the deliberations of the convention, and administer to each delegate, before taking his seat in the convention, the oath of allegiance to the United States in the form above prescribed.

SEC. 7. And be it further enacted, That the convention shall declare, on behalf of the people of the state, their submission to the constitution and laws of the United States, and shall adopt the following provisions, hereby prescribed by the United States in the execution of the constitutional duty to guarantee a republican form of government to every state, and incorporate them in the constitution of the state, that is to say:

> First. No person who has held or exercised any office, civil or military, except offices merely ministerial, and military offices below the grade of colonel, state or confederate, under the usurping power, shall vote for or be a member of the legislature, or governor.
>
> Second. Involuntary servitude is forever prohibited, and the freedom of all persons is guaranteed in said state.
>
> Third. No debt, state or confederate, created by or under the sanction of the usurping power, shall be recognized or paid by the state.

SEC. 8. And be it further enacted, That when the convention shall have adopted those provisions, it shall proceed to re-establish a republican form of government, and ordain a constitution containing those provisions, which, when adopted the convention shall by ordinance provide for submitting to the people of the state, entitled to vote under this law, at an election to be held in the manner prescribed by the act for the election of delegates; but at a time and place named by the convention, at which election the said electors, and none others, shall vote directly for or against such constitution and form of state government, and the returns of said election shall be made to the provisional governor, who shall canvass the same in the presence of the electors, and if a majority of the votes cast shall be for the constitution and form of government, he shall certify the same, with a copy thereof, to the President of the United States, who, after obtaining the assent of congress, shall, by proclamation, recognize the government so established, and none other, as the constitutional government of the state, and from the date of such recognition, and not before, Senators and Representatives, and electors for President and Vice President may be eleected in such state, according to the laws of the state and of the United States.

SEC. 9. And be it further enacted, That if the convention shall refuse to reestablish the state government on the conditions aforesaid, the provisional governor shall declare it dissolved; but it shall be the duty of the President, whenever he shall have reason to believe that a sufficient number of the people of the state entitled to vote under this act, in number not less than a majority of those enrolled, as aforesaid, are willing to reestablish a state government on the conditions aforesaid, to direct the provisional governor to order another election of delegates to a convention for the purpose and in the manner prescribed in this act, and to proceed in all respects as hereinbefore provided, either to dissolve the convention, or to certify the state government reestablished by it to the President.

SEC. 10. And be it further enacted, That, until the United States shall have recognized a republican form of state government, the provisional governor in each of said states shall see that this act, and the laws of the United States, and the laws of the state in force when the state government was overthrown by the rebellion, are faithfully executed within the state ; but no law or usage whereby any person was heretofore held in involuntary servitude shall be recognized or enforced by any court or officer in such state, and the laws for the trial and punishment of white persons shall extend to all persons, and jurors shall have the qualifications of voters under this law for delegates to the convention. The President shall appoint such officers provided for by the laws of the state when its government was overthrown as he may find necessary to the civil administration of the slate, all which officers shall be entitled to receive the fees and emoluments provided by the state laws for such officers.

SEC. 11. And be it further enacted, That until the recognition of a state government as aforesaid, the provisional governor shall, under such regulations as he may prescribe, cause to be assessed, levied, and collected, for the year eighteen hundred and sixty-four, and every year thereafter, the taxes provided by the laws of such state to be levied during the fiscal year preceding the overthrow of the state government thereof, in the manner prescribed by the laws of the state, as nearly as may be ; and the officers appointed, as aforesaid, are vested with all powers of levying and collecting such taxes, by distress or sale, as were vested in any officers or tribunal of the state government aforesaid for those purposes. The proceeds of such taxes shall be accounted for to the provisional governor, and be by him applied to the expenses of the administration of the laws in such state, subject to the direction of the President, and the surplus shall be deposited in the treasury of the United States to the credit of such state, to be paid to the state upon an appropriation therefor, to be made when a republican form of government shall be recognized therein by the United States.

SEC. 12. And be it further enacted, that all persons held to involuntary servitude or labor in the states aforesaid are hereby emancipated and discharged therefrom, and they and their posterity shall be forever free. And if any such persons or their posterity shall be restrained of liberty, under pretence of any claim to such service or labor, the courts of the United States shall, on habeas corpus, discharge them.

SEC. 13. And be it further enacted, That if any person declared free by this act, or any law of the United States, or any proclamation of the President, be restrained of liberty, with intent to be held in or reduced to involuntary servitude or labor, the person convicted before a court of competent jurisdiction of such act shall be punished by fine of not less than fifteen hundred dollars, and be imprisoned not less than five nor more than twenty years.

SEC. 14. And be it further enacted, That every person who shall hereafter hold or exercise any office, civil or military, except offices merely ministerial, and military offices below the grade of colonel, in the rebel service, state or confederate, is hereby declared not to be a citizen of the United States.

1. According to the Wade-Davis Bill once the Union had suppressed military resistance in the rebellious states, it would

   a. force those states to submit their slaves.
   b. require that those states pay a tax.
   c. force slaves in those states to move to northern states.
   d. demand that white male citizens in those states take an oath.

2. What is one probable reason why Wade and Davis wanted a more stringent Bill?

   a. They feared the rebellious southern states.
   b. They were proud of their victory.
   c. They wanted allegiance.
   d. all of the above

3. The convention was enacted so as to help create

   a. a provisional governor.
   b. new state constitutions.
   c. freed slave representation.
   d. allegiance to the Union.

4. Why did the bill refuse the vote of those white male voters who had taken the oath?

   a. They had did not aid the Union.
   b. They had owned slaves.
   c. They had fought against the Union.
   d. They had helped the rebel states.

5. What would happen if the convention refused to follow the statutes of the bill?

   a. They would be forced into involuntary labor.
   b. The commissioners would lose their jobs.
   c. The president would remove the rights of the state.
   d. The state would be disbanded.

6. Did the oath secure the allegiance to the United States? Why or why not? What is one possible reason why Lincoln might have been opposed to demanding that a high percentage of white males in the south take the oath? Explain.

Articles of Agreement Relating to the Surrender of the Army of Northern Virginia (1865)

The surrender formalities to end the Civil War lasted 4 days. On April 9, 1865, Generals Ulysses S. Grant and Robert E. Lee met in the parlor of a house in Appomattox Court House, Virginia, to discuss the surrender of the Army of Northern Virginia. The terms were generous: The men of Lee's army could return home in safety if they pledged to end the fighting and deliver their arms to the Union Army.

On April 12, 1865, in a quiet but emotional ceremony, the infantry of Lee's army surrendered their arms, folded their battle flags, and received their parole papers, which guaranteed them safe passage home.

Correspondence between Gen. Lee and Gen. Grant.

April 7, 1865
Gen. R. E. Lee, Commanding C.S.A.:

General: The result of the last week must convince you of the hopelessness of further resistance on the part of the Army of Northern Virginia in this struggle. I feel that it is so and regard it as my duty to shift from myself the responsibility of any further effusion of blood, by asking of you the surrender of that portion of the Confederate States Army, known as the Army of Northern Virginia.

Very Respectfully,
Your obedient servant,
U.S. Grant,
Lieutenant-General,
Commanding Armies of the United States.

April 7, 1865

General: I have received your note of this date.
Though not entirely of the opinion you express of the hopelessness of further resistance on the part of the army of Northern Virginia, I reciprocate your desire to avoid useless effusion of blood, and therefore, before considering your proposition, ask the terms you will offer, on condition of its surrender.

R. E. Lee, General
To Lieut.-Gen. U. S. Grant, Commanding Armies of the United States.

April 8, 1865
To Gen. R. E. Lee, Commanding C.S.A.

General: Your note of last evening in reply to mine of same date, asking the conditions on which I will accept the surrender of the Army of Northern Virginia, is just received.

In reply, I would say that peace being my first desire, there is but one condition that I insist upon, viz.:

That the men surrendered shall be disqualified for taking up arms again against the Government of the United States until promptly exchanged.

I will meet you, or designate officers to meet any officers you may name, for the same purpose, at any point agreeable to you, for the purpose of arranging definitely the terms upon which the surrender of the Army of Northern Virginia will be received.

Very respectfully, your obedient servant,
U.S. Grant, Lieut.-General, Commanding armies of the United States.

April 8, 1865

General: I received, at a late hour, your note of to-day, in answer to mine of yesterday.

I did not intend to propose the surrender of the Army of Northern Virginia, but to ask the terms of your proposition. To be frank, I do not think the emergency has arisen to call for the surrender.

But as the restoration of peace should be the sole object of all, I desire to know whether your proposals would tend to that end.

I cannot, therefore, meet you with a view to surrender the Army of Northern Virginia, but as far as your proposition may affect the Confederate States forces under my command, and tend to the restoration of peace, I should be pleased to meet you at 10 A.M., to-morrow, on the old stage road to Richmond, between the picket lines of the two armies.

Very Respectfully, your obedient servant,
R. E. Lee
General, C.S.A.

To Lieut.-Gen. Grant, Commanding Armies of the United States
April 9, 1865
General R. E. Lee, commanding C.S.A.:

General: Your note of yesterday is received. As I have no authority to treat on the subject of peace, the meeting proposed for 10 A. M. to-day could lead to no good. I will state, however, General, that I am equally anxious for peace with yourself; and the whole North entertain the same feeling. The terms upon which peace can be had are well understood. By the South laying down their arms, they will hasten that most desirable event, save thousands of human lives, and hundreds of millions of property not yet destroyed.

Sincerely hoping that all our difficulties may be settled without the loss of another life, I subscribe myself,

Very respectfully,
Your obedient servant,
U.S. Grant,
Lieutenant-General United States Army.

Sunday April 9, 1865,

General—I received your note of this morning, on the picket line, whither I had come to meet you and ascertain definitely what terms were embraced in your preposition of yesterday with reference to the surrender of this army.

I now request an interview in accordance with the offer contained in your letter of yesterday for that purpose.

Very respectfully, your obedient servant,
R. E. Lee, General.

To Lieut.-Gen. Grant, Commanding United States Armies.
Sunday, April 9, 1865
Gen. R. E. Lee, Commanding Confederate States Armies.

Your note of this date is set this moment, 11:50 A.M., received.

In consequence of my having passed from the Richmond and Lynchburgh road to the Farmville and Lynchburgh road, I am at this writing about four miles West of Walter's church, and will push forward to the front for the purpose of meeting you.

Notice sent to me, on this road, where you wish the interview to take place, will meet me.

Very respectfully, your ob'd't servant,
U.S. Grant,
Lieutenant-General

Court House, April 9, 1865.
General R. E. Lee, Commanding C. S. A.:

In accordance with the substance of my letters to you of the 8th inst., I propose to receive the surrender of the Army of Northern Virginia on the following terms, to wit:

Rolls of all the officers and men to be made in duplicate, one copy to be given to an officer designated by me, the other to be retained by such officers as you may designate.

The officers to give their individual paroles not to take arms against the Government of the United States until properly exchanged, and each company or regimental commander sign a like parole for the men of their commands.

The arms, artillery and public property to be packed an[d] stacked and turned over to the officers appointed by me to receive them.

This will not embrace the side-arms of the officers, nor their private horses or baggage.

This done, each officer and man will be allowed to return to their homes, not to be disturbed by United States authority so long as they observe their parole and the laws in force where they reside.

Very respectfully,
U.S. Grant, Lieutenant-General.

Headquarters Army of Northern Virginia,
April 9, 1865
Lieut. Gen. U.S. Grant, Commanding U.S.A.:

General: I have received your letter of this date, containing the terms of surrender of the army of northern Virginia, as proposed by you; As they are substantially the same as those expressed in your letter of the 8th inst., they are accepted. I will proceed to designate the proper officers to carry stipulations late effect.

Very Respectfully, Your Obedient Servant, R. E. Lee, General.

Headquarters Armies of the United States, 4:30 P.M., April 9.

Hon. Edwin M. Stanton, Secretary of War:

GEN. LEE SURRENDERED THE ARMY OF NORTHERN VIRGINIA THIS AFTERNOON, upon the terms proposed by myself. The accompanying additional correspondence will show the conditions fully.

(signed)
U.S. Grant, Lieut. Gen'l.

Appomattox Court House Virginia
April 10, 1865

Agreement entered into this day in regard to the surrender of the Army of Northern Virginia to the United States Authorities.

1st The troops shall march by Brigades and Detachments to a designated point, stock their Arms, deposit their flags, Sabres, Pistols, etc. and from thence march to their homes under charge of their Officers, superintended by their respective Division and Corps Commanders, Officers, retaining their side Arms, and the authorized number of private horses.

2. All public horses and public property of all kinds to be turned over to Staff Officers designated by the United States Authorities.

3. Such transportation as may be agreed upon as necessary for the transportation of the Private baggage of Officers will be allowed to accompany the Officers, to be turned over at the end of the trip to the nearest U.S. Quarter Masters, receipts being taken for the same.

4. Couriers and Wounded men of the artillery and Cavalry whose horses are their own private property will be allowed to retain them.

5. The surrender of the Army of Northern Virginia shall be construed to include all the forces operating with that Army on the 8th inst., the date of commencement of negociation for surrender, except such bodies of Cavalry as actually made their escape previous to the surrender, and except also such forces of Artillery as were more than Twenty (20) miles from Appomattox Court House at the time of Surrender on the 9th inst.

1. In the April 7th exchange between Grant and Lee, what was the main topic of the message?

   a. surrender of the Confederate Army to Northern Virginia
   b. battle plans at Appomattox Court House in Virginia
   c. agreement on the terms and conditions of surrender
   d. surrender of General Lee's army to General Grant

2. In an exchange on April 8th, General Grant calls for

   a. aid from the Army of Northern Virginia.
   b. guidance from the president.
   c. the disqualification of Lee's men.
   d. General Lee to meet him at Richmond.

3. In the exchange of April 9th why was Grant unable to meet General Lee between the picket lines?

   a. Grant was unable to surrender his arms at that time.
   b. Grant did not have the power to negotiate a peace.
   c. Grant was uncertain of General Lee's plans at the battlefield.
   d. Grant did not want to anger the Northern troops on the field.

4. The final exchange between Grant and Lee showed that

   a. both men were fierce and strongly against surrender.
   b. Lee had an upper hand in the battle.
   c. both men wanted to negotiate a peace quickly.
   d. the armies were weak from the fighting.

5. In the agreement at Appomattox,

   a. the Confederate Army was imprisoned.
   b. General Lee surrendered his weapons.
   c. wounded men were allowed to keep their privately-owned horses.
   d. the Confederate army was allowed to keep their flags, but not their sabers.

6. Throughout the correspondence it seems that Lee does not believe that his army needed to surrender. Do you think this was true? Do you think that Lee had no intention of surrendering? Please explain.

7. Are the terms of the surrender fair? Do you think that Grant should have asked for more from Lee? If so, what and why?

Ex Parte MILLIGAN (1865)

A democracy, even at war, must retain its basic democratic character, or else it loses that for which its citizens fight. War, however, places great strains on the body politic, and occasionally individual liberties and the needs of the state come into conflict. The Civil War had its share of overbearing governmental actions, including Lincoln's questionable suspension of habeas corpus—the "great writ" of Anglo-American law that provided for the release of people wrongfully imprisoned. Few of the government's actions came under the scrutiny of the courts during the war, but once the Union had achieved victory, the Supreme Court proved willing to hear some cases arising out of the conflict.

Lambden P. Milligan had been sentenced to death by an army court in Indiana for allegedly disloyal activities. Lincoln delayed his execution, but after Lincoln's assassination, the new president, Andrew Johnson, approved the sentence. Milligan's attorney appealed for his release under the 1863 Habeas Corpus Act, and the federal circuit court split on the question of whether civilian courts had jurisdiction over appeals from military tribunals. Although this seems only a technical matter, the case gave the Supreme Court a chance—now that the fighting was over—to comment on the limits of the government's war powers.

In what many scholars hail as a landmark in constitutional protection of civil liberties, the Court decided that military rule could not supersede the civil courts in areas where the civil courts and government remained open and operational. Indiana had been a loyal state, and its regular government and courts had functioned throughout the war. In such a situation, the military courts had no jurisdiction over civilians.

Certainly the language of Milligan allows the courts to interpose themselves between the citizenry on the one hand, and Congress, the president and the armed forces on the other. There is little doubt that the Lincoln administration overreacted to threats of potential disorder in the northern states, and the arbitrary use of executive authority—often without congressional approval—could only be justified by the unique conditions surrounding the Civil War. The Court's rebuff, however, came late, and its primary value was as a precedent for future governmental action.

Justice Davis delivered the opinion of the Court:

On the 10th day of May, 1865, Lambden P. Milligan presented a petition to the Circuit Court of the United States for the District of Indiana, to be discharged from an alleged unlawful imprisonment . . .

Milligan insists that said military commission had no jurisdiction to try him upon the charges preferred, or upon any charges whatever; because he was a citizen of the United States and the State of Indiana, and had not been, since the commencement of the late Rebellion, a resident of any of the States whose citizens were arrayed against the government, and that the right of trial by jury was guaranteed to him by the Constitution of the United States . . .

The importance of the main question presented by this record cannot be overstated; for it involves the very framework of the government and the fundamental principles of American liberty.

During the late wicked Rebellion, the temper of the times did not allow that calmness in deliberation and discussion so necessary to a correct conclusion of a purely judicial question. Then, considerations of safety were mingled with the exercise of power; and feelings and interests prevailed which are happily terminated. Now that the public safety is assured, this question, as well as all others, can be discussed and decided without passion or the admixture of any element not required to form a legal judgment. We approach the investigation of this case, fully sensible of the magnitude of the inquiry and the necessity of full and cautious deliberation . . .

The controlling question in the case is this: Upon the facts stated in Milligan's petition, and the exhibits filed, had the military commission mentioned in it jurisdiction, legally, to try and sentence him? Milligan, not a resident of one of the rebellious states, or a prisoner of war, but a citizen of Indiana for twenty years past and never in the military or naval service, is, while at his home, arrested by the military power of the United States, imprisoned, and, on certain criminal charges preferred against him, tried, convicted, and sentenced to be hanged by a military commission, organized under the direction of the military commander of the military district of Indiana. Had this tribunal the legal power and authority to try and punish this man?

No graver question was ever considered by this court, nor one which more nearly concerns the rights of the whole people; for it is the birthright of every American citizen when charged with crime, to be tried and punished according to law. The power of punishment is, alone through the means which the laws have provided for that purpose, and if they are ineffectual, there is an immunity from punishment, no matter how great an offender the individual may be, or how much his crimes may have shocked the sense of justice of the country, or endangered its safety. By the protection of the law human rights are secured; withdraw that protection, and they are at the mercy of wicked rulers, or the clamor of an excited people. If there was law to justify this military trial, it is not our province to interfere; if there was not, it is our duty to declare the nullity of the whole proceedings. The decision of this question does not depend on argument or judicial precedents, numerous and highly illustrative as they are. These precedents inform us of the extent of the struggle to preserve liberty and to relieve those in civil life from military trials. The founders of our government were familiar with the history of that struggle; and secured in a written constitution every right which the people had wrested from power during a contest of ages. By that Constitution and the laws authorized by it this question must be determined. The provisions of that instrument on the administration of criminal justice are too plain and direct, to leave room for misconstruction or doubt of their true meaning. Those applicable to this case are found in that clause of the original Constitution which says, "That the trial of all crimes, except in case of impeachment, shall be by jury"; and in the fourth, fifth, and sixth articles of the amendments . . .

Have any of the rights guaranteed by the Constitution been violated in the case of Milligan? and if so, what are they?

Every trial involves the exercise of judicial power; and from what source did the military commission that tried him derive their authority? Certainly no part of the judicial power of the country was conferred on them; because the Constitution expressly vests it "in one supreme court and such inferior courts as the Congress may from time to time ordain and establish," and it is not pretended that the commission was a court ordained and established by Congress. They cannot justify on the mandate of the President; because he is controlled by law, and has his appropriate sphere of duty, which is to execute, not to make, the laws; and there is "no unwritten criminal code to which resort can be had as a source of jurisdiction."

But it is said that the jurisdiction is complete under the "laws and usages of war."

It can serve no useful purpose to inquire what those laws and usages are, whence they originated, where found, and on whom they operate; they can never be applied to citizens in states which have upheld the authority of the government, and where the courts are open and their process unobstructed. This court has judicial knowledge that in Indiana the Federal authority was always unopposed, and its courts always open to hear criminal accusations and redress grievances; and no usage of war could sanction a military trial there for any offence whatever of a citizen in civil life, in nowise connected with the military service. Congress could grant no such power; and to the honor of our national legislature be it said, it has never been provoked by the state of the country even to attempt its exercise. One of the plainest constitutional provisions was, therefore, infringed when Milligan was tried by a court not ordained and established by Congress, and not composed of judges appointed during good behavior . . .

It is claimed that martial law covers with its broad mantle the proceedings of this military commission. The proposition is this: that in a time of war the commander of an armed force (if in his opinion the exigencies of the country demand it, and of which he is to judge), has the power, within the lines of his military district, to suspend all civil rights and their remedies, and subject citizens as well as soldiers to the rule of his will; and in the exercise of his lawful authority cannot be restrained, except by his superior officer or the President of the United States.

If this position is sound to the extent claimed, then when war exists, foreign or domestic, and the country is subdivided into military departments for mere convenience, the commander of one of them can, if he chooses, within his limits, on the plea of necessity, with the approval of the Executive, substitute military force for and to the exclusion of the laws, and punish all persons, as he thinks right and proper, without fixed or certain rules.

The statement of this proposition shows its importance; for, if true, republican government is a failure, and there is an end of liberty regulated by law. Martial law, established on such a basis, destroys every guarantee of the Constitution, and effectually renders the "military independent of and superior to the civil power"—the attempt to do which by the King of Great Britain was deemed by our fathers such an offence, that they assigned it to the world as one of the causes which impelled them to declare their independence. Civil liberty and this kind of martial law cannot endure together; the antagonism is irreconcilable; and, in the conflict, one or the other must perish.

This nation, as experience has proved, cannot always remain at peace, and has no right to expect that it will always have wise and humane rulers, sincerely attached to the principles of the Constitution. Wicked men, ambitious of power, with hatred of liberty and contempt of law, may fill the place once occupied by Washington and Lincoln; and if this right is conceded, and the calamities of war again befall us, the dangers to human liberty are frightful to contemplate. If our fathers had failed to provide for just such a contingency, they would have been false to the trust reposed in them. They knew—the history of the world told them—the nation they were founding, be its existence short or long, would be involved in war; how often or how long continued, human foresight could not tell; and that unlimited power, wherever lodged at such a time, was especially hazardous to freemen. For this, and other equally weighty reasons, they secured the inheritance they had fought to maintain, by incorporating in a written constitution the safeguards which time had proved were essential to its preservation. Not one of these safeguards can the President, or Congress, or the Judiciary disturb, except the one concerning the writ of habeas corpus.

It is essential to the safety of every government that, in a great crisis, like the one we have just passed through, there should be a power somewhere of suspending the writ of habeas corpus. In every war, there are men of previously good character, wicked enough to counsel their fellow-citizens to resist the measures deemed necessary by a good government to sustain its just authority and overthrow its enemies; and their influence may lead to dangerous combinations. In the emergency of the times, an immediate public investigation according to law may not be possible; and yet, the peril to the country may be too imminent to suffer such persons to go at large. Unquestionably, there is then an exigency which demands that the government, if it should see fit in the exercise of a proper discretion to make arrests, should not be required to produce the persons arrested in answer to a writ of habeas corpus. The Constitution goes no further. It does not say after a writ of habeas corpus is denied a citizen, that he shall be tried otherwise than by the course of the common law; if it had intended this result, it was easy by the use of direct words to have accomplished it. The illustrious men who framed that instrument were guarding the foundations of civil liberty against the abuses of unlimited power; they were full of wisdom, and the lessons of history informed them that a trial by an established court, assisted by an impartial jury, was the only sure way of protecting the citizen against oppression and wrong. Knowing this, they limited the suspension to one great right, and left the rest to remain forever inviolable. But, it is insisted that the safety of the country in time of war demands that this broad claim for martial law shall be sustained. If this were true, it could be well said that a country, preserved at the sacrifice of all the cardinal principles of liberty, is not worth the cost of preservation. Happily, it is not so.

It will be borne in mind that this is not a question of the power to proclaim martial law, when war exists in a community and the courts and civil authorities are overthrown. Nor is it a question what rule a military commander, at the head of his army, can impose on states in rebellion to cripple their resources and quell the insurrection. The jurisdiction claimed is much more extensive. The necessities of the service, during the late Rebellion, required that the loyal states should be placed within the limits of certain military districts and commanders appointed in them; and, it is urged, that this, in a military sense, constituted them the theatre of military operations; and, as in this case, Indiana had been and was again threatened with invasion by the enemy, the occasion was furnished to establish martial law. The conclusion does not follow from the premises. If armies were collected in Indiana, they were to be employed in another locality, where the laws were obstructed and the national authority disputed. On her soil there was no hostile foot; if once invaded, that invasion was at an end, and with it all pretext for martial law. Martial law cannot arise from a threatened invasion. The necessity must be actual and present; the invasion real, such as effectually closes the courts and deposes the civil administration.

It is difficult to see how the safety of the country required martial law in Indiana. If any of her citizens were plotting treason, the power of arrest could secure them, until the government was prepared for their trial, when the courts were open and ready to try them. It was as easy to protect witnesses before a civil as a military tribunal; and as there could be no wish to convict, except on sufficient legal evidence, surely an ordained and established court was better able to judge of this than a military tribunal composed of gentlemen not trained to the profession of the law.

It follows, from what has been said on this subject, that there are occasions when martial rule can be properly applied. If, in foreign invasion or civil war, the courts are actually closed, and it is impossible to administer criminal justice according to law, then, on the theatre of active military operations, where war really prevails, there is a necessity to furnish a substitute for the civil authority, thus overthrown, to preserve the safety of the army and society; and as no power is left but the military, it is allowed to govern by martial rule until the laws can have their free course. As necessity creates the rule, so it limits its duration; for, if this government is continued after the courts are reinstated, it is a gross usurpation of power. Martial rule can never exist where the courts are open, and in the proper and unobstructed exercise of their jurisdiction. It is also confined to the locality of actual war.

1. Why did Milligan petition the Circuit Court?

   a. The Supreme Court would not hear his case.
   b. The military courts were biased and unlawful.
   c. He wanted to be discharged from prison.
   d. He was fearful that a trial by jury would not favor him.

2. What was one of the court's reasons for considering Milligan's imprisonment unlawful?

   a. He had never been in the military.
   b. He was a citizen of the United States.
   c. The military did not have jurisdiction.
   d. He did not participate in the Rebellion.

3. What is one reason why Milligan was arrested?

   a. He was not a citizen of Indiana.
   b. He was in the military.
   c. He was a resident of one of the rebellious states.
   d. none of the above

4. According to the Constitution, in this case, it was important that the framers secured the right to

   a. bear arms.
   b. a trial by jury.
   c. free speech.
   d. emancipate slaves.

5. Though Milligan was tried in a martial court, why was it possible, during the war, for Milligan's case to have been heard in the Indiana court system?

   a. The Indiana judicial system was in full operation during the war.
   b. A judge in the Indiana court system testified that he had been willing to hear the case.
   c. Milligan was living in Indiana at the time.
   d. The military was stationed in Indiana and could have waited there for the trial to come to a close.

6. Why could martial law be considered dangerous to civil liberties?

   a. It gives power to the president of the United States.
   b. It allows the chief of an armed force to suspend civil privileges.
   c. The law gives a state control over many judicial bodies.
   d. Martial law endows men with the power to use weapons against the government.

7. According to Justice Davis, the reasons for suspending habeas corpus and invoking martial law are to

   a. ascertain where the present danger lies.
   b. ensure the rights of the citizens during a time of crisis.
   c. guarantee that the executive is being checked by a strong military.
   d. ensure the safety of the country during war.

8. When can martial law be put into action according to Justice Davis?

   a. whenever the country needs the power to be invoked
   b. whenever the president calls for it
   c. only when the necessity is present
   d. when an invasion is perceived or likely to occur

9. Is martial law a good idea? When do you think it could be useful? In your own words, explain how such a law can be abused.

10. Explain this phrase in your own words: "The illustrious men who framed that instrument were guarding the foundations of civil liberty against the abuses of unlimited power . . . "

PROCEEDINGS OF THE SENATE SITTING FOR THE TRIAL OF ANDREW JOHNSON, PRESIDENT OF THE UNITED STATES

On Articles of Impeachment exhibited by the House of Representatives

On Monday, February the 24th, 1868, the House of Representatives of the Congress of the United States resolved to impeach Andrew Johnson, President of the United States, of high crimes and misdemeanors, of which the Senate was apprised and arrangements were made for the trial. On Monday the 2d of March, articles of impeachment were agreed upon by the House of Representatives, and on the 4th they were presented to the Senate by the managers on the part of the House, who were accompanied by the House, the grand inquest of the nation, as a Committee of the Whole on the state of the Union. Mr. BINGHAM, chairman of the managers, read the articles as follows:

Articles exhibited by the House of Representatives of the United States, in the name of themselves and all the people of the United States, against Andrew Johnson, President of the United States, in maintenance and support of their impeachment against him for high crimes and misdemeanors.

ARTICLE I.

That said Andrew Johnson, President of the United States, on the 21st day of February, in the year of our Lord, 1868, at Washington, in the District of Columbia, unmindful of the high duties of his office, of his oath of office, and of the requirement of the Constitution that he should take care that the laws be faithfully executed, did unlawfully and in violation of the Constitution and laws of the United States issue and order in writing for the removal of Edwin M. Stanton from the office of Secretary for the Department of War, said Edwin M. Stanton having been theretofore duly appointed and commissioned, by and with the advice and consent of the Senate of the United States, as such Secretary, and said Andrew Johnson, President of the United States, on the 12th day of August, in the year of our Lord 1867, and during the recess of said Senate, having been suspended by his order Edwin M. Stanton from said office, and within twenty days after the first day of the next meeing of said Senate, that is to say, on the 12th day of December, in the year last aforesaid, having reported to said Senate such suspension, with the evidence and reasons for his action in the case and the name of the person designated to perform the duties of such office temporarily until the next meeting go the Senate, and said Senate thereafterward, on the 13th day of January, in the year of our Lord 1868, having duly considered the evidence and reasons reported by said Andrew Johnson for said suspension, and having been refused to concur in said suspension, whereby and by force of the provisions of an act entitled "An act regulating the tenure of certain civil offices," passed March 2, 1867, said Edwin M. Stanton did forthwith resume the functions of his office, whereof the said Andrew Johnson had then and there due notice, and said Edwin Stanton, by reason of the premises, on said 21st day of February, being lawfully entitled to hold said office of Secretary for the Department of War, which said order for the removal of said Edwin M. Stanton is, in substance, as follows, that is to say:

EXECUTIVE MANSION,
WASHINGTON, D.C., February 21, 1868

SIR: By virtue of the power and authority vested in me, as President by the Constitution and laws of the United States, you are hereby removed from the office of Secretary for the Department of War, and your functions as such will terminate upon receipt of their communication. You will transfer to Brevet Major-General L. Thomas, Adjutant-General of the Army, who has this day been authorized and empowered to act as Secretary of War ad interim, all books, paper and other public property now in your custody and charge.

Respectfully yours, ANDREW JOHNSON.

Hon. E. M. Stanton, Secretary of War

Which order was unlawfully issued, and with intent then are there to violate the act entitled "An act regulating the tenure of certain civil office," passed March 2, 1867; and, with the further intent contrary to the provisions of said act, and in violation thereof, and contrary to the provisions of the Constitution of the United States, and without the advice and consent of the Senate of the United States, the said Senate then and there being in session, to remove said Edwin M. Stanton from the office of Secretary for the Department of War, the said Edwin M. Stanton being then and there Secretary of War, and being then and there in the due and lawful execution of the duties of said office, whereby said Andrew Johnson, President of the United States, did then and there commit, and was guilty of a high misdemeanor in office.

ARTICLE II.

That on the 21st day of February, in the year of our Lord 1868, at Washington, in the District of Columbia, said Andrew Johnson, President of the United States, unmindful of the high duties of his office, of his oath of office, and in violation of the Constitution of the United States, and contrary to the provisions of an act entitled "An act regulating the tenure of certain civil offices," passed March 2, 1867, without the advice and consent of the Senate of the United States, said Senate then and there being in session, and without authority of law, did, with intent to violate the Constitution of the United States and the act aforesaid, issue and deliver to one Lorenzo Thomas a letter of authority, in substance as follows, that is to say:

EXECUTIVE MANSION,
WASHINGTON, D.C., February 21, 1868

SIR: The Hon. Edwin M. Stanton having been this day removed from office as Secretary for the Department of War, you are hereby authorized and empowered to act as Secretary of War ad interim, and will immediately enter upon the discharge of the duties pertaining to that office.

Mr. Stanton has been instructed to transfer to you all the records, books, papers and other public property now in his custody and charge.

Respectfully yours, ANDREW JOHNSON

To Brevet Major-General Lorenzo Thomas, Adjutant General United States Army, Washington, D.C.

then and there being no vacancy in said office of Secretary for the Department of War: whereby said Andrew Johnson, President of the United States, did then and there commit, and was guilty of a high misdemeanor in office.

ARTICLE III.

That said Andrew Johnson, President of the United States, on the 21st day of February,in the year of our Lord 1868, at Washington in the District of Columbia, did commit, and was guilty of a high misdemeanor in office, in this, that, without authority of law, while the Senate of the United States was then and there in session, he did appoint one Lorenzo Thomas to be Secretary for the Department of War, ad interim, without the advice and consent of the Senate, and with intent to violate the Constitution of the United States, no vacancy having happened in said office of Secretary for the Department of War during the recess of the Senate, and no vacancy existing in said office at the time, and which said appointment so made by Andrew Johnson, of said Lorenzo Thomas is in substance as follows, that is to say:

EXECUTIVE MANSION,
WASHINGTON, D.C., February 21, 1868

SIR: The Hon. Edwin M. Stanton having been this day removed from office as Secretary for the Department of War, you are hereby authorized and empowered to act as Secretary of War ad interim, and will immediately enter upon the discharge of the duties pertaining to that office.

Mr. Stanton has been instructed to transfer to you all the records, books, papers and other public property now in his custody and charge.

Respectfully yours, ANDREW JOHNSON

To Brevet Major-General Lorenzo Thomas, Adjutant General United States Army, Washington, D.C.

ARTICLE IV.

That said Andrew Johnson, President of the United States, unmindful of the high duties of his office, and of his oath of office, in violation of the Constitution and laws of the United States, on the 21st day of February, in the year of our Lord 1868, at Washington, in the District of Columbia, did unlawfully conspire with one Lorenzo Thomas, and with other persons to the House of Representatives unknown, with intent by intimidation and threats unlawfully to hinder and prevent Edwin M. Stanton, then and there, the Secretary for the Department of War, duly appointed under the laws of the United States, from holding said office of Secretary for the Department of War, contrary to and in violation of the Constitution of the United States, and of the provisions of an act entitled "An act to define and punish certain conspiracies," approved July 31, 1861, whereby said Andrew Johnson, President of the United States, did then and there commit and was guilty of high crime in office.

ARTICLE V.

That said Andrew Johnson, President of the United States, unmindful of the high duties of his office and of his oath of office, on the 21st of February, in the year of our Lord 1868, and on divers others days and time in said year before the 2d day of March, A.D. 1868, at Washington, in the District of Columbia, did unlawfully conspire with one Lorenzo Thomas, and with other persons in the House of Representatives unknown, to prevent and hinder the execution of an act entitled "An act regulating the tenure of certain civil office," passed March 2, 1867, and in pursuance of said conspiracy, did attempt to prevent Edwin M. Stanton, then and there being Secretary for the Department of War, duly appointed and commissioned under the laws of the United States, from holding said office, whereby the said Andrew Johnson, President of the United States, did then and there commit and was guilty of high misdemeanor in office.

ARTICLE VI.

That said Andrew Johnson, President of the United States, unmindful of the high duties of his office and of his oath of office, on the 21st day of February, in the year of our Lord 1868, at Washington, in the District of Columbia, did unlawfully conspire with one Lorenzo Thomas, by force to seize, take, and possess the property of the United Sates in the Department of War, and then and there in the custody and charge of Edwin M. Stanton, Secretary for said Department, contrary to the provisions of an act entitled "An act to define and punish certain conspiracies," approved July 31, 1861, and with intent to violate and disregard an act entitled "An act regulating the tenure of certain civil offices," passed March 2, 1867, whereby said Andrew Johnson, President of the United States, did then and there commit a high crime in office.

ARTICLE VII.

That said Andrew Johnson, President of the United States, unmindful of the high duties of his office, and of his oath of office, on the 21st day of February, in the year of our Lord 1868, at Washington, in the District of Columbia, did unlawfully conspire with one Lorenzo Thomas with intent unlawfully to seize, take, and possess the property of the United States in the Department of War, in the custody and charge of Edwin M. Stanton, Secretary of said Department, with intent to violate and disregard the act entitled "An act regulating the tenure of certain civil offices," passed March 2, 1867, whereby said Andrew Johnson, President of the United States, did then and there commit a high misdemeanor in office.

ARTICLE VIII.

That said Andrew Johnson, President of the United States, unmindful of the high duties of his office and of his oath of office, with intent unlawfully to control the disbursements of the moneys appropriated for the military service and for the Department of War, on the 21st day of February, in the year of our Lord 1868, at Washington, in the District of Columbia, did unlawfully and contrary to the provisions of an act entitled "An act regulating the tenure of certain civil offices," passed March 2, 1867, and in violation of the Constitution of the United States, and without the advice and consent of the Senate of the United States, and while the Senate was then and there in session, there being no vacancy in the office of Secretary for the Department of War, with intent to violate and disregard the the act aforesaid, then and there issue and deliver to one Lorenzo Thomas a letter of authority in writing, in substance as follows, that is to say:

EXECUTIVE MANSION,
WASHINGTON, D.C., February 21, 1868

SIR: The Hon. Edwin M. Stanton having been this day removed from office as Secretary for the Department of War, you are hereby authorized and empowered to act as Secretary of War ad interim, and will immediately enter upon the discharge of the duties pertaining to that office.

Mr. Stanton has been instructed to transfer to you all the records, books, papers and other public property now in his custody and charge.

Respectfully yours, ANDREW JOHNSON

To Brevet Major-General Lorenzo Thomas, Adjutant General United States Army, Washington, D.C.

Whereby said Andrew Johnson, President of the United States, did then and there commit and was guilty of a high misdemeanor in office . . .

ARTICLE X.

That said Andrew Johnson, President of the United States, unmindful of the high duties of his office and the dignity and proprieties thereof, and of the harmony and courtesies which ought to exist and be maintained between the executive and legislative branches of the Government of the United States, designing and intending to set aside the rightful authorities and powers of Congress, did attempt to bring into disgrace, ridicule, hatred, contempt and reproach the Congress of the United States, and the several branches thereof, to impair and destroy the regard and respect of all the good people of the United States for the Congress and legislative power thereof, (which all officers of the government ought inviolably to preserve and maintain,) and to excite the odium and resentment of all good people of the United States against Congress and the laws by it duly and constitutionally enacted; and in pursuance of his said design and intent, openly and publicly and before divers assemblages of citizens of the United States, convened in divers parts thereof, to meet and receive said Andrew Johnson as the Chief Magistrate of the United States, did, on the 18th day of August, in the year of our Lord 1866, and on divers other days and times, as well before as afterward, make and declare, with a loud voice certain intemperate, inflammatory, and scandalous harangues, and therein utter loud threats and bitter menaces, as well against Congress as the laws of the United States duly enacted thereby, amid the cries, jeers and laughter of the multitudes then assembled in hearing, which are set forth in the several specifications hereinafter written, in substance and effect, that it to say:

Specification First. In this, that at Washington, in the District of Columbia, in the Executive Mansion, to a committee of citizens who called upon the President of the United States, speaking of and concerning the Congress of the United States, heretofore, to wit: On the 18th day of August, in the year of our Lord, 1866, in a loud voice, declare in substance and effect, among other things, that is to say:

> "So far as the Executive Department of the government is concerned, the effort has been made to restore the Union, to heal the breach, to pour oil into the wounds which were consequent upon the struggle, and, to speak in a common phrase, to prepare, as the learned and wise physician would, a plaster healing in character and co-extensive with the wound. We thought and we think that we had partially succeeded, but as the work progresses, as reconstruction seemed to be taking place, and the country was becoming reunited, we found a disturbing and moving element opposing it. In alluding to that element it shall go no further than your Convention, and the distinguished gentleman who has delivered the report of the proceedings, I shall make no reference that I do not believe, and the time and the occasion justify.
>
> "We have witnessed in one department of the government every endeavor to prevent the restoration of peace, harmony and union. We have seen hanging upon the verge of the government, as it were, a body called or which assumes to be the Congress of the United States, while in fact it is a Congress of only part of the States. We have seen this Congress pretend to be for the Union, when its every step and act tended to perpetuate disunion and make a disruption of States inevitable.
>
> "We have seen Congress gradually encroach, step by step, upon constitutional rights, and violate day after day, and month after month, fundamental principles of the government. We have seen a Congress that seemed to forget that there was a limit to the sphere and scope of legislation. We have seen a Congress in a minority assume to exercise power which, if allowed to be consummated, would result in despotism or monarchy itself."

Specification Second. In this, that at Cleveland, in the State of Ohio, heretofore to wit: On the third day of September, in the year of our Lord, 1866, before a public assemblage of citizens and others, said Andrew Johnson, President of the United States, speaking of and concerning the Congress of the United States, did, in a loud voice, declare in substance and effect, among other things, that is to say:

> "I will tell you what I did do? I called upon your Congress that is trying to break up the Government."

* * * * * * * * * * * *

"In conclusion, beside that Congress had taken much pains to poison the constituents against him, what has Congress done? Have they done anything to restore the union of the States? No: On the contrary, they had done everything to prevent it: and because he stood now where he did when the rebellion commenced, he had been denounced as a traitor. Who had run greater risks or made greater sacrifices than himself? But Congress, factions and domineering, had undertaken to poison the minds of the American people . . . "

Which said utterances, declarations, threats and harangues, highly censurable in any, are peculiarly indecent and unbecoming in the Chief Magistrate of the United States, by means whereof the said Andrew Johnson has brought the high office of the President of the United States into contempt, ridicule and disgrace, to the great scandal of all good citizens, whereby said Andrew Johnson, President of the United States, did commit, and was then and there guilty of a high misdemeanor in office.

ARTICLE XI.

That the said Andrew Johnson, President of the United States, unmindful of the high duties of his office and of his oath of office, and in disregard of the Constitution and laws of the United States, did, heretofore, to wit: On the 18th day of August, 1866, at the city of Washington, and in the District of Columbia, by public speech, declare and affirm in substance, that the Thirty-Ninth Congress of the United States was not a Congress of the United States authorized by the Constitution to exercise legislative power under the same; but, on the contrary, was a Congress of only part of the States, thereby denying and intending to deny, that the legislation of said Congress was valid or obligatory upon him, the said Andrew Johnson, except in so far as he saw fit to approve the same, and also thereby denying the power of the said Thirty-Ninth Congress to propose amendments to the Constitution of the United States. And in pursuance of said declaration, the said Andrew Johnson, President of the United States, afterwards, to wit: On the 21st day of February, 1868, at the city of Washington, D.C., did, unlawfully and in disregard of the requirements of the Constitution that he should take care that the laws be faithfully executed, attempt to prevent the execution of an act entitled "An act regulating the tenure of certain civil office," passed March 2, 1867, by unlawfully devising and contriving and attempting to devise and contrive means by which he should prevent Edwin M. Stanton from forthwith resuming the functions of the office of Secretary for the Department of War, notwithstanding the refusal of the Senate to concur in the suspension therefore made by the said Andrew Johnson of said Edwin M. Stanton from said office of Secretary for the Department of War; and also by further unlawfully devising and contriving, and attempting to devise and contrive, means then and there to prevent the execution of an act entitled "An act making appropriations for the support of the army for the fiscal year ending June 30, 1868, and for other purposes," approved March 2, 1867. And also to prevent the execution of an act entitled "An act to provide for the more efficient government of the rebel States," passed March 2, 1867. Whereby the said Andrew Johnson, President of the United States, did then, to wit: on the 21st day of February, 1868, at the city of Washington, commit and was guilty of a high misdemeanor in office.

1. Edwin Stanton had been appointed as the

   a. Chairman of the Managers.
   b. representative to Congress.
   c. judge presiding over the impeachment trial.
   d. secretary of the Department of War.

2. Why did Congress impeach President Andrew Johnson?

   a. He removed Edwin Stanton from office.
   b. He neglected to inform Congress of his intentions.
   c. He vetoed the Congress's acts.
   d. He did not agree with Congress on matters concerning Reconstruction.

3. According to Congress, President Johnson's decision regarding Secretary Stanton was

   a. improper.
   b. greedy.
   c. illegal.
   d. none of the above.

4. How did Johnson violate the "Act regulating the tenure of certain civil offices"?

   a. He did not know about the act when it passed Congress.
   b. After the act had been passed, he dismissed someone who was in a civil office.
   c. He vetoed the act numerous times.
   d. He ignored the act and, when a new position opened up, he hired someone Congress did not approve of.

5. Lorenzo Thomas was appointed to the position of

   a. High Secretary.
   b. Secretary of State.
   c. Secretary of War.
   d. High Treasurer.

6. Why didn't the Senate approve of the appointment of Lorenzo Thomas?

   a. Johnson had appointed him without the Senate's consent.
   b. Johnson had appointed him to anger Edwin Stanton.
   c. Thomas did not have enough experience for the position.
   d. Thomas was not eager for the post.

7. If, according to the Senate, Johnson could not legally appoint Thomas, then by hiring him, Johnson was essentially committing

   a. an act of war.
   b. treason.
   c. conspiracy.
   d. perjury.

8. According to Johnson, the legislative branch was

   a. aiding his opponents.
   b. not helping the Reconstruction.
   c. working for a peaceful settlement.
   d. violating his awesome powers as president.

9. Do you think that the "Act regulating the tenure of certain civil offices" was constitutional? Why or why not?

10. In President Johnson's remarks he said, "We have witnessed in one department of the government every endeavor to prevent the restoration of peace, harmony and union." What, in your own words, did Johnson mean by those remarks?

Treaty of Fort Laramie (1868)

The history of Native Americans in North America dates back thousands of years. Exploration and settlement of the United States by Americans and Europeans wreaked havoc on the Native American peoples living there. In the 19th century the American drive for expansion clashed violently with the Native American resolve to preserve their lands, sovereignty, and ways of life. The struggle over land has defined relations between the U.S. government and Native Americans.

From the 1860s through the 1870s the American frontier was filled with Native American wars and skirmishes. In 1865 a congressional committee began a study of the Native American uprisings and wars in the West, resulting in a "Report on the Condition of the Indian Tribes," which was released in 1867. This study and report by the congressional committee led to an act to establish an Indian Peace Commission to end the wars and prevent future Native American conflicts. The U.S. government set out to establish a series of Native American treaties that would force them to give up their lands and move further west onto reservations. In the spring of 1868, a conference was held at Fort Laramie, in present-day Wyoming, which resulted in a treaty with the Sioux. This treaty was to bring peace between the whites and the Sioux who agreed to settle within the Black Hills reservation in the Dakota Territory.

The Black Hills of Dakota are sacred to the Sioux. In the 1868 treaty, signed at Fort Laramie and other military posts in Sioux country, the United States recognized the Black Hills as part of the Great Sioux Reservation, set aside for exclusive use by the Sioux people. In 1874, however, Gen. George A. Custer led an expedition into the Black Hills accompanied by miners who were seeking gold. Once gold had been found in the Black Hills, miners were soon moving into the Sioux hunting grounds and demanding protection from the U.S. Army. Soon, the Army was ordered to move against wandering bands of Sioux hunting on the range in accordance with their treaty rights. In 1876, Custer, leading an army detachment, encountered the encampment of Sioux and Cheyenne at the Little Bighorn River. Custer's detachment was annihilated, but the United States would continue its battle against the Sioux in the Black Hills until the government confiscated the land in 1877. To this day, ownership of the Black Hills remains the subject of a legal dispute between the U.S. government and the Sioux.

ARTICLES OF A TREATY MADE AND CONCLUDED BY AND BETWEEN

Lieutenant General William T. Sherman, General William S. Harney, General Alfred H. Terry, General O. O. Augur, J. B. Henderson, Nathaniel G. Taylor, John G. Sanborn, and Samuel F. Tappan, duly appointed commissioners on the part of the United States, and the different bands of the Sioux Nation of Indians, by their chiefs and headmen, whose names are hereto subscribed, they being duly authorized to act in the premises.

ARTICLE I.

From this day forward all war between the parties to this agreement shall for ever cease. The government of the United States desires peace, and its honor is hereby pledged to keep it. The Indians desire peace, and they now pledge their honor to maintain it . . .

ARTICLE VII.

In order to insure the civilization of the Indians entering into this treaty, the necessity of education is admitted, especially of such of them as are or may be settled on said agricultural reservations, and they, therefore, pledge themselves to compel their children, male and female, between the ages of six and sixteen years, to attend school, and it is hereby made the duty of the agent for said Indians to see that this stipulation is strictly complied with; and the United States agrees that for every thirty children between said ages, who can be induced or compelled to attend school, a house shall be provided, and a teacher competent to teach the elementary branches of an English education shall be furnished, who will reside among said Indians and faithfully discharge his or her duties as a teacher. The provisions of this article to continue for not less than twenty years.

ARTICLE VIII.

When the head of a family or lodge shall have selected lands and received his certificate as above directed, and the agent shall be satisfied that he intends in good faith to commence cultivating the soil for a living, he shall be entitled to receive seeds and agricultural implements for the first year, not exceeding in value one hundred dollars, and for each succeeding year he shall continue to farm, for a period of three years more, he shall be entitled to receive seeds and implements as aforesaid, not exceeding in value twenty-five dollars. And it is further stipulated that such persons as commence farming shall receive instruction from the farmer herein provided for, and whenever more than one hundred persons shall enter upon the cultivation of the soil, a second blacksmith shall be provided, with such iron, steel, and other material as may be needed . . .

ARTICLE XIII.

The United States hereby agrees to furnish annually to the Indians the physician, teachers, carpenter, miller, engineer, farmer, and blacksmiths, as herein contemplated, and that such appropriations shall be made from time to time, on the estimate of the Secretary of the Interior, as will be sufficient to employ such persons.

ARTICLE XIV.

It is agreed that the sum of five hundred dollars annually for three years from date shall be expended in presents to the ten persons of said tribe who in the judgment of the agent may grow the most valuable crops for the respective year.

ARTICLE XV.

The Indians herein named agree that when the agency house and other buildings shall be constructed on the reservation named, they will regard said reservation their permanent home, and they will make no permanent settlement elsewhere; but they shall have the right, subject to the conditions and modifications of this treaty, to hunt, as stipulated in Article XI hereof.

ARTICLE XVI.

The United States hereby agrees and stipulates that the country north of the North Platte river and east of the summits of the Big Horn mountains shall be held and considered to be unceded Indian territory, and also stipulates and agrees that no white person or persons shall be permitted to settle upon or occupy any portion of the same; or without the consent of the Indians, first had and obtained, to pass through the same; and it is further agreed by the United States, that within ninety days after the conclusion of peace with all the bands of the Sioux nation, the military posts now established in the territory in this article named shall be abandoned, and that the road leading to them and by them to the settlements in the Territory of Montana shall be closed.

ARTICLE XVII.

It is hereby expressly understood and agreed by and between the respective parties to this treaty that the execution of this treaty and its ratification by the United States Senate shall have the effect, and shall be construed as abrogating and annulling all treaties and agreements heretofore entered into between the respective parties hereto, so far as such treaties and agreements obligate the United States to furnish and provide money, clothing, or other articles of property to such Indians and bands of Indians as become parties to this treaty, but no further.

In testimony of all which, we, the said commissioners, and we, the chiefs and headmen of the Brule band of the Sioux nation, have hereunto set our hands and seals at Fort Laramie, Dakota Territory, this twenty-ninth day of April, in the year one thousand eight hundred and sixty-eight.

N. G. TAYLOR,
W. T. SHERMAN,
Lieutenant General
WM. S. HARNEY,
Brevet Major General U.S.A.
JOHN B. SANBORN,
S. F. TAPPAN,
C. C. AUGUR,
Brevet Major General
ALFRED H. TERRY,
Brevet Major General U.S.A.

Attest:
A. S. H. WHITE, Secretary.

Executed on the part of the Brule band of Sioux by the chiefs and headman whose names are hereto annexed, they being thereunto duly authorized, at Fort Laramie, D.T., the twenty-ninth day of April, in the year A.D. 1868.

MA-ZA-PON-KASKA, his X mark, Iron Shell.
WAH-PAT-SHAH, his X mark, Red Leaf.
HAH-SAH-PAH, his X mark, Black Horn.
ZIN-TAH-GAH-LAT-WAH, his X mark, Spotted Tail.
ZIN-TAH-GKAH, his X mark, White Tail.
ME-WAH-TAH-NE-HO-SKAH, his X mark, Tall Man.
SHE-CHA-CHAT-KAH, his X mark, Bad Left Hand.
NO-MAH-NO-PAH, his X mark, Two and Two.
TAH-TONKA-SKAH, his X mark, White Bull.
CON-RA-WASHTA, his X mark, Pretty Coon.
HA-CAH-CAH-SHE-CHAH, his X mark, Bad Elk.
WA-HA-KA-ZAH-ISH-TAH, his X mark, Eye Lance.
MA-TO-HA-KE-TAH, his X mark, Bear that looks behind.
BELLA-TONKA-TONKA, his X mark, Big Partisan.
MAH-TO-HO-HONKA, his X mark, Swift Bear.
TO-WIS-NE, his X mark, Cold Place.
ISH-TAH-SKAH, his X mark, White Eye.
MA-TA-LOO-ZAH, his X mark, Fast Bear.
AS-HAH-HAH-NAH-SHE, his X mark, Standing Elk.
CAN-TE-TE-KI-YA, his X mark, The Brave Heart.

SHUNKA-SHATON, his X mark, Day Hawk.
TATANKA-WAKON, his X mark, Sacred Bull.
MAPIA SHATON, his X mark, Hawk Cloud.
MA-SHA-A-OW, his X mark, Stands and Comes.
SHON-KA-TON-KA, his X mark, Big Dog.

Attest:
ASHTON S. H. WHITE, Secretary of Commission.
GEORGE B. WITHS, Phonographer to Commission.
GEO. H. HOLTZMAN.
JOHN D. HOWLAND.
JAMES C. O'CONNOR.
CHAR. E. GUERN, Interpreter.
LEON T. PALLARDY, Interpreter.
NICHOLAS JANIS, Interpreter.

Executed on the part of the Ogallalla band of Sioux by the chiefs and headmen whose names are hereto subscribed, they being thereunto duly authorized, at Fort Laramie, the 25th day of May, in the year A. D. 1868.

TAH-SHUN-KA-CO-QUI-PAH, his mark, Man-afraid-of-his-horses.
SHA-TON-SKAH, his X mark, White Hawk.
SHA-TON-SAPAH, his X mark, Black Hawk.
EGA-MON-TON-KA-SAPAH, his X mark, Black Tiger
OH-WAH-SHE-CHA, his X mark, Bad Wound.
PAH-GEE, his X mark, Grass.
WAH-NON SAH-CHE-GEH, his X mark, Ghost Heart.
COMECH, his X mark, Crow.
OH-HE-TE-KAH, his X mark, The Brave.
TAH-TON-KAH-HE-YO-TA-KAH, his X mark, Sitting Bull.
SHON-KA-OH-WAH-MEN-YE, his X mark, Whirlwind Dog.
HA-KAH-KAH-TAH-MIECH, his X mark, Poor Elk.
WAM-BU-LEE-WAH-KON, his X mark, Medicine Eagle.
CHON-GAH-MA-HE-TO-HANS-KA, his X mark, High Wolf.
WAH-SECHUN-TA-SHUN-KAH, his X mark, American Horse.
MAH-KAH-MAH-HA-MAK-NEAR, his X mark, Man that walks under the ground.
MAH-TO-TOW-PAH, his X mark, Four Bears.
MA-TO-WEE-SHA-KTA, his X mark, One that kills the bear.
OH-TAH-KEE-TOKA-WEE-CHAKTA, his X mark, One that kills in a hard place.
TAH-TON-KAH-TA-MIECH, his X mark, The Poor Bull.
OH-HUNS-EE-GA-NON-SKEN, his X mark, Mad Shade.
SHAH-TON-OH-NAH-OM-MINNE-NE-OH-MINNE, his X mark, Whirling hawk.
MAH-TO-CHUN-KA-OH, his X mark, Bear's Back.
CHE-TON-WEE-KOH, his X mark, Fool Hawk.
WAH-HOH-KE-ZA-AH-HAH, his X mark,
EH-TON-KAH, his X mark, Big Mouth.
MA-PAH-CHE-TAH, his X mark, Bad Hand.
WAH-KE-YUN-SHAH, his X mark, Red Thunder.
WAK-SAH, his X mark, One that Cuts Off.
CHAH-NOM-QUI-YAH, his X mark, One that Presents the Pipe.
WAH-KE-KE-YAN-PUH-TAH, his X mark, Fire Thunder.
MAH-TO-NONK-PAH-ZE, his X mark, Bear with Yellow Ears.

CON-REE-TEH-KA, his X mark, The Little Crow.
HE-HUP-PAH-TOH, his X mark, The Blue War Club.
SHON-KEE-TOH, his X mark, The Blue Horse.
WAM-BALLA-OH-CONQUO, his X mark, Quick Eagle.
TA-TONKA-SUPPA, his X mark, Black Bull.
MOH-TOH-HA-SHE-NA, his X mark, The Bear Hide.

Attest:
S. E. WARD.
JAS. C. O'CONNOR.
J. M. SHERWOOD.
W. C. SLICER.
SAM DEON.
H. M. MATHEWS.
JOSEPH BISS
NICHOLAS JANIS, Interpreter.
LEFROY JOTT, Interpreter.
ANTOINE JANIS, Interpreter.

Executed on the part of the Minneconjou band of Sioux by the chiefs and headmen whose names are hereunto subscribed, they being thereunto duly authorized.

HEH-WON-GE-CHAT, his X mark, One Horn.
OH-PON-AH-TAH-E-MANNE, his X mark, The Elk that Bellows Walking.
HEH-HO-LAH-ZEH-CHA-SKAH, his X mark, Young White Bull.
WAH-CHAH-CHUM-KAH-COH-KEEPAH, his X mark, One that is Afraid of Shield.
HE-HON-NE-SHAKTA, his X mark, The Old Owl.
MOC-PE-A-TOH, his X mark, Blue Cloud.
OH-PONG-GE-LE-SKAH, his X mark, Spotted Elk.
TAH-TONK-KA-HON-KE-SCHUE, his X mark, Slow bull.
SHONK-A-NEE-SHAH-SHAH-ATAH-PE, his X mark, The Dog Chief.
MA-TO-TAH-TA-TONK-KA, his X mark, Bull Bear.
WOM-BEH-LE-TON-KAH, his X mark, The Big Eagle.
MATOH, EH-SCHNE-LAH, his X mark, The Lone Bear.
MA-TOH-OH-HE-TO-KEH, his X mark, The Brave Bear.
EH-CHE-MA-KEH, his X mark, The Runner.
TI-KI-YA, his X mark, The Hard.
HE-MA-ZA, his X mark, Iron Horn.

Attest:
JAS. C O'CONNOR,
WM. D. BROWN,
NICHOLAS JANIS,
ANTOINE JANIS,
Interpreters.

Executed on the part of the Yanctonais band of Sioux by the chiefs and headmen whose names are hereto subscribed, they being thereunto duly authorized:

MAH-TO-NON-PAH, his X mark, Two Bears.
MA-TO-HNA-SKIN-YA, his X mark, Mad Bear.
HE-O-PU-ZA, his X mark, Louzy.

AH-KE-CHE-TAH-CHE-KA-DAN, his X mark, Little Soldier.
MAH-TO-E-TAN-CHAN, his X mark, Chief Bear.
CU-WI-TO-WIA, his X mark, Rotten Stomach.
SKUN-KA-WE-TKO, his X mark, Fool Dog.
ISH-TA-SAP-PAH, his X mark, Black Eye.
IH-TAN-CHAN, his X mark, The Chief.
I-A-WI-CA-KA, his X mark, The One who Tells the Truth.
AH-KE-CHE-TAH, his X mark, The Soldier.
TA-SHI-NA-GI, his X mark, Yellow Robe.
NAH-PE-TON-KA, his X mark, Big Hand.
CHAN-TEE-WE-KTO, his X mark, Fool Heart.
HOH-GAN-SAH-PA, his X mark, Black Catfish.
MAH-TO-WAH-KAN, his X mark, Medicine Bear.
SHUN-KA-KAN-SHA, his X mark, Red Horse.
WAN-RODE, his X mark, The Eagle.
CAN-HPI-SA-PA, his X mark, Black Tomahawk.
WAR-HE-LE-RE, his X mark, Yellow Eagle.
CHA-TON-CHE-CA, his X mark, Small Hawk, or Long Fare.
SHU-GER-MON-E-TOO-HA-SKA, his X mark, Fall Wolf.
MA-TO-U-TAH-KAH, his X mark, Sitting Bear.
HI-HA-CAH-GE-NA-SKENE, his X mark, Mad Elk.
Arapahoes.
LITTLE CHIEF, his X mark.
TALL BEAR, his X mark.
TOP MAN, his X mark.
NEVA, his X mark.
THE WOUNDED BEAR, his X mark.
WHIRLWIND, his X mark.
THE FOX, his X mark.
THE DOG BIG MOUTH, his X mark.
SPOTTED WOLF, his X mark.
SORREL HORSE, his X mark.
BLACK COAL, his X mark.
BIG WOLF, his X mark.
KNOCK-KNEE, his X mark.
BLACK CROW, his X mark.
THE LONE OLD MAN, his X mark.
PAUL, his X mark.
BLACK BULL, his X mark.
BIG TRACK, his X mark.
THE FOOT, his X mark.
BLACK WHITE, his X mark.
YELLOW HAIR, his X mark.
LITTLE SHIELD, his X mark.
BLACK BEAR, his X mark.
WOLF MOCASSIN, his X mark.
BIG ROBE, his X mark.
WOLF CHIEF, his X mark.

Witnesses:
ROBERT P. MCKIBBIN,
Captain 4th Infantry, and Bvt. Lieut. Col. U. S. A.,

Commanding Fort Laramie.
WM. H. POWELL,
Brevet Major, Captain 4th Infantry.
HENRY W. PATTERSON,
Captain 4th Infantry.
THEO E. TRUE,
Second Lieutenant 4th Infantry.
W. G. BULLOCK.
FORT LARAMIE, WYOMING TERRITORY
November 6, 1868.
MAH-PI-AH-LU-TAH, his X mark, Red Cloud.
WA-KI-AH-WE-CHA-SHAH, his X mark, Thunder Man.
MA-ZAH-ZAH-GEH, his X mark, Iron Cane.
WA-UMBLE-WHY-WA-KA-TUYAH, his X mark, High Eagle.
KO-KE-PAH, his X mark, Man Afraid.
WA-KI-AH-WA-KOU-AH, his X mark, Thunder Flying Running.

1. Articles I and II of the treaty call for

   a. loyalty and sovereignty in the Black Hills.
   b. commissions and committees to be appointed.
   c. peace and education.
   d. a laying down of arms on both sides.

2. How did the U.S. government determine the number of blacksmiths to send to the reservations?

   a. by the amount of Native Americans living on the reservations
   b. by the amount of Native Americans living on cultivated soil
   c. by the number of number of Native American children enrolled in school
   d. by the number of horses living on the reservation

3. Why did the U.S. government agree to abandon the military posts in the reservation?

   a. They did not need to have the military stationed there.
   b. as a show of good faith
   c. in order to ensure that the settlers and the Native Americans did not come into contact
   d. all of the above

4. Why did this treaty have a completely binding affect?

   a. It annulled all other treaties.
   b. It was the last treaty made between the Native Americans and the white settlers.
   c. It was signed by the Sioux.
   d. none of the above

5. Do you think that these reservations for Native Americans were a good idea? Why or why not? Think of another way peace could have been settled between the Native Americans and the white settlers and explain it thoroughly.

14TH AMENDMENT TO THE U.S. CONSTITUTION: CIVIL RIGHTS (1868)

Following the Civil War, Congress submitted to the states three amendments as part of its Reconstruction program to guarantee equal civil and legal rights to black citizens. The major provision of the 14th amendment was to grant citizenship to "All persons born or naturalized in the United States," thereby granting citizenship to former slaves. Another equally important provision was the statement that "nor shall any state deprive any person of life, liberty, or property, without due process of law; nor deny to any person within its jurisdiction the equal protection of the laws." The right to due process of law and equal protection of the law now applied to both the Federal and state governments. On June 16, 1866, the House Joint Resolution proposing the 14th amendment to the Constitution was submitted to the states. On July 28, 1868, the 14th amendment was declared, in a certificate of the Secretary of State, ratified by the necessary 28 of the 37 States, and became part of the supreme law of the land.

Congressman John A. Bingham of Ohio, the primary author of the first section of the 14th amendment, intended that the amendment also nationalize the Federal Bill of Rights by making it binding upon the states. Senator Jacob Howard of Michigan, introducing the amendment, specifically stated that the privileges and immunities clause would extend to the states "the personal rights guaranteed and secured by the first eight amendments." He was, however, alone in this assertion. Most senators argued that the privileges and immunities clause did not bind the states to the Federal Bill of Rights.

Not only did the 14th amendment fail to extend the Bill of Rights to the states; it also failed to protect the rights of black citizens. One legacy of Reconstruction was the determined struggle of black and white citizens to make the promise of the 14th amendment a reality. Citizens petitioned and initiated court cases, Congress enacted legislation, and the executive branch attempted to enforce measures that would guard all citizens' rights. While these citizens did not succeed in empowering the 14th amendment during the Reconstruction, they effectively articulated arguments and offered dissenting opinions that would be the basis for change in the 20th century.

Section 1.

All persons born or naturalized in the United States, and subject to the jurisdiction thereof, are citizens of the United States and of the State wherein they reside. No State shall make or enforce any law which shall abridge the privileges or immunities of citizens of the United States; nor shall any State deprive any person of life, liberty, or property, without due process of law; nor deny to any person within its jurisdiction the equal protection of the laws.

Section 2.

Representatives shall be apportioned among the several States according to their respective numbers, counting the whole number of persons in each State, excluding Indians not taxed. But when the right to vote at any election for the choice of electors for President and Vice-President of the United States, Representatives in Congress, the Executive and Judicial officers of a State, or the members of the Legislature thereof, is denied to any of the male inhabitants of such State, being twenty-one years of age, and citizens of the United States, or in any way abridged, except for participation in rebellion, or other crime, the basis of representation therein shall be reduced in the proportion which the number of such male citizens shall bear to the whole number of male citizens twenty-one years of age in such State.

Section 3.

No person shall be a Senator or Representative in Congress, or elector of President and Vice-President, or hold any office, civil or military, under the United States, or under any State, who, having previously taken an oath, as a member of Congress, or as an officer of the United States, or as a member of any State legislature, or as an executive or judicial officer of any State, to support the Constitution of the United States, shall have engaged in insurrection or rebellion against the same, or given aid or comfort to the enemies thereof. But Congress may by a vote of two-thirds of each House, remove such disability.

Section 4.

The validity of the public debt of the United States, authorized by law, including debts incurred for payment of pensions and bounties for services in suppressing insurrection or rebellion, shall not be questioned. But neither the United States nor any State shall assume or pay any debt or obligation incurred in aid of insurrection or rebellion against the United States, or any claim for the loss or emancipation of any slave; but all such debts, obligations and claims shall be held illegal and void.

Section 5.

The Congress shall have the power to enforce, by appropriate legislation, the provisions of this article.

1. In section 1 of this amendment, who has a right to reduce the privileges of the citizens of the United States?

   a. the states
   b. the federal government
   c. no one
   d. It does not specify.

2. How does this amendment differ from the Constitution?

   a. It protects life and liberty.
   b. It enumerates state rights.
   c. It defines who are the citizens of the United States.
   d. It specifies that all citizens have rights to due process of law.

3. Only if the voter ________ could his rights be reduced.

   a. works for the government
   b. committed a crime
   c fought in a war
   d. refused to speak in his own defense

4. In your own words, what is the definition of a citizen of the United States? Is this a broad or narrow view? Why?

15TH AMENDMENT TO THE U.S. CONSTITUTION: VOTING RIGHTS (1870)

To former abolitionists and to the Radical Republicans in Congress who fashioned Reconstruction after the Civil War, the 15th amendment, enacted in 1870, appeared to signify the fulfillment of all promises made to African Americans. Set free by the 13th amendment, with citizenship guaranteed by the 14th amendment, black males were given the vote by the 15th amendment. From that point on, the freedmen were generally expected to fend for themselves. In retrospect, it can be seen that the 15th amendment was in reality only the beginning of a struggle for equality that would continue for more than a century before African Americans could begin to participate fully in U.S. public and civic life.

African Americans exercised the franchise and held office in many Southern states through the 1880s, but in the early 1890s, steps were taken to ensure subsequent "white supremacy." Literacy tests for the vote, "grandfather clauses" excluding from the franchise all whose ancestors had not voted in the 1860s, and other devices to disenfranchise African Americans were written into the constitutions of former Confederate states. Social and economic segregation were added to black America's loss of political power. In 1896 the Supreme Court decision Plessy v. Ferguson legalized "separate but equal" facilities for the races. For more than 50 years, the overwhelming majority of African American citizens were reduced to second-class citizenship under the "Jim Crow" segregation system. During that time, African Americans sought to secure their rights and improve their position through organizations such as National Association for the Advancement of Colored People and the National Urban League, and through the individual efforts of reformers like Booker T. Washington, W.E.B. DuBois, and A. Philip Randolph.

The most direct attack on the problem of African-American disfranchisement came in 1965. Prompted by reports of continuing discriminatory voting practices in many Southern states, President Lyndon B. Johnson, himself a southerner, urged Congress on March 15, 1965, to pass legislation "which will make it impossible to thwart the 15th amendment." He reminded Congress that "we cannot have government for all the people until we first make certain it is government of and by all the people." The Voting Rights Act of 1965, extended in 1970, 1975, and 1982, abolished all remaining deterrents to exercising the franchise and authorized Federal supervision of voter registration where necessary.

Fortieth Congress of the United States of America;

At the third Session, Begun and held at the city of Washington, on Monday, the seventh day of December, one thousand eight hundred and sixty-eight.

A Resolution Proposing an amendment to the Constitution of the United States.

Resolved *by the Senate and House of Representatives of the United States of America in Congress assembled,* (two-thirds of both Houses concurring) that the following article be proposed to the legislature of the several States as an amendment to the Constitution of the United States which, when ratified by three-fourths of said legislatures shall be valid as part of the Constitution, namely:

Article XV.

Section 1. The right of citizens of the United States to vote shall not be denied or abridged by the United States or by any State on account of race, color, or previous condition of servitude—

Section 2. The Congress shall have the power to enforce this article by appropriate legislation.

1. What portion of the legislature has to ratify a proposal in order for it to become an amendment?

   a. two -fifths
   b. one-half
   c. three-fourths
   d. one-quarter

2. Why was the fifteenth amendment needed?

   a. Some people had been denied the vote.
   b. Congress wanted to punish the southern states.
   c. Abolitionists were not satisfied with the fourteenth amendment.
   d. none of the above

3. Why is the right to vote an important part of being a U.S. citizen?

Made in the USA
Middletown, DE
02 July 2022

68342730R00124